Being Mindful, Easing Suffering

of related interest

Journeys into Palliative Care
Roots and Reflections
Edited by Christina Mason
ISBN 1 84310 030 4

Music Therapy in Palliative Care
New Voices
Edited by David Aldridge
ISBN 1 85302 739 1

Complementary Therapies in Context
The Psychology of Healing
Helen Graham
ISBN 1 85302 640 9

Good Grief 1
Exploring Feelings, Loss and Death with Under Elevens, 2nd edition
Barbara Ward and Associates
ISBN 1 85302 324 8

Good Grief 2
Exploring Feelings, Loss and Death with Over Elevens and Adults
Barbara Ward and Associates
ISBN 1 85302 340 X

The Inspiration of Hope in Bereavement Counselling
John Cutcliffe
ISBN 1 84310 082 7

Counsellors in Health Settings
Edited by Kim Etherington
Foreword by Tim Bond
ISBN 1 85302 938 6

Being Mindful, Easing Suffering

Reflections on Palliative Care

Christopher Johns

Jessica Kingsley Publishers
London and New York

First published in the United Kingdom in 2004
by Jessica Kingsley Publishers Ltd
116 Pentonville Road
London N1 9JB, England
and
29 West 35th Street, 10th fl.
New York, NY 10001-2299, USA
www.jkp.com

Copyright © Christopher Johns 2004

Library of Congress Cataloging in Publication Data
Johns, Christopher.
    Being mindful, easing suffering : reflections on palliative care / Christopher Johns.— 1st American pbk. ed.
        p. cm.
    Includes bibliographical references.
    ISBN 1-84310-212-9 (pbk.)
    1. Palliative treatment. 2. Terminal care. I. Title.
    R726.8.J64 2004
    616′.029—dc22

                                                                2003027301

British Library Cataloguing in Publication Data
A CIP catalogue record for this book is available from the British Library

ISBN 1 84310 212 9

Printed and Bound in Great Britain by
Athenaeum Press, Gateshead, Tyne and Wear

Contents

Preface   7

Acknowledgements   12

Part 1   Mindful practice   13

Part 2   Being mindful, easing suffering: The narrative   35

Part 3   Postscript: Reflections from a Buddhist perspective   251
    Bert Leguit

Appendices

Appendix 1: The Being available template   255

Appendix 2: Glossary of drugs   261

References   263

Subject Index   267

Author Index   272

Preface

As a palliative care nurse, complementary therapist and Buddhist working in a hospice, my intent is to ease suffering and nurture the growth of those people with whom I meet who face death and dying. Perhaps it is the person themselves, a family member or a friend. Yet what is it I do that makes a caring difference to these peoples' lives? How can I become more skilful in what I do?

In response to these questions I kept a journal in which I reflected on my practice experiences between September 2000 and September 2002. From these experiences, I wove the narrative presented in this book; a treatise on mindful practice working with people towards easing suffering and nurturing growth through the dying experience. Reflection offers an opportunity for palliative care practitioners to enlighten the essential nature of palliative care by 'delving into the less articulated structures of knowing how to journey with the patient with a terminal illness and his or her family' (Dunniece and Slevin 2002).

Reflection offers a subjective and contextual view of the world through my lens; partial glimpses of the subtle nuances of the nature of palliative care and my work as a complementary therapist and nurse. It is who I am as a person, my feelings, frustrations, concerns and compassion that dominate the way I see and respond to the world and determine how effective a practitioner I can be. Yet I know through sharing my stories in diverse settings that such stories trigger other people's. All those who work within palliative care and beyond will, if open to the possibility, recognise my stories in themselves. If closed to this possibility they must inevitably wither and perish, for as Remen (1996) wistfully reminds each of us:

> Objectivity makes us far more vulnerable emotionally than compassion or a simple humanity. Objectivity separates us from the life around us and within us. We are wounded from life all the same; it is only the healing which cannot reach us … in the objective stance no one can draw on their human strengths, no one can cry, or accept comfort, or find meanings or pray, or understand the life around us. (p.78)

Reflection is a process of self-inquiry and transformation towards realising desirable practice as a lived reality. As such, reflection is both the research and developmental tool. By reflecting on my everyday practice I become increasingly mindful of myself within everyday practice. I become more aware of the way I think, feel and respond to situations as they unfold. I become more sensitive to the people within those situations, whether patients, their friends or relatives, or my colleagues. As a consequence, I can respond more in tune with my values and more skilfully with my patients and others. In other words, through reflection I become a more mindful practitioner. This is not an end-state, it is a constant reflexive and dynamic movement that I accept as my responsibility as a carer and therapist. The idea of *being mindful* also reflects my own spiritual journey that coincides with the narrative time span. Over this time I have embraced Buddhism and illuminate through the narrative the way I have endeavoured to live out Buddhism within my clinical practice. I view my practice as a path to ease suffering and nurture growth in the other person and for myself. It is a story of sense making, of pulling back the curtains of self-distortion to reveal my authentic self and ease the contradictions within my own life.

Book structure

The book is presented in three parts. Part 1 – Mindful practice provides a background to position me in context of the narrative and offers an appreciation of palliative care and the reflective process, to help the reader understand my mindset and approach to narrative form. This part can be skipped or returned to because the narrative stands alone as a piece of reflective writing.

Part 2 – Being mindful, easing suffering: The narrative sets out the narrative and forms the substantive part of the book.

Part 3 is a brief commentary by Bert Leguit, a Dutch Buddhist and nurse. I met him in November 2001 and asked him to reflect on my words and illustrate the narrative. Like me, Bert weaves his Buddhist practice with his nursing practice. I am the more experienced nurse while he is the more experienced Buddhist. Together through our words and illustrations we weave a pattern together. My thanks also for his illustrations which add a new dimension for reflection.

Appendix 1 sets out the Being available template as a framework to mark my reflexive development towards realising my vision of caring as a lived reality. Appendix 2 is a glossary of the different drugs referred to in the text.

Writing as a research process

The reflexive narrative is presented as an exemplar of researching self as a process of self-inquiry and transformation. The word 'researching' is emphasised because it is not the usual type of research that health care practitioners have traditionally undertaken. I have been developing this methodology in working with students researching themselves at undergraduate, masters and MPhil/PhD level. An outline of this emerging methodology and examples of narratives are presented in *Guided Reflection: Advancing Practice* (Johns 2002).

I felt it was not good enough for me to guide others to construct a reflexive narrative without having undertaken the journey myself, or from a purely theoretical perspective. That felt a contradiction with my own values of being a credible practitioner if you are going to teach practice. However, I also wanted to tell my story and write the narrative as a reflection of the way I normally practise reflection rather than primarily as an intellectual pursuit. I must also confess I have not pursued a theoretical literature to the extent I might insist a research student should do so. In addition, my own guidance has lacked the discipline and presence I would expect to see within a research narrative. My own horizons have been limited and would certainly have benefited from a greater challenge.

As a research methodology, my approach to guided reflection research as a process of self-inquiry and transformation has been and continues to be widely influenced by diverse sources. These were discussed in *Guided Reflection: Advancing Practice*, but in the year since that book was finally edited, the influences have been refined.

Such work as the narrative I present reveals facets of suffering and my responses. Morse (2001) emphasises 'the need to research suffering from a number of research perspectives, examine suffering within the clinical context, and evaluate nurse-patient interactions with patients who are suffering' (p.48). Morse would like an accurate behavioural description of suffering which she will never attain. Like caring, suffering has an elusive shifting quality that defies abstraction in its complexity. The sensitive nurse, able to fathom the complexity of suffering, will appreciate and respond to the person's suffering in its unique pattern manifestation (Cowling 2000). Narrative research gives insight into these dimensions of practice yet without the need to distil the narrative in terms of defining schemes or attributes. Narrative writing responds to Benner's (1984) challenge:

> What's missing are systematic observations of what nurse clinicians
> learn from their clinical practice. Nurses have not been careful record

keepers of their own clinical learning. The failure to chart our practices and clinical observations has deprived nursing theory of the uniqueness and richness of the knowledge embedded in expert clinical practice. Well charted practices and observations are essential for theory development. (pp.1–2)

I would not make any claims to theory development although I would emphasise that the rich description of narrative highlights the exquisite nature of caring, lifting it out of the mundane into something sacred and the way caring makes a difference to peoples' lives. This is especially so at a time of death with its losses and anguish. Reflection as a process of self-inquiry and transformation is an approach to research that will interest any practitioner concerned with being and becoming an effective practitioner in their particular field of practice. There can be no more meaningful way of undertaking research than researching self, although a guide is recommended as it is not easy to travel alone on such journeys.

Reading the text

It is not necessary to read Part 1 before the main narrative. Indeed the reader may benefit from reading the narrative first and then the introduction. However, in reading my narrative I ask the reader to be open to what my text has to say. Perhaps some readers will not like my interpretations or wonder how I could make such assumptions. So I ask you, the reader, to be still, and to consider the assumptions or assertions that give offence. It has not been my intention to be authoritative about the nature of palliative care so please do not become irritated with the text if you do not agree with something. See the narrative as a gift to trigger your own reflection and examine your own prejudices. Perhaps you have become closed to new ideas and locked into habitual ways of feeling, thinking and responding within your practice and life. Open the shutters of your own soul and feel the light flood in and the shadows dance.

The stories reflect images of caring for all practitioners who work with dying patients; whether in hospitals, hospices or in the community. The messages within the stories are relevant to all carers in whatever setting to help the reader reflect on the meaning of living and dying, not just for patients and families, but for self. Indeed the quest to know self is paramount for those who work with dying people and their families. This also applies to lay carers, those relatives and friends who live with and care for people who are dying. It is not necessarily easy to tune into the thoughts and feelings of people experiencing dying. They may be self-conscious of what to say, they might have mixed emotions, they may suffer. I hope the stories inspire and give confidence, and offer nuggets for reflection and personal insight.

The names of patients, relatives and colleagues have been changed in order to protect their anonymity. Where I talk in general terms of a practitioner I use the feminine form of representation, either 'she' or 'her', simply because most of my therapist and nurse colleagues are women. One name I have not changed is Sister Kathleen Moore. She is a Roman Catholic nun and hospice volunteer, whose presence at the hospice radiates like a shining light giving love, courage and humility to all. My love and thanks to her.

Acknowledgements

There are many people I need to acknowledge and thank. To the patients and their families whose lives infuse this book: needless to say without them the book would not have been possible. It is both a deep privilege and humbling to work with people experiencing their own dying. They have nurtured my inner flame. To my colleagues at the hospice and in the community where I practise who have allowed me to join with them in a collective journey to realise wise and compassionate caring. To work at the hospice is such a joy because they have created such a mutually caring environment. To my friends at the Cambridge Buddhist Centre as they guide me along the Buddhist path. To Carol Picard, for her choreographic work interpretation of Gabrielle Roth's work which has inspired my own interpretations of the caring dance using this work, and to Jean Watson, for her continuous inspiration and friendship, and her caring work. To my family for their forbearance and love. To Sue Duke and Denise Rankin-Box for reviewing the manuscript and their helpful and supportive comments.

And finally to everyone at Jessica Kingsley Publishers...

PART I

Mindful practice

The world is what the world is and I will work in the best way I can to do the healing I can, to take loving actions.

(Glassman 2001, p.38)

The narrative that forms the substantial part of this book has been constructed from a series of reflections on my practice as a palliative care nurse and complementary therapist working within a hospice between September 2000 and September 2002. Each reflection illuminates the unique experience of working with patients and families experiencing death and dying, revealing the meaning of suffering and the caring response to ease suffering.

The narrative commences with my chance meeting with Iris, a woman with advanced and incurable cancer in day care. Our relationship spans the whole narrative period, culminating shortly after her death, and gives the narrative a sense of continuity. Between my experiences with Iris I weave other experiences with patients in the inpatient unit of the hospice or in the community.

This introduction sets the background for the narrative by placing myself within the context of palliative care and mindful practice.

Palliative care

The hospice in which I practise was founded in 1991. It is managed as a charity, raising the majority of its running costs from public donation. It has ten inpatient beds and a day care unit that takes patients four days a week. The hospice admits patients for symptom management, respite care and terminal illness, especially those whose dying at home is difficult for whatever reason.

Hospice care is founded on the core tenet that patients should be helped to live until they die and that dying is a natural part of living despite the general taboo of dying within society (Twycross 1986). Hospices have a strong ideal of the 'good death'; a death in which the patient drifts off peacefully, with dignity at the right time, in comfort with symptoms well controlled, with their right for self-determination respected as far as possible, with open communication and acceptance by the whole family, without encroachment of unnecessary medical intervention (Lawton 2000; McNamara, Waddel and Colvin 1994). We experience the good death when afterwards both staff and family can look back with satisfaction, and when the family express gratitude and sweet memory.

The World Health Organisation (1992) defines palliative care as:

> The active total care of patients whose disease is not responsive to curative treatment. Control of pain, of other symptoms and of psychological, social and spiritual problems is paramount. The goal of palliative care is achievement of the best possible quality of life for patients and their families. Many aspects of palliative care are also applicable earlier in the course of the illness, in conjunction with anticancer treatment (cited in The National Council for Hospice and Specialist Palliative Care Services, Briefing Paper 9, May 2001).

Words develop subtle shades of meaning which bend in the breeze of experience. For example, what does 'total care' mean? What does 'spiritual' mean? What does 'active' mean? Does it suggest there is also 'passive' care? Without intending to be definitive the narrative throws light on such questions. The fundamental vision that guides my practice is to ease suffering and nurture the growth of the other through their illness experience.

Easing suffering

Suffering manifests on a physical, emotional, psychological, existential or spiritual plane. Much palliative care work is centred on symptom management to alleviate what can be termed 'physical suffering'. Efforts to relieve non-physical suffering (and here I am tempted to use an adjective like 'existential' to try and capture the idea that suffering is implicitly related to the way the suffering person views the world) are not so easily determined because the source of the suffering cannot be directly observed. It requires a sensitive practitioner able to tune into the other person to fathom the depth of the other's suffering and respond appropriately. It is the existential plane that has most intrigued me and stimulated my reflection. Hence the narrative can be viewed as my search for meaning in suffering and how best to ease it.

Morse (2001) asserts 'nurses are the caretakers of suffering' (p.47). Morse, in an attempt to grasp the essence of suffering, suggests that suffering has two broad and divergent behavioural states: enduring and emotional suffering. In Morse's words:

> Enduring occurs as a response to a threat to integrity of self. It results in a shutting down of emotional responses while the person 'comes to grips' with a situation. (p.50)

In this behavioural manifestation of suffering, Morse claims the sufferer *must* (her emphasis) experience an emotional release if healing is to occur. In contrast, emotional suffering is when emotions are released. In my experience, suffering is complex and defies reduction into a conceptual scheme.

Alongside my colleagues, I work in the shadow of death, a shadow that cloaks people in suffering. While suffering may be inevitable in a modern society that fears death, it is also a source of compassion for those who work within the shadow.

Nurturing growth of the other

The idea that suffering and caring are opportunities for growth resonates with proponents of the hospice movement (Lawton 2000). Saunders (1988) describes this opportunity for growth as 'the chance of a creative moment' (cited by Lawton 2000, p.14). More broadly, caring philosophers such as Milton Mayeroff (1971), and nurse philosophers such as Jean Watson (1988) and Margaret Newman (1994) highlight this opportunity for growth. Mayeroff states: 'To care for another person, in the most significant sense, is to help him grow and actualise himself'(p.1).

To actualise self is to fulfil one's human potential, whatever that might mean. Newman (1994) describes her approach as 'health as expanded consciousness'. Her work illuminates the way suffering creates the opportunity to stand back and take stock of self, especially when suffering becomes life-threatening. Then, one's taken-for-granted mortality is shaken, forcing self to contemplate life as impermanent. Forced out of our complacency we may question the very essence of our existence and the things that are really important to us. In other words people experiencing health crisis will ease their suffering by finding meaning, yet meaning is to be found at a higher level of consciousness. My caring intent is to help the person appreciate their life pattern – revealing the ways they normally feel, think and respond within their world in such a way that they can contemplate new ways of being to resolve the crisis that threat of death inevitably creates. In the face of cancer diagnosis and prognosis the person can be thrown off-balance such that normal ways of managing self no longer seem to work, resulting in fear and anxiety. It is often said that life-threatening illness is life changing.

A spiritual focus

The WHO vision of palliative care notes the significance of responding to the spiritual problems of people. Perhaps the word 'problems' is inappropriate because it suggests the spiritual is something that can be fixed, whereas I feel it is the very essence of being human. In the narrative I use the word 'spiritual' to connect with the meaning and experience that people give to their dying and beyond. This is profound work that takes my relationship with patients and families below the surface of symptoms into the mysterious and uncharted areas of self. It is a journey of discovery in relationship with the other where there is no prescription to respond in certain ways. Being spiritual is not about applying technique; it is a way of being for the practitioner.

As I go about my hospice practice I observe that the spiritual is generally a neglected area of clinical practice and represents a contradiction within palliative care ideology that espouses a holistic approach to care, and like all contradiction does not sit comfortably. The topic of spirituality has been widely addressed in the nursing literature, usually with a singular aim to know it. Spirituality has an elusive quality that researchers find perplexing and challenging (for example, see McSherry and Draper 1998). Reed (1992) notes that: 'The study of spirituality is like walking "a tightrope of trying to avoid a misleading reductionism while being sufficiently effective to fulfil scientific and practical needs"' (p.355). Reed captures the tension as researchers try and objectively define spirituality, resulting in a list of attributes or themes that can never reveal the meaning of spirituality for the individual or provide a schedule to assess spiritual needs, at least not without turning both practitioners and their patients into objects. The decline of religion and the rise of the secular society coincided with the rise of science. Perhaps, then, it is not surprising that scientists struggle with things that cannot be easily observed by the senses. I do not attempt to define spirituality. However, its nature ripples through the narrative like an elusive shadow or a pulsating drum beat. Ever present, it can be sensed by those tuned into a spiritual wavelength, but not grasped as some conceptual scheme.

Self-growth

Just as palliative care is a response to the patient's spiritual needs, so it is also for myself as caregiver. Through reflection, caring is an opportunity for self-growth, as a pathway to transforming self towards realising my vision of practice. Transformation can be viewed in different ways. Fay (1987), from a critical social science perspective, suggests transformation (or liberation from a state of oppression) as having three phases: enlightenment, empowerment and emancipation. Enlightenment (I prefer to say 'understanding') is coming to understand why things are as they are, not just things out there in the environment but also things in here, embodied within self, that determine the way I think, feel and respond to situations. Enlightenment also means developing a clear vision or purpose to guide the emancipatory journey.

From a Buddhist perspective, enlightenment is the end result of an evolutionary path from conditioned existence (samsara) towards unconditioned existence (nirvana). The path is an ethical pathway that guides the person to become more skilful by shedding negative emotions and nurturing positive emotions such as love, generosity, equanimity and goodwill.

Stephen Batchelor (1990) notes that the Zen tradition often speaks of three factors that need to be cultivated along the path (to transformation): great doubt, great courage and great faith. Great doubt is the core of being mindful – most basically put as 'what does it mean to be?' – a constant yet compassionate confrontation with self and practice in terms of responding in tune with our vision. And courage: 'courage is the strength needed to be true to ourselves under all conditions, to cast aside the obstacles that are constantly thrown in our way' (pp.16–17). Courage is the vital force that moves us from bleating like lambs for the slaughter to lions whose roar is heard across the landscape. Great faith is having the confidence and commitment to take action as necessary to realise our vision within our everyday practice.

My spiritual exploration is reflected in the different titles I have given to conference papers based on my experience with Mary (see p.49). In May 2002 I gave a paper at the International Association for Human Caring Conference in Boston entitled 'Easing into the light'. The paper told my story of sitting one evening on a late shift with Mary who was sedated and dying of cancer. I sat with her for about two hours before the night staff took over. As I sat with her, I visualised easing her spirit into the light of 'God'. Easing is letting go of resistance; to give way with grace and flow with each unfolding moment. The title was apt because, perhaps for the first time, I had really reflected on my spiritual self. I realised that to enable Mary to ease into the light then I would need to ease myself.

I had given this paper previously in May 2001 at the University of Akureyri, Iceland. On that occasion, I entitled the paper 'Dancing with the shadows'. The idea of dance as a metaphor for caring was inspired by the Native American ritual of dance to mark life's passages (Johns 2001). For a nurse, caring is ritual, and it seemed that caring was like a dance, whereby the nurse tunes into the rhythm of the patient and learns to flow with the patient – a theme I pursue in the narrative through the work of Gabrielle Roth. The shadow represents the unknown side of self. It also represents the shadow of death lurking in the wings of life, waiting to take the stage. I felt that I danced in the shadows because I was uncertain of my dance steps. I have never been taught to dance the spiritual steps of caring. The secular and technological nature of health care practice leaves little room for spiritual engagement, even in a hospice, with its religious undertones.

The spiritual focus of the narrative is sharpened because during the time span of the narrative I was and indeed remain engaged on a Buddhist spiritual path. As such, the narrative reveals the way I interpret and respond to patients' and families' spiritual needs from my particular Buddhist stance. My approach is always tentative, ever cautious of being intrusive, but also infused with a growing confidence. I pursue a path that lifts my spiritual self into conscious relief. Without some glimmer of my own spiritual self, how can I help another gaze at their own? The reader will sense how Buddhism has influenced the way I view and respond to the patient and family. This is sometimes controversial as I endeavour to find meaning in using Buddhist ideas in being with the patient. I have found much congruence between my hospice and teaching beliefs and Buddhist philosophy. Because of my hospice practice, Buddhist ideas are real and reflected within my everyday practice and increasingly influence the way I teach and lead my life. Buddhism inspires me and gives greater meaning to what I do. I have become more mindful within each moment and able to nurture and focus my compassion in my caring and teaching work.

Mindful practice

While the narrative is written as a stream of unfolding reflections on my practice, I have largely written it in the present tense in order to capture something of the immediacy of the moment and the nature of mindful practice. Being mindful is the exquisite ability to pay attention to self within the unfolding moment in such a way that one remains fully available to ease suffering and nurture growth. Goldstein (2002) describes mindfulness as the quality of mind that notices what is present, without judgement, without interference. It is like a mirror that clearly reflects what comes before it (p.89). Being mindful guides me to see things as they truly are, rather than as a projection of myself.

So, mindful practice is the conscious dwelling of self with patients and families with the intention to ease suffering and nurture their growth through the illness experience towards realising a more harmonious sense of well-being. It is also the conscious dwelling with other care practitioners towards harmonising the caring effort and to grow through the care experience. It creates the essential ground for caring practice, a clearing where I am conscious of myself in relationship with the other, a clearing where I can tune my compassion and pause so as to respond wisely to what is unfolding.

The Buddhist vision of the Bodhisattva ideal inspires my vision of being mindful – the balance of wisdom and compassion to help ease the suffering of others and guide them towards enlightenment. Like a gentle flowing stream the Bodhisattva ideal threads through the narrative, finding its level within the nooks and crannies of everyday caring to reveal the profound significance of caring; where the mundane becomes sacred. What a vision to guide my practice! My effort through reflection is to become more wise and compassionate in my practice. Without a deep compassion I cannot truly care for the other. Compassion is unconditional; it is room in my heart for whatever the other is experiencing (Levine 1986). Levine contrasts compassion with pity, which he suggests is a response to our discomfort with whatever the other is experiencing. To be compassionate requires a deep self-knowing. Sharon Salzberg (1995) states: 'The first step in developing true compassion is being able to recognise, to open to, and to acknowledge that pain and sorrow (suffering) exists' (p.104).

Wisdom is being free from ignorance. From a Buddhist perspective this means understanding and living out the Buddha's teaching (the Dharma). However, I refer to wisdom in a more mundane way in respect of approaching each moment with an open mind, approaching each situation from a perspective of not-knowing. If I approach a situation knowing how best to respond then I have closed my senses to reading the signs, seeking out only the signs that confirm my knowing. As a consequence people are at risk of being diminished. I risk responding inappropriately and manipulating people as if they were merely objects in my game plan. Therefore, as a mindful practitioner, I do not pretend to know. Indeed, I eschew knowing, because once I think I know then I am at risk of closing my mind to other ways of seeing and being. Worse, I may become attached to my knowing and resist attempts to view in other ways. Worse still, I may impose my restrictive frameworks on others, especially if I set myself up as an expert and teacher. This is the difference between knowing and wisdom. A wise person does not prejudge, but weighs up the situation in tune with his or her values, and makes a judgement based on the situation as it presents itself, having taking into account the perspectives of all involved, including his or her own. Of course, the wise person is cognisant of his or her own value judgements and assumptions. In other words, wisdom is ethical action. How can one know beforehand how *best* to respond? Certainly we may have had similar experiences and have knowledge of certain theories but these can only inform the mindful practitioner. They cannot prescribe the response. Paramanda (2001) puts this succinctly:

> Awareness brings an understanding that even the most common sight is never to be repeated and that to see something, as it really is, we must be free from the habitual tendency to label and categorise. Only then can we truly recognise things for what they are. (pp.138–139)

Being mindful is the antidote to habitual practice. Nothing is taken for granted. Everything has meaning, even the most mundane event like pulling a patient's curtains in the morning to reveal the new day or greeting a colleague with warmth. As the narrative will reveal, it is such 'small things' that make such a difference in the way caring is perceived.

Being mindful is not passive; it is a dynamic way of being within practice that requires firstly an awareness of self, and then requires an awareness of awareness of self, within each unfolding moment. It is as if I witness myself – the way that I am thinking, feeling and responding in each unfolding moment is held up for scrutiny within a clear vision of what I seek to achieve and in the knowledge of those factors that are influencing me.

Being mindful requires commitment to become the most effective practitioner I can be; to know and work towards realising what is desirable as a lived reality. I accept this responsibility to myself as a nurse. I owe my patients nothing less. Beckett (1969) puts it like this:

> We are entrusted by our patients with their needs and their hopes. Impossible or not, our task is to help them become all that they are capable of becoming. If we have not met our responsibilities to ourselves, we cannot be capable of sharing the responsibility for another's becoming. (p.170)

Running in place

Mindful practice is being aware of one's experience as it unfolds in its unpredictable and unique way. What does it mean to care? How does it feel to care? How does the patient or relative experience caring? How are such things known? It was when I read Joko Beck's (1989) sense of *running in place* that I glimpsed the path towards becoming mindful. She writes:

> Suppose we want to know how a marathon runner feels; if we run two blocks, or two miles or five miles, we will know something about running these distances, but we won't yet know anything about running a marathon. We can recite theories about marathons; we can describe tables about the physiology of marathon runners; we can pile up endless information about marathon running; but it doesn't mean we know what it is. We can only know when we are the one doing it. We only know our lives when we experience them directly...this we can call running in place, being present as we are, right here and now. (p.123)

Beck suggests that there are three stages to running in place in our practice. By practice Beck refers to *zazen* or Zen meditation practice. However, I feel this can mean any mindful practice such as the mindful way I go about my daily clinical practice. Beck's words require no commentary.

> *The first stage* in practice is to recognise that we're not running in place, we're always thinking about how our lives might be (or how they once were). What is there in our life right now that we don't want to run in place with? Whatever is repetitive, dull, painful or miserable: we don't want to run in place with that. No indeed! The first stage in practice is to recognise that we are rarely present: we're not experiencing life, we are thinking about it, conceptualising it, having opinions about it. It is frightening to run in place. A major component of practice is to realise how this fear and unwillingness dominates us.

> If we practice with patience and persistence, we (can) enter *the second stage*. We slowly begin to be conscious of the ego barriers of our life: the thoughts, the emotions, the evasions, the manipulations can now be observed and objectified more easily. This objectification is painful and revealing; but if we continue, the clouds obscuring the scenery become thinner.

> And what is the crucial, healing *third stage*? It is the direct experience of whatever the scenery of our life is at any moment as we run in place. Is it simple? Yes. Is it easy? No.

We grow by being where we are and experiencing what our life is right now. We must experience our anger, our sorrow, our failure, our apprehension; they can all be our teachers, when we do not separate ourselves from them. When we escape what is given, we cannot learn, we cannot grow. (pp.123–124)

So I can say that the narrative presented in this book is my journey of learning to run in place, to become more mindful towards easing suffering. It is a journey that I feel I have only just begun and that has no ending once I committed myself to the path. It is a lifelong quest.

Assumptions

As I reflect and draw insights, I make assumptions about the nature of my practice. Assumptions are intuitive hunches. Intuition is the hallmark of the expert practitioner (Dreyfus and Dreyfus 1986), characterised by an engaged and holistic appreciation of a situation. Intuition taps the embodied level of tacit knowing (Polanyi 1966). It is the sort of knowing we use when we ride a bike or tie up shoelaces; our bodies have learnt to do such things without the need to think about it. However, assumptions or intuitive hunches are often dismissed by a world that demands explanation – how do you justify this assumption? As Benner (1984) suggests, our intuition sense is largely accurate. It is as if we have a deeper, embodied level of knowing beyond the conscious grasp that accurately influences our perception.

The assumptions I make are revealed within the narrative. I cannot be certain they accurately reflect the truth of the situation. While I try and check out their truth value within the unfolding practice situation, it is not always possible, especially when I get caught up in the drama of the moment. Perhaps it is only afterwards, reflecting on the event, that I can contemplate the assumption and the factors that influenced my perception.

Accepting other peoples' assumptions can be difficult for readers, especially if their own experience or understanding differs. We live in a rational world where everything must be explained to have any validity. Hence it may be difficult to accept my 'subjective' experience as valid, especially experiences of a spiritual and emotional nature.

Accessing reflection

Reflection is the path to becoming mindful. It is a mirror to gaze at self, to contemplate the ways I think, feel and respond within situations and their consequences, and to consider other ways of responding that might lead to more effective practice. Through reflection I surface the contradictions within my practice between what I desire or achieve and my actual practice, and work towards resolving those contradictions within future practice. Through understanding the nature of contradiction I gain insight into myself and my practice, like planting seeds in my fertile mind to influence how I think, feel and respond in future experiences. It is rather like an unfolding a serial drama – will the insights be realised in future practice? If not, what factors 'out there' or 'in here' constrain me? Have I been able to overcome those factors in order to practise in tune with my beliefs? Indeed, are my beliefs true or strong enough? As Blackwolf and Gina Jones (1996) say:

> Before we can give our energy to another, we must first acknowledge and understand that we have two sides to our own existence. We have written a song with both high and low notes. We must understand and befriend our complete being before we can dance with someone else. We must love and accept our own reflection, before we can gaze deep into the heart of another. (p.148)

As I reflect, I am aware of the risk that I may have distorted reality or that parts of the actual experience are missing. I do not pretend to accurately recall the experience as it was. People snipe at reflection, insinuating it is a flawed process for these reasons. Perhaps reflection cannot accurately capture the experience as it was. Yet this is to miss the point. It is the spirit of the event that is most significant to capture and that reveals the meanings buried within the experience.

Confession

Reflection can be likened to a confessional, baring my mind and soul to unburden my sins and rejoice in my triumphs. From a Buddhist perspective the confessional has profound spiritual significance for the attainment of higher levels of consciousness (Sangharakshita 1995). Yet reflection only has value if I intend to be open and authentic with myself. What value is there in deceiving myself? It is natural to reflect on negative feelings, self-doubt and guilt because these feelings create anxiety due to the contradictions between the way we have responded and our beliefs. It is this sense of inner conflict we pay attention to. Our inclination is to defend against the anxiety, to disperse the conflict in whatever we can by drawing on defence mechanisms such as rationalisation or projection. Perhaps we learn to care less so we are not so vulnerable to suffering. Yet balancing anxiety requires energy that is depleting and makes us tired and less available for caring. It is better to face up to the anxiety and learn through it so we no longer respond with anxiety but with equanimity. Of course, we can also pay attention to positive feelings and experiences that are self-affirming.

I pay attention to my practice because it matters to me. Indeed, every day I work at the hospice is a gift to me. It nourishes my soul and fills me with joy. However, paying attention to positive feelings does not seem to be as natural as being aware of negative feelings. Perhaps this is a reflection of a culture that emphasises blame and shame rather than learning through experience. To hide from the perpetual fear of blame nurses inhabit the shadows, to be invisible to suffer alone with their self-blame and guilt. When others do not affirm our worth then we may also learn to discount ourselves and diminish what we do because it seems not to be valued. To reiterate, reflection is a way of honouring self and others, to reaffirm self as caring and that caring makes a significant difference to peoples' lives.

Reflective writing is well suited to capture the contextual richness and nuances of practice, revealing the significance of caring within the mundane as well as the dramatic situations that face health care practitioners everywhere. Stories reveal the beauty of caring even within the suffering that accompanies death and dying. In storytelling all things become possible. Indeed beauty is each caring moment, each moment of the caring dance unfolding revealed in its simplicity. As Paramanda (2001) says: 'To walk in beauty means to walk with an awareness that is open and appreciative of the world around us' (p.111). Yet when our minds are full of *stuff* it is sometimes difficult to see this beauty. *Stuff* is the clatter of thought that continuously bombards or clouds the mind. Reflection gives us distance from our minds to see the *stuff* for what it is, to bring the mind home to dwell in the simplicity and beauty of each caring moment. In a practice world where caring is diminished in the face of technology and the heroes of medicine, we who purport to care need to constantly remind ourselves of the significance of caring, and to nurture our caring self. Otherwise, our caring self may inadvertently slip away without our realisation, caught up in the distractions of the world out there. Reflection and stories open us to caring. We need stories as we need breath.

> Just as the writer only learns a spontaneous freedom of expression after years of often gruelling study, and just as the simple grace of the dancer is achieved only with enormous patient effort, so when you begin to understand where reflection will lead you, you will approach it as the

greatest endeavour of your life, one that demands of you the deepest perseverance, enthusiasm, intelligence, and discipline. (Rinpoche 1992, p.59. I have replaced the original word 'meditation' with 'reflection'.)

Journal writing

During the narrative period I kept a journal, recording what I considered to be significant experiences along this journey of realisation. I usually reflect and write in the evening after my work at the hospice. I know, with experience, that it is vital (at least for me) to write my reflection within 24 hours after the event in order to *adequately* recapture the sense of the situation. I (nearly) always have my journal within easy reach at work to make notes and record dialogue between the patient and myself, rather like a disciplined ethnographic researcher with her fieldwork journal.

Writing a journal may not be easy for people, especially for those educated in an arid academic culture where 'objectivity' is paramount, or in an organisational culture where the 'facts' rule; cultures where the 'I' has been denied, and where feelings, opinions and beliefs have been minimised as relatively insignificant. It may also be uncomfortable to face self. Street (1995) notes that: 'Facing ourselves on paper is sometimes a painful process and requires the support of others, particularly someone experienced to help us move beyond' (p.156).

The journal is a space, like an eddy within a fast moving stream, where I can pause from the often hectic and reactive effort of stream life in order to reflect and see things for what they are. It may be useful to commence a reflection by writing down any negative feeling. Writing it down will help me let go of the feeling. So, for example, I might write 'I feel angry!!!!' (number of exclamation marks optional). I can then look at this feeling objectively, prod it – Why do I feel angry? Why do I keep feeling angry? How can I shift it? What needs to change?

As I reflect and write, responding to these questions gives me some control over the feeling and possibilities for responding differently in similar situations. Reflection is like planting seeds that when we next experience a similar situation, we are more aware and hopefully respond in better ways.

Reflective writing begins with thick description and is laced with responses to a set of implicit reflective cues offered sequentially along a reflective curve:

- What issues seem significant to pay attention to?
- How was I feeling and what made me feel that way?
- What was I trying to achieve?
- Did I respond effectively and in tune with my values?
- What were the consequences of my actions on the patient, others and myself?
- How were others feeling?
- What made them feel that way?
- What factors influenced the way I was feeling, thinking or responding?
- What knowledge did or might have informed me?
- To what extent did I act for the best?
- How does this situation connect with previous experiences?
- How might I respond more effectively given this situation again?
- What would be the consequences of alternative actions for the patient, others and myself?
- How do I *now* feel about this experience?
- Am I now more able to support myself and others better as a consequence?
- What have I learnt?

(These cues form the Model for Structured Reflection, Johns 2002)

Such cues are *not* a prescription for reflection, they are merely a guide to help access the mystery of experience. In a technological world, reflection might easily become simply another technology towards producing a specific outcome – an effective practitioner. Reflection would be judged on this merit. But an emphasis on technology would diminish the meditative quality of reflection and the development of mindfulness.

The reflective cues inevitably arouse the practitioner's curiosity into her practice, challenging the practitioner to question how they think, feel and act about situations and imagining new ways more congruent with desirable practice. Stephen Batchelor (1990) puts the idea of questioning poetically into perspective:

Questioning is a quest: it takes the first step into the dark and proceeds to build a path from ignorance to clarity, from bewilderment to recognition, from estrangement to intimacy. It creates the initial fissure in the veil of the unknown. It forms an opening through which the light of wisdom is able to shine and penetrate. Questioning simultaneously reveals our limitations and our urge to go beyond them. (p.38)

Guidance

Part of the aim of our spiritual practice is to clarify our own motives. To achieve that, we need help and guidance, and companions on the way, who can reflect us back to ourselves. (Subhuti 2001, p.6)

Through the narrative I draw attention to the times I share my stories with others. Without doubt, I have benefited from the guidance of my peers at the hospice and students on the care of the dying courses I teach. No matter how mindful I feel I am, like everyone else I have blind spots. Another person may be able to see what I cannot see in myself, to take me deeper, into the darker aspects of the mind where many secrets are stored, places I fear to tread, but which strongly influence the way I see and respond to the world.

It is difficult to see beyond ourselves and envisage new ways of being. We can easily get locked into viewing the world in habitual and complacent ways, resistant to new ideas and change, tired and burnt out because we have failed to nurture and sustain ourselves. As John O'Donohue (1997) says, 'People get trapped at one window.' A guide helps me to open new shutters to 'reveal new vistas of possibility, presence and creativity' (pp.163–164). A guide challenges and supports me to 'pull back the shutters' to see beyond my normal ways of perceiving, thinking, feeling and responding to situations and reveal new possibilities. I like to think that I am open to my experience, curious and deeply committed to my practice. Fay (1987) considers these attributes as prerequisite to reflection. Of these, perhaps commitment is the most significant because people pay attention to things because they matter to them. Of course, you might expect that every health care practitioner cares deeply about her practice and wants to become the best practitioner she could be. Alas, somewhere along the line, the caring edge becomes blunted, the passion for practice merely a spark rather than a roaring fire. Like others, I am sure I sometimes cling to the familiar and resist new ideas. Practitioners may turn their heads away from the mirror of reflection because it is uncomfortable to face themselves. The reflected image may be disturbing. Perhaps it is better to live in ignorance and self-delusion. Tortured by their angst, these practitioners are likely to project their negativity into others, both patients and colleagues, creating rather than easing suffering.

Without doubt, it takes a certain kind of courage to face and be critical of self; to admit and accept that sometimes our actions are less than caring, that sometimes we make mistakes, that we get angry, that we cannot cope at times, and that we dislike patients and relatives we find difficult and demanding. Sometimes we are selfish and put our needs first; after all we are only human, and susceptible to the frailties of what that means. Facing up to anxiety can be tough because it goes against our natural fight or flight response.

Dialogue

The essence of guidance is dialogue. Dialogue is the way the mindful practitioner communicates with others. Dialogue is listening to and understanding the other's perspective without distorting it through a filter of the listener's own concerns, prejudices, prejudgements and so forth. In order to dialogue effectively with another person(s) or with texts, the practitioner must first dialogue with their 'objective' self in order to know and suspend their own perspectives, and to weigh up how best to respond within situations. Bohm (1996) describes this as proprioception of thought – being aware of our thoughts just as we are aware of our bodies in space when our eyes are shut. It is also being conscious and critical of our thinking patterns so we can move beyond ways of thinking that constrain our realising desirable practice. By suspending judgement we are more likely to perceive things for what they really are. In other words, reflection holds intuition in balance; it holds it up for scrutiny and yet without losing the spontaneity of the actual moment. To do this it is necessary to 'watch your mind action all the time' (Krishnamurti 1996, p.177) so as to observe the way you are thinking and free self from conditioning. Krishnamurti writes:

> Then only can there be freedom from conditioning, and, therefore, the total stillness of the mind in which alone it is possible to find out what is truth. If there is not that stillness, which is the outcome of a total understanding of conditioning, your search for truth has no meaning at all, it is merely a trap. (p.177)

The trap is set by an ego which listens in terms of its own cravings, judgements and prejudices.

Again, Krishnamurti:

We have formulations, opinions, judgements, beliefs through which we listen, so we actually never really listen at all; we are only listening in terms of our own particular prejudices, conclusions, or experiences. We are always interpreting what we hear, and obviously that does not bring about understanding. (p.178)

Dialogue is always focused towards reaching consensus and creating a more just and humane world (Bohm 1996). In other words dialogue is the natural expression of mindfulness.

Dialogue with literature

Besides dialogue with a guide I also dialogue with literature that has inspired me or helped me to frame my experience within broader contexts. Through dialogue with the literature I juxtapose and assimilate the author's ideas with my personal ways of knowing; the weaving together of different voices towards constructing my own informed and passionate voice (Belenky, Clinchy, Goldberger and Tarule 1986). For example, at a particular time of writing the narrative, I was reading *A deeper beauty* by Paramanda (2001) from which I have taken a number of ideas. Paramanda does not necessarily say anything I have not already glimpsed, but he adds a dimension in such a way that gives substance to my own emerging ideas besides inspiring my text. Paramanda's words add a poetic quality and richness of description. This is not embellishment for the sake of it but heightens and reflects the profound nature of caring.

However, from a reflective perspective, the words of others are never accepted on face value. Words can sometimes be seductive. Rather like assumptions, the use of literature is always critiqued for its relevance *to fit* with my own emerging ideas.

Narrative

The narrative strings together and edits my unfolding series of reflections into a *coherent* form (Johns 2002). Coherence is important in giving the text integrity. Narrative is constructed as a *drama unfolding* over time towards realising the plot. The sense *of drama unfolding* is imperative to grip and stir the reader's imagination. It also highlights that the narrative is always reflexive; the sense of one thing emerging out of the previous thing evident by looking back over the narrative and clearly seeing the way self has been transformed through the series of experiences. In the narrative I have used the Being available template to plot my transformation (see Appendix 1, p.255).

Narrative must reflect the nature of experience. As such, narrative can never be a neat linear progression of clearly defined events. But like life itself, it is contradictory, stories unfolding within stories without clear beginnings or endings, and has multiple sub-plots that go off on tangents. Issues are left unresolved, left hanging in the air yet always within a sense of progression towards some ultimate purpose.

Ask yourself – what makes a good story? You might say a strong plot, vivid description, coherent form. But most importantly, a good story will take readers to places in their minds where the imagination stirs; where they are confronted with their own experiences. Ben Okri (1997) describes this as the joy of storytelling. He argues that storytelling is about transgression, of taking readers beyond normal boundaries. He writes:

> Of taking readers to places they wouldn't willingly go…dragging readers in spite of themselves to places deep in them where wonders lurk beside terrors, this delicate art of planting delayed repeat explosions and revelations in the reader's mind, and doing this while enchanting them – this is one of the mysterious joys of all. (p.65)

Okri's idea of transgression; of breaking free from those forces that have contained, inspires my approach to narrative. Within the narrative I engage in dialogue with Okri in the context of my experience of being with Mary (see pp.60–63). The idea of transgression resonates with the idea that reflection is a counter movement to oppression. Certainly, the narrative within this book is an account of my own effort to liberate and transform myself to realise myself as a 'spiritual' practitioner so I can best respond to ease the patient's suffering. The theme of liberation and transformation flows within the narrative.

The narrative has a number of turns that reflect different stages in its construction. When I commenced writing the journal I had no vision of publishing it. I simply felt I ought to practise what I preach to students – to keep a reflective journal simply because it creates the opportunity to reflect daily and develop my practice.

The early narrative is a reflection of my work with Iris, a woman I met with on a regular basis for reflexology as an outpatient. Working with clients with cancer was new work for me as a reflexologist and aromatherapist, and reflection offered a way to evaluate my practice. My work with Iris is a continuous thread through the narrative. My reflections on working with Iris offer a powerful and poignant insight into one woman's struggle with a life-threatening cancer spanning 23 months within the context of my work as a complementary therapist and nurse.

My journal then expands to include reflections on my work as both a nurse and therapist with patients within the inpatient unit alongside my continuing work with Iris. The journal also shifts in style, moving from a more descriptive to reflective mode. I become more reflective as I begin to explore the spiritual side of myself and practice in context of a wider literature. I anticipated that some of these stories could be developed for journal publication, which gives the narrative a more discursive feel. The later part of the narrative (from 22 August 2001, p.112) was written with this book in mind. As such I became more conscious of writing in narrative form.

As I noted in the preface, all names of patients and nurses have been changed to respect their anonymity. Writing in narrative form is an ethical endeavour that must respect peoples' rights to privacy.

Expression and imagination

In writing the narrative I have endeavoured to be dramatic without embellishing the truth. I have tried to be poignant, beautiful, even poetic, as well as stark and confronting, simply because that is what practice is like. Clinical practice must always be vital, imaginative and creative. We owe nothing less to our patients and families. Then the narrative must adequately reflect this vitality. It must be descriptive of the truth, as free as possible from ambiguities, although the text is always open for multiple interpretations.

Okri's (1997) idea of the artist as creative play is inspirational:

> The artist should never lose the spirit of play. It is curious how sometimes the biggest tasks are best approached tangentially, with a smile in the soul. Much has been written about the seriousness with which important work has to be undertaken. I believe that seriousness and rigour are invaluable, and hard work indispensable – but I want to speak a little for the mysterious and humble might of a playful creative spirit. Playfulness lightens all terrifying endeavours. It humanises them, and brings them within the realm of childhood. The playfulness becomes absorbing, engrossing, all-consuming, serious even. The spirit warms. Memory burns brightly. The fires of intelligence blaze away, and self-consciousness evaporates. Then – wonderfully – the soul finds the sea; and the usually divided selves function, luminously as one. (p.23)

There are so many truths wrapped up in Okri's words. Hopefully they are obvious to the reader when reading the narrative. The first truth is the spirit of play – of releasing the soul to express itself without censorship and self-consciousness and yet with discipline and rigour. Play is fun and creative and yet so often education is seen as a chore. I can only write as I do because my soul smiles. My spirit warms because I am writing myself. My intelligence burns brightly because writing is self-revealing and insightful.

Writing is not predictable. As I write I explore new roads and discover new parts of myself, and in doing so astonish myself. It is as if my spirit has broken free to reclaim itself, a self torn apart by other peoples' perspectives. I hope my stories bound with a joyful, creative and playful attitude – it may be hard work and indeed it was, yet it also transcends the mundane; transforms the mundane into something sacred. And realising the sacred within everyday practice is perpetual delight. To be with someone who is dying and suffers greatly is profound and humbling. It is as if I tremble in knowing this. I wear a blessed smile because I feel as if I have liberated myself to care.

However, the form of expressing the truth is poetic license. In particular, I have been influenced by the work of Hélène Cixous (1996). She urges women, and here I might also say men, to express their freedom rather than be contained and sanitised, to recover their bodies, their minds and their souls that have been confiscated. She writes:

> Woman writing herself, will go back to this body that has been worse than confiscated, a body replaced with a disturbing stranger, sick or dead, who so often is a bad influence, the cause and place of inhibitions … Write yourself: your body must make itself heard. Then the huge resources of the unconscious will burst out. (p.97)

When I ask myself, what is palliative care, I must break out of a confined and sanitised place to feel the edges to this question; to feel and express the raw data of myself, both masculine and feminine. Yet would I recognise it even if I felt it? Cixous emphasises women because she believes it is men who have confiscated the women's bodies, and who have dictated its expressive form. However, I believe that she also encourages women to express their masculine side, to break out of their passive subjugation, yet in ways that honour their feminine side. From a feminist slant the practitioner's gaze and attention is turned towards those subtle aspects of caring; those everyday acts of caring which are apparently mundane yet which exemplify the profound nature of caring hidden behind the heroic 'masculine' scenes of medicine.

I sense a perpetual schism between what might be construed as the feminine and the masculine. Harmony is a synthesis (not a balance) as expressed in the Bodhisattva ideal; compassion, the exquisite unconditional sense of connection and love for the other; wisdom, the exquisite opening of self to what is unfolding without imposition. Narrative expression must endeavour to realise this synthesis; to realise the Bodhisattva ideal; or more simply – to realise self as caring. I try and write with wisdom and compassion, with imagination and freedom. If I ask myself, what is the spiritual nature of myself, I have no option but to go deep within myself. I find myself in a desert with few markers to guide me. I imagine I live in a Tipi on the desert's edge. Each day I contemplate the desert. Reflection and writing the narrative is a path that takes me deeper into the desert, and only then can I feel freedom and know its beauty. I am conscious of every step and marvel at the hot sand underneath my feet. It is as if I have tuned into my deeper self. My words are the cry of a lone wolf standing on a lofty promontory silhouetted against the full moon. She cries to her mate. This may seem a strange symbol, but it is something like I feel when I express myself in writing – calling for my spiritual mate deep within. Blackwolf and Gina Jones (1996) put it like this:

> Flow with time, but be present with each moment. Consider the vibration of the humming bird's wings. Which of its flutter is flight? Is flight the past fluttering of its wings? Or is flight the next flap of the wing? Come to see that flight is all of this. Transcend and flow with time, yet be present with the movement. Like all the winged, in order to transcend, we, too, must be in movement. We must vibrate. Truth after truth after truth reveals itself at each fluttering of our spiritual wings. Like the gradual shading of blue to green, we become, we live the transformations. It is as though we are in a cocoon within a cocoon, within a cocoon. The more truths we experience, the more we are set free in colourful flight. Always in movement, the different levels of consciousness we experience lead us to the next level. This is how we come to soar! (p.54)

Writing, like caring and healing, is vibrational. Vibrate! Soar!

PART 2

Being mindful, easing suffering:
The narrative

We need to hold ourselves open to the truth as the flower holds itself open to the sun.

(Sangharakshita 1999, p.132)

Friday 15 September 2000

Iris

I am working as the complementary therapist in the day care unit as Stella, the regular volunteer complementary therapist, is unwell. One of the patients calls me by name: 'Chris? Hello, I'm Iris. You asked who would like a therapy today?' Clutching my towels I sit down with her and feel her attraction. She vibrates with energy. I ask what therapy would she like? She chooses reflexology. Her enthusiasm is catching. She's ready now if I am.

We move into the treatment room. First, I need to know this woman. I must tune into her to understand the pattern of her life. I ask, 'How are you?' She reveals a number of problems; she's not sleeping well, she has been feeling a bit depressed, waking early in the morning with her head full of thoughts.

Iris fills me in with her medical and social history. She is 38 years old, married to Robert with two young children. Charlotte is five years old and James is seven. She has a primary breast cancer that has been treated by mastectomy, and now with chest wall, liver and bone metastases. She is being treated with herseptin, a trial drug that has so far contained the growth of the liver tumour. She says her shoulders are painful, worse in the right shoulder. She wears a fentanyl patch for the pain and takes sevredol regularly in the evening for breakthrough pain. Rippling below the cheerful exterior is a troubled woman. However, at this time I do not probe beneath the surface. It is enough to respond to the surface signs on this first encounter.

I commence the reflexology by placing each hand on each of her feet. My intention is to centre myself through breathing and to tune into Iris, to feel her wavelength and to become one with her. As I do this, I ask Iris to close her eyes and to follow her breath in and follow her breath out. After four breaths in and out I ask her to imagine she is surrounded in a soft and loving light. I invite her to breathe in the light until every cell of her body is bathed in light. I suggest that this feels good. I then ask her to breathe out any concerns or fears of the day; that she can let them go now. I then guide her through a body scan; moving from her scalp to her toes focusing and relaxing each part in turn; and then to imagine she is a fluffy cloud floating in a clear blue sky. The powerful drone of Rusty Crutcher's CD 'Chaco Canyon' vibrates between us. She seems very relaxed.

Commencing the reflexology Iris is quickly asleep. I am in awe that she has surrendered to my hands with such trust. My compassion burns for this woman! Compassion is the healing energy. There is nothing remarkable about the actual reflexology treatment. Her feet are pale suggesting she lacks some vital energy. Some hard patches suggest she would benefit from more attention. I finish the reflexology by holding her feet for about five minutes as I again focus my breathing in harmony with her body, radiating Reiki[1] healing energy through my hands.

Afterwards she says the reflexology was deeply relaxing. She asks if I can see her for more treatments?

I ask myself, 'Can I resist when people have such need?' We make an appointment for the following Thursday. As I say goodbye I touch her shoulder and say 'take care' – she thanks me and gives me a hug.

On deeper reflection – a first meeting between a young woman with advanced cancer fighting for survival, positive and determined to beat the cancer despite her poor prognosis, and a therapist. In itself the meeting was commonplace yet meeting a new patient experiencing life-threatening illness is always remarkable, more so when she is young with such young children. I immediately sensed her vulnerability and hope that reflexology might help her beat cancer. I was very mindful of connecting with Iris

---

1   Reiki is a laying on of hands touch healing system. The Reiki practitioner receives attonements that connect them in an increased way to the universal healing energy (Ki). The receiver becomes a channel for this energy. (Stein 1995, pp.8-17.)

through my physical touch. To massage someone is deeply intimate. While the feet are recognised as a 'safe touching zone' (Chung Ok Sung 2001), it is a way of touching and vibrating every part of her body, helping to energise and balance her energetic system. As I consciously move my hands across her feet, this is a very powerful healing visualisation. For example, when tripping the adrenal glands I bathe them in a healing light and imagine the adrenal medulla and cortex secreting their steroids and adrenaline.

Using the Burford Model cues (Johns 1994) I write my notes; I sense who Iris is and the meanings she gives to having advanced cancer. My effort is to read and appreciate her pattern of wholeness (Cowling 2000) rather than reduce her to a series of parts that characterise most nursing models. Her vulnerability ripples across her, the signs are evident although I did not pursue them at this time. Pattern appreciation is an unfolding process over time. Yet I can read she is fearful of an uncertain future and my empathy senses the poignancy of losing her two children.

Thursday 21 September 2000

Iris

As I arrive in day care, Iris greets me wearing a big smile. She looks radiant. We move into the treatment room. It is already 14.10 and I must leave by 14.45 to pick up my daughter from school. I feel the pressure of time and apologise that the treatment will be truncated. Iris simply smiles and says she is grateful for any time I can give her.

Iris says she has been okay. Picking up her signs, I ask if she thinks about the future. She says it's gloomy although the various treatments she has had have kept things at bay. She says she must have hope. I ask if she has any particular religious beliefs. She hasn't. I ask if she would like anything 'spiritual' to read. I sense her caution and quickly add that I have nothing to sell. She laughs. 'I wondered...but I could do with something on positive thinking. I'm not sleeping well, my thoughts spin around keeping me awake. I often wake early thinking and worrying about the future although I've slept better since the last treatment.' The use of Bach flower remedies comes to mind, but I'm conscious of overwhelming her.

As part of my reflexology assessment I observe the colour of Iris's feet. They are dark blue-red, suggesting a build-up of negative feelings. I feel her liver, a white patch in the middle of her feet. It is soft and cold. I gingerly touch this area and imagine her tumour there.

After the treatment she says how relaxing the treatment is. I say her heels tell me she is full of feelings that she has difficulty expressing. She looks knowingly at me and admits she must be cheerful at all costs. She wears a cheerful mask that is her face to the world. I can see by the way she dresses and uses make-up that her face to the world is important to her. But behind her brave and cheerful face lurks a deep fear. She says she has a lot of support although she cannot easily talk about these things. That is why Fridays at day care are so important to her, so she can talk to other people who share and understand her predicament. That strikes a chord – how can nurses really empathise and understand what someone like Iris thinks and feels about her illness? Perhaps the company of fellow travellers is where greatest solace is found.

I suggest we use a meditation tape next time to guide her breathing to help her relax more between treatments. She says she is starting t'ai chi this evening. I applaud, yet I also sense her desperation at grasping at treatments as if grasping for hope. Despite the chaos that ripples through her, I find it easy to tune into and flow with her rhythm because she is so open and accepting. For the moment I just flow along her surface yet already she is revealing deeper parts of herself. Who knows what lies deeper? I must simply flow with her and resist any urge to 'fix it' for her. I imagine myself as a raft for her. Words from Palace Music's song 'Lost Blues' comes to mind, where they sing about following the flow of the ocean line. *Follow the flow* is to follow the rhythm of the caring dance. Newman (1999) says, 'we need to join in partnership with clients and dance their dance … the partnership demands that we develop tolerance with uncertainty' (p.228).

I think of Iris's rhythm as a cluster of atonal music. Discordant guitars. When we hear atonal music, it is often unfamiliar and confusing. The dissonance hits us all at once, right in the chest like a blast of catastrophe. Newman notes that the risk is a defensive response, to protect us from being annihilated by the (musical) chaos; to cover our ears from the dreadful sound and to flee to safety. Most of us prefer nice melodies to hum along to. Yet the fact is that when people face life-threatening illness the music is often far from melodic. Iris needs to find meaning in her atonal rhythms so she can find harmony in the chaos that unfolds within and about her day by day. My work is to guide her to explore the edges of her predicament; where she can learn through the chaos rather than cling to known ways of being that clearly do not work for her anymore. I am an alchemist in her life, a creative and supportive presence to guide her towards harmony and turn her fear into stillness. Newman (1999) is so right when she says: 'A sensitive, aware nurse provides clients with an opportunity to resonate through a period of uncertainty until a new rhythm emanating from the client's own centre of consciousness emerges' (p.229).

I am conscious of not knowing about women's experience of living with breast cancer. Colyer (1996), using a feminist methodology, interviewed three women with breast cancer to appreciate their living experience. She notes in her abstract: 'the stories convey the catastrophic nature of a diagnosis of cancer, which leads to a painful, existential crisis and feelings of bewilderment, powerlessness and isolation' (p.496). If this was true for Iris she contains it well with her cheerful public face although, as I suggest, her surface signs suggest a deeper existential crisis. How does she cope? Benedict, Williams and Baron (1994) study the way women with breast cancer cope. They identify five themes:

- diversionary (staying physically busy and mentally occupied)
- spiritual (relinquishing the problem to a higher being)
- interpersonal (seeking reassurance and information through sharing and talking with others)
- hopeful (thinking positive)
- avoidance (blocking the experience from the mind).

I sense the first coping method is paramount for Iris…she makes her life so busy. Indeed she makes her illness a career in itself but, as she suggested when I first met her, she does not sleep well at night when her fears come to haunt her. She has no spiritual or higher purpose to life to sustain or comfort her. She attends day care and finds considerable support in being with other patients. She says she has developed strong relationships with fellow sufferers. She tries to be hopeful but it is a thin veneer and certainly she cannot avoid her uncertain future. Although my search of the literature has been minimal, it helps me frame Iris within a bigger picture.

Wednesday 4 October 2000

Iris

I arrive at 13.00. Iris is waiting for me. She looks well. We wait a few minutes while the doctor examines another patient in the treatment room. I ask Iris, 'How are you?'

She is distressed – 'I have a new lump on the other side. A few weeks ago I had a new lump on the mastectomy side removed…What does this new lump mean?'

She recaps the history of her breast cancer; the original nodes under her left armpit and then two years later the primary shows up in her left breast. She had a mastectomy and then new tumours along the scar line requiring a deep chest resection that removed two ribs. Then they discovered liver and bone metastases. However, her lungs are clear. She sighs. 'Small mercies… does this mean another deep resection?' I don't know. She regrets not having both breasts removed. 'If onlys' drift between us. As I listen attentively to her story I am reminded of Treya's journal in *Grace and Grit*:

> Oh hell I knew it. Those dammed little bumps, just like mosquito bites except they weren't red and didn't itch. They were just too odd and in too incriminating a location to be anything but cancer and I knew it. (Wilber 1991, p.105)

Treya, too, had regretted not having a mastectomy. The word 'recurrence' spun in her head as if she was standing on the edge of a crater staring into a deep void.

Iris tells me about the healer she sees. She feels he saved her life when she had had a liver obstruction. She is seeing him this evening and hopes he will be able to deal with the new tumour. I am curious about what he does but don't intrude. I ask her about her diet. She says she tries to be healthy. I ask if she has ever considered a homeopathic doctor? She says she has thought about it but balks at the cost, not much money to spare. The healer doesn't charge. I can see that people love her and give themselves to her, as I do willingly. She seeks hope to sustain her and is determined to find respite from this cancer's inexorable advance. The survival instinct is powerful, not just for herself, but for her two young children. I ask if her children understand what is happening to her? Yes, she talks to them and they understand. I feel the poignancy.

The room is free. Iris lies on the couch. She rejects the offered blanket as she feels warm enough. Hot flushes are now part of her life. She asks, 'Did you bring the meditation tape?' Damn, I have forgotten. A quick pang of guilt pierces me, but she shrugs it off – 'Next time?' I promise to remember. In fact I have forgotten to bring any music so I choose a relaxation CD from the day care selection. It's bland and lacks vibration. I feel it's important to play music that vibrates and ripples through people. Such music helps establish a healing environment.

I am amazed at how quickly Iris falls asleep and pleased that she can relax so totally, especially today with her news and new fears. Yet she did not react so fearfully as with her last lump (Lena, the day care leader, confirms this later), so perhaps her responses are shifting, as the disease becomes more a part of who she is.

Her heels are not so congested. Perhaps the reflexology is helping her to rid toxins from her body. Her liver area is still cold, pale and shiny. I sense the tumour there as I work the area, visualising the liver and blasting it with healing energy. Afterwards the liver area is warmer with more colour. I feel the energy has returned. I cannot detect the new tumour in her chest wall although I doubt my ability to read the signs well enough. We finish. She says she is so relaxed; that it's wonderful! It's good to get such positive feedback.

Off the cuff, I ask her about her bowels. She is constipated – probably as a side effect of morphine, and the co-danthrusate laxative doesn't work well. I give her a glass of water as after-care treatment and suggest she tries to drink more. I suggest replacing a cup of coffee with a glass of water. She smiles and says she will try. On a positive note she says she's sleeping better. We hug and arrange to meet next Wednesday.

On reflection I am conscious of the unpredictable and shifting nature of Iris's disease trajectory causing fluctuations in her mood and optimism. It is a roller coaster which I am beginning to understand and ride so I can be available to her.

Wednesday 11 October 2000

Iris

Iris greets me with her usual warm smile. I ask her if the reflexology has helped? She says she feels more relaxed, reflected in the way she has accepted the news of her new breast lump. She again says she's sleeping better. I ask her about her pain – 'Is it any better in the evening?' She feels it has been. She seems surprised as if she hadn't thought about that.

Since she has upped her co-danthrusate to double dosage her bowels are working better. Perhaps the reflexology has helped. I ask about her appetite – 'I'm putting on weight!' She laughs – 'I need to go on a diet!' She has a sore gum.

I have remembered the meditation music – 'Peace of mind' CD produced by Brahma Kumaris. Her heels are less congested. She says she's not so full of emotion now. She quickly goes to sleep. As I work on her feet I pay more attention to her shoulder and liver areas. Her liver area is pinker, less clammy and cold…it feels better. I work carefully on the bowel, visualising moving the faeces along the bowel. Afterwards, Iris says she was so relaxed. She feels marvellous. She says, 'I felt the music in my sleep. It was very good.'

I was very conscious of the music, especially the track about forgiveness: 'Imagine you have been told you do not have long for this world.' Iris hadn't picked up on this lyric.

Iris and I have now met for four sessions. We have moved into a sacred space where healing becomes possible. The word 'sacred' may seem rather pretentious but it is a word to capture the sense of healing offered by energy therapies such as reflexology. Healing, in this sense, is not 'cure' in the traditional medical model but bringing the person into right or balanced relationship with his or her own body so healing is possible (Quinn 1992). The practitioner is the healing space.

Sacred reflects the shift of consciousness to another creative level between the therapist and patient. In this space I harmonise my own being with Iris with the intention of helping her ease suffering; to loosen the fear that binds her. Sleeping better is a good marker.

Wednesday 18 October 2000

Iris

Iris's huge smile greets me. She is so grateful for these treatments. Her gratitude is humbling. She has had a couple of dark days. Behind the smile she reveals her vulnerability. I imagine her effort to keep her happy mask in place. However, she has been sleeping well although disturbed by a dream that has remained with her, haunting her. In the dream there was a serpent after her. She asks, 'What can it mean?' I give the question back to her and ask her what she thinks it means. She is uncertain but feels it is unpleasant. I think of the serpent as death stalking her but I cannot tell her this. She says her pain is barely controlled…she still needs the breakthrough sevredol in the evenings although she takes it reluctantly because she interprets any worsening of her symptoms as signs of her downward spiral. I feel she plays down the worsening of the pain.

Her feet are warm, more energy than before although her heels are again congested. Her emotions are like a roller coaster. The reflexology is slow and rhythmic. I am in tune and it feels good. Iris is quickly asleep. She is woken once by her mobile phone…she knew it was her father as she had planned to meet him at 13.30. It's nearly 14.00. I finish the treatment with Reiki and visualise her bathed in a soft light. My compassion wraps her in gossamer threads. Afterwards she feels very relaxed and energised. I suggest she use lavender essential oil in her burner/pillow/bath to help her sleep and relax, with some bergamot to ease her anxiety.

My conversations with patients are very different in my therapist role than as a nurse. Of course I am a nurse but being a therapist has expanded my sense of being with patients. Therapy opens up spaces to explore deeper aspects of the patient's self. I feel I develop a more intimate relationship, perhaps through using relaxation and physical touch but perhaps most significantly by the conscious use of myself as a healing space. It feels as if I am metaphorically touching her soul with my own. This sense of intimacy is reflected in my use of words: 'My compassion wraps her in gossamer threads' an effort to capture the essence and significance of compassion that is absolutely fundamental to all healing work.

Perhaps compassion is the greatest gift I can give someone. Perhaps compassion is the greatest gift I can give myself.

Wednesday 8 November 2000

Iris

I have not met Iris for three weeks due to her various hospital appointments. Iris's disease management is a full-time career. Today she is very upset. Her little son had asked her if she would be a grandmum – she had tried to answer around the question but confessed it was unlikely she would make being a grandmum. On a positive note, she is pleased that her scan results showed her liver is stable. Crumbs of comfort, or so it felt.

We talk about living in the moment as a way of releasing some of the deep fear she feels when she thinks about the future; to put some distance between herself and her fear so she can witness her fear rather than let it sweep over her like storm clouds. This is not to deny the future but to put it into some perspective...to treat each new day as precious. She listens carefully and says, 'I'll try.' I wonder how I would respond if I was her. Could I put such ideas into practice?

I give Iris Therapeutic Touch[2](TT) to help ease the tense muscles in her neck and shoulders and ease the shoulder pain. She shrugs her shoulders and says they feel much easier.

---

2   The practice of Therapeutic Touch involves the use of oneself (that is one's own localised energy field) as an instrument to help rebalance areas within the patient's field that have become obstructed and disordered by disease. The practitioner must establish the intent to become a calm, focused conduit for the universal life energy and to direct to the patient (Macrae 1996, pp.18–19).

I am conscious of not absorbing Iris's suffering as my own, especially when she shares such poignant moments as her son's question. Yet I wonder to what extent I do absorb her suffering? How would I know? I certainly felt 'light' after treating Iris, reflecting how therapy is energising and joyful and helps to ease my own suffering.

Wednesday 15 November 2000

Iris

Lena gives me feedback that Iris had been in good spirits on Friday; that the reflexology had lightened her dark mood. I felt energised to get such positive feedback. Iris arrives and says she's more relaxed today. Her recent bone scan results showed no worsening bone disease (since her previous scan six months ago). She is holding her own.

After the reflexology, Iris tells me about finding her first lymph node lump under her left armpit. This was removed and she was told 'all clear'. Not until a year later did she find the breast lump. She again talks about her regret at not having a double mastectomy, but I gently confront her – she says that now with hindsight but at the time she made the choice that seemed right. Again Treya's words from *Grace and Grit* ring in my ears: 'A mastectomy seemed the only choice. I was too frightened to take the risk of leaving more of those grade four cancer cells inside my body' (p.108).

In the meantime, Iris has cashed in an endowment policy because they were short of money, but then she couldn't get insurance which means the house will not be paid off when she dies…a burden for her husband. Worry layered on worry, fear feeding itself.

To distract herself she fills her days with activity. When we discuss her appointment time next week she wonders if I could fit it around her Pilates – 'I need to work at keeping fit.' I suggest a walk in the woods. She likes this idea because that wouldn't cost her anything whereas Pilates is expensive.

Her pain is much the same although she felt very calm after the TT last week. No pain at the moment in her shoulder, just some twinges. She thinks the TT solved that: 'After the treatment last week I didn't need the sevredol in the evening…so I think it really helped. I've upped my laxatives again, though.'

I suggest she ask Stella, the therapist in day care, to give her a bowel massage next Friday.

Each time I meet Iris she reveals more and more about herself, reflecting the way knowing someone unfolds over time. It makes me realise how superficial most caring relationships really are. Yet knowing her is not simply seeing her as an object or a pattern to be appreciated. Knowing her is intersubjective – I know her in an embodied sense, not easily expressed in words. I am not, at least deliberately, trying to mystify our relationship but perhaps trying to convey the sense of mystery in knowing someone within a healing relationship.

The therapies I offer complement each other besides complementing Iris's conventional medical treatment. Reiki is a calm way to finish a reflexology treatment while Therapeutic Touch helps with more specific physical symptoms besides helping the person to feel very calm – a deeper sense of being than relaxation. I often supplement reflexology with aromatherapy by adding essential oils to my reflex base cream or advise on oils for people to use based on their specific healing properties.

Wednesday 29 November 2000

Iris

Iris is radiant in a red top. She says she has been feeling good, too good almost, considering what goes on inside her. She says how much focusing on the 'now' has helped, and that each new day is a new joy. Yet there are moments when she is caught off-guard when she thinks of the future as a dark shadow that sweeps across her brow. I encourage her not to resist these thoughts but to witness them and consider what messages they bring. She says she is sleeping well now, although her persistent constipation remains unresolved. During the treatment I note that her transverse bowel feels hot. She says her faeces have been a 'bit squidgy' with all the co-danthrusate. I suggest that movicol might be a better solution. I suggest she ask the day care nurses to ring her GP and change the prescription.

Iris is moving. Perhaps her relationship with me is only a respite from the storm that batters her. But it may also be something deeper, shifting who she is inside towards a greater harmony with herself. We can only dwell in the moment. My work as a therapist is not simply as a technician to give reflexology or TT but to touch and help her touch her soul. The caring dance; to move across the floor in tune with the music, to feel held by someone who knows how to dance well and to feel safe in case she should trip.

Iris's story resonates with the following poem by Rumi:

> I was going to tell you my story
> But waves of pain drowned my voice.
> I tried to utter a word but my thoughts
> Became fragile and shattered like glass.
> Even the largest ship can capsize
> In the stormy sea of love;
> Let alone my feeble boat
> Which shattered to pieces leaving me nothing
> But a strip of wood to hold onto.
> Small and helpless, rising to heaven
> On one wave of love and falling with the next
> I don't even know if I am or I am not.
> When I think I am, I find myself worthless,
> When I think I am not, I find my value.
> Like my thoughts, I die and rise again each day
> So how can I doubt the resurrection?
> Tired of hunting for love in this world,
> At last I surrender in the valley of love
> And become free.
>
> (Rumi 2001)

Wednesday 17 January 2001

Iris

A new year. Iris is anxious that we had lost contact as we hadn't met for three weeks. Christmas was for the kids an emotional time – her daughter had asked her if this would be their last Christmas together. Another emotional bombshell. Yet Iris feels strong and took her daughter's comment in her stride. She says how much it helps her to talk about these things with me; that I give her a positive spiritual focus but don't push it. It is balance – Iris learning how to control the flow. Going with the flow is not passive but a skilful weaving within the tumultuous currents of life that threaten to crash against the rocks. In being available to Iris I must give her space when it could be so easy to crowd her with solutions in my need to fix her problems.

Thursday 1 February 2001

Iris

Iris shares her positive news from the liver scan: like her recent bone scan there is no evidence of disease progression. She is waiting for more radiotherapy for repeated chest wall lumps which makes me think again of Treya's words in *Grace and Grit* which portray both a beautiful and horrific perspective on her journey thorough breast cancer; horrific in the unfolding tragedy and yet beautiful in her realisation of self. It helps me understand what Iris is experiencing. That life-threatening illness can be a time for significant growth is an important message for Iris if she can step outside her fear. She tells me about her son's dream of a burglar coming to take his mother away. Premonition dreams – again we feel the poignancy of such remarks.

My thumb trips over her liver – it is cold and pale. As before, I visualise a soft healing light bathe the cells. I trip across her chest wall and imagine the lumps dissolving. I flood her body with chakra colours (see p.232) as I trip along her spine. Visualisation adds another dimension to reflexology practice and has been shown to facilitate healing (Simonton, Matthews-Simonton and Creighton 1978). I would ask Iris to visualise the cancer cells dying and the healthy cells regenerating but she is always asleep!

Maisey

Leaving Iris, I visit the inpatient unit and ask whether any of the patients would like some complementary therapy? Brenda, one of the senior staff nurses, suggests Maisey might like me to visit her. Maisey is 30 years old and has breast cancer with widespread secondary bone spread. She has been admitted for symptom management. She has a brain scan booked for Friday because of her persistent headaches on top of the constant headache she suffers from due to temporal bone invasion. She has had a recent course of radiotherapy to reduce this pain but despite medication it persists. The question being asked – does she have cerebral secondaries?

I pop my head around her door. Her moon-shaped steroid face greets me. She looks so small sitting in her chair. Her mother is sitting by her bedside there with Maisey's young daughter. I greet her and inform her that I am a complementary therapist. She asks, 'What can you do?' She is eager. I display my wares and she says she would love some reflexology. 'Kay used to do it…she used to visit me at my home when I was having chemotherapy. She could pinpoint the pain I had and know I was constipated.'

It is nearly 13.30 and Maisey is still waiting for her lunch. It is delayed because of the drugs she is having. I suggest I visit her at 14.00 and that in the meantime I'll find her lunch. She agrees, smiling. Maisey has a huge appetite, a consequence of her steroid medication. As Maisey tucks into her lunch I read her notes and plot the trajectory of her disease and symptom management. She is prescribed anti-emetics and laxatives for the nausea and constipation that typically accompany morphine prescription. She scores 6 on the pain chart, suggesting a high level of pain.

It is 14.20 before she is ready. She says, 'You're eager.' I smile at the irony, but she does makes me wonder whether I am offering the treatment for my benefit rather than for her. It's good to check out my motivation. People should love what they do, especially healing work, because without love compassion could not exist. I feel slightly anxious because time has slipped away and I have another appointment booked for 14.30. I will be late but I have committed myself to Maisey's reflexology. I shall have to modify it. Maisey raises her feet on the electric chair. I kneel on the floor. She has small feet. Good colour. I place my hands on her feet to tune into her wavelength. I suggest she closes her eyes and concentrate on her breathing but she starts talking, telling me her illness story. The cancer was diagnosed in February last year. She had a lumpectomy followed by radiotherapy. Then it spread to her bones this year. She had chemotherapy. She says her headache is constant but the nausea has stopped. She sleeps okay. She tells me about her therapeutic abortion with the twins and her husband having an affair when she was having chemotherapy. She has now divorced him. Amy, her daughter, is five years old, the same name as my eldest daughter. A level of connection. I say it must be hard when things are so uncertain. She picks up the cue and says, 'Yes – Amy knows about the cancer. If I have two years then Amy will be seven…it will be enough.'

I am intrigued at the way she has struck a bargain. Yet two years is grossly optimistic. I have been told Maisey is very anxious but I do not sense it. If true, she contains it well. I prefer to make my own appreciation rather than accept on face value what other staff say. She says that with her home life she doesn't have time to reflect on her illness and her approaching death. Yet she feels its presence hovering. I gaze at this remarkable woman and think to myself, 'It must be extraordinarily tough to contemplate your dying when you have a five-year-old daughter.'

I listen carefully to Maisey's story and when she reaches a pause I insist she tries to relax…no more words…to surrender and flow into the treatment. She quietens. My hands melt into her body. I become one with her body. We are connected and I work away. I gingerly feel my way along her lymph system. My cautious thumb or finger treads along the pathways of her body carefully sensing the cancer's presence. I say, 'Your constipation is clear.' She says, 'Yes.' She looks at me with surprise and recognition. I have passed the 'Kay test'. I am always pleased to give people this type of feedback because it increases their confidence with the treatment.

I suggest to Maisey that she drink more water. Another knowing look. She says she knows she should but has been neglectful. I offer to see her again if she would like that? If so, to send me a message via the nursing staff. She said the treatment was deeply relaxing. She is like a cat, a little drowsy but content. I think of the past hour as an interlude for her to find some stillness and balance.

Afterwards in day care I tell Lena about Maisey's 'two years left'. Lena says, 'Once Maisey had been told that she had three months to live. She was very angry about that.' We speculate how long – how can we know…yet better to say two years and give her some hope, whereas less time would distress her. Lena says that Maisey has been prescribed an anti-depressant to take the edge off her despair.

Later, writing my journal, I ask myself, 'Who is Maisey and what meaning does she give to being in the hospice at this time?' I had expected to pick up the signs of anxiety but I hadn't. I searched her face for tears but they were not present. Instead I found a smile, thankful that I had stepped into her life with the offer of reflexology, which she had positively experienced before. The denial of her immediate death is her salvation; clinging to the illusion that she has two years with her daughter is her life raft. Nothing is predictable. Each moment must be approached with openness and curiosity to whatever unfolds.

Sunday 4 March 2001

Mary

The hospice phones – can I work a late shift today? I agree and arrive by 16.00. Brenda, the senior nurse, gives me a report of the patients. Mary had become agitated when she had haemorrhaged from her buccal tumour earlier in the day. She had been semi-conscious then. The staff feared she would die. Topical adrenaline had stemmed the blood flow and midazolam had sedated her. Now she has a midazolam pump going, keeping her heavily sedated. Her social death is complete. Now we all wait for her physical body death.

Mary is sequestrated in a hospice side room. I have not met her before and feel slightly shocked but fascinated to see her fungating tumour protruding from her mouth. It occludes her whole mouth. Just from the very corners of her mouth, she sucks in air through a tiny gap like a fish's gills. Her nostrils are flared and flattened. Her breath carries a *very unpleasant* odour. Polite words that mask the offensive. Mary's husband David sits by her bed. He is struggling to stay with Mary and the 'monster' – as they have called it. He recoils from the smell even as he bears it with equanimity. He is apologetic, reflecting his embarrassment that we have to put up with this stench. He is struggling with ambivalent feelings of disgust and distress, feeling helpless as his wife dies. Reluctant tears leak from his eyes. Reluctant, because he tries to contain the tears in his effort to be brave. But he is torn apart. The text of his life has gone wrong. Mixed emotions playing out along his surface. Death should be peaceful and it's not. It is violent and repulsive.

Lawton (2000) discusses the idea that people whose bodies had become unbounded were sequestrated within hospices, no longer able to be tolerated within the bounds of home and society. The hospice fabric, which includes myself, is the new boundary that contains. In the single room Mary is contained although the stench seeps out, refusing to be contained. The stench drifts along the corridors. I had noticed it when I arrived. I had thought it must be very unpleasant for other patients, relatives and for the staff although no one comments in a negative way. Fallowfield (1993) notes that one of the symptoms which isolates patients is odour:

> The trauma of witnessing your own body rotting before your eyes, as happens with fungating tumours, is bad enough; having to live constantly with the smell and to see the disgust on the face of others is almost too awful for most of us to contemplate. (p.196)

Knowing this, we all mask our disgust. Sitting with Mary, she is apparently impervious to my presence. But is she? She is unable to make eye contact with me even though her left eye remains open. I was informed that Mary had been very distressed by the monster's growth. Now her breathing is compromised, her mouth forced open. It is a grotesque posture, undignified. I try to imagine what she felt. No wonder she was agitated. Gazing at her, I wonder, 'What does she think between the pulse of the midazolam pump?' I sense she knows she is dying. I also sense that she needs to comfort David as he suffers at her bedside even through the midazolam mist.

David is encouraged by Brenda to take time out. He apologises to me for not staying, as if he is deserting Mary. I say some fresh air would be good. I feel it is important for us both to be authentic and not pretend about the stench and his distress at his wife's dying. A knowing smile. More a grimace. David goes.

I sit with Mary, gently massaging her hand with a drop or two of the lemon grass and orange oil mix that another complementary therapist had mixed for the aroma stone last Friday. It is now Sunday and the mix is clearly ineffectual at neutralising the stench. In response, I set up a second aroma stone with a stronger mix. Gradually the two odours clash; the stench of Mary's tumour breath and the sweet citrus oils, swirling as if competing for dominance. Sitting close to Mary the smell is inescapable. Lawton's (2000) words come to mind:

> I was always struck by the smell when I first walked into the [hospice] building. It was not the typical antiseptic smell one would expect of a hospital setting; it was more pungent and nauseating: a combination of essential oils such as lemon and cinnamon, interlaced with the odour of vomit and excreta. Sometimes the smell was very strong, on other occasions it was much weaker; nonetheless, it was always there. (p.77)

My naivete is exposed in a moment of recognition – one smell does not neutralise the other. They simply swirl together. The smell makes me feel heady. I feel slightly uncomfortable, that as an aromatherapist, I do not know enough about neutralising such strong smells.

After half an hour David returns. He sits next to me as I massage Mary's hand. I explain what we had done to combat the odour. Sensing his need I ask if he wanted to sit next to Mary. He says, 'Yes,' so I move away.

Later, Mary again becomes restless. David has gone home for a while so I sit with her. The time is 20.10. We are alone. Mary's breathing pattern is abnormal. She has periods of apneoa followed by a short burst of inhalations gathering in strength until subsiding. I hear her muted anguished cry through the violence of her breathing. The stench hovers over and about us. I turn my head to escape the frontal force of the smell. Taking Mary's hand I inform her I am going to sit with her while David has a break. I ask her, 'How best can I be with you, Mary?' I catch her open left eye and smile at her. Is there a glimmer of recognition beneath the subdued consciousness? No giveaway signs. How can I best respond? I am uncertain and feel the anxiety that uncertainty brings. I am conscious of my frayed edge, of the yarn unwinding, of chaos even as I seek to impose order. Yet there is no thread to pick up. We are strangers. We had woven no pattern. In this dark void we must weave a pattern even at this late hour when the light is low. We must learn to dance well together in the gathering gloom beneath death's shadow to reveal the light. Dance the caring dance. She must trust me to do this for her. I am a light for her to see in her darkness. We are two souls bobbing on a perilous sea.

> As a nurse, I maybe just sit, or just breathe with the person, or use therapeutic touch. Basically, I'm trying to read what the person is saying on so many subtle levels of their being, whether it's in the intonation of their voice, their nuances, or their breathing pattern. Sometimes that's all you need to hear. (Longaker 1997, p.63)

Holding her hand I tell her that she can let go of her fear, that there is no need to struggle, that she can melt into the light and find peace. Why do I say these words? I sense her struggle and anguish. My role is to help ease her passage into another dimension. I sense my Buddhist beliefs influencing me – and here I am in this place putting into practice beliefs which I have never really put into practice before. On one hand life is an unfolding journey of opportunity, yet on the other hand, is it ethical to impose such beliefs and see Mary as 'an opportunity'? Perhaps I should go to 'dancing school', but how do you teach someone to use himself in a spiritual way? I have read the texts and now I must apply and reflect on the experience. In Mary's suffering I dwell and seek a way for both of us to move on in harmony.

I decide to sing her 'Deep peace', a mantra taken from Donovan's album 'Sutras' (American recordings 1996), as if helping a restless child to relax and sleep. Suffering child, rest your soul in my bosom and let the deep peace of the running wave, the flowing air and the quiet earth flow into you. The words nurture my compassion and focus my intention to help Mary find peace at this momentous moment in her life as death's tendrils move to embrace her. Using Reiki touch, I hold Mary at this time of transition, that she is not alone but part of a greater whole. I sense that being held must be essentially comforting when boundaries are melting. Again, the idea of containment. I then work with Mary using Therapeutic Touch – sitting in my chair using my left hand in wave like motions sweeping from her crown down to her legs. My right hand continues to hold her hand. I feel the presence of her primary glottis cancer in the etheric energy field, the energy field closest to the body where the physical body can be sensed. Its presence is strong like a magnet perhaps sensing its host is dying and so must die itself. The energy field is hot so, as I continue to sing and hum 'Deep peace', I visualise a blue waterfall to cool her. I feel at peace with her. I have tuned into her wavelength and flow easily with her, and yet shifting her wavelength to ease the tension. I know this because her breathing has settled into an easy normal rhythm. The stench becomes less offensive until I can barely discern it.

Another nurse comes into the room and, without a word, lifts the bedclothes and touches Mary's legs. Mary simply disembodied. The nurse exclaims her surprise that Mary's legs had become warm when they had been so cold two hours before. Mary's peripheries had shut down. Now her body is balanced. The nurse asks if I want relief but I decline. I need to stay with Mary now.

22.00 – the night shift is taking over. It was Yvonne who came in. I told her about the Therapeutic Touch but felt uneasy about saying this – would she appreciate it? She accepts what I say although I do not disclose my Reiki or singing 'Deep peace'.

Mary is very peaceful. She seems to be sleeping. David has not returned so I cannot say goodbye to him. I wish Mary a good journey and with a tinge of regret I leave her. That night my thoughts turn to Mary and I include her in my prayers and imagine she is being held by her God.

On Tuesday I return to the hospice. Mary had died at 13.00 on Monday after another haemorrhage. I share my thoughts about managing the odour with Leona, one of the nurses. Talking it through, I feel my embodied tension lift. I feel neither sadness nor elation, just a sense of tension. Afterwards I feel lighter. I realise I had absorbed some of Mary's and David's suffering as my own. I know I cannot resist suffering but must flow with it. Then suffering becomes the opportunity to grow, or as Joko Beck (1989) cites from the Shoyo Roku, 'On the withered tree, a flower blooms' (p.34).

Marie de Hennezel (1998) notes the impact that one caring assistant has with patients at night:

> Creating this atmosphere of warmth and calm around a sick person who is in torment is unquestionably the most beneficial thing one can do for him or her. Chantal has known this for a long time. The doctors have always been astonished to note so few tranquillisers or anxiety-reducing drugs are given on nights when she's on duty. She just prefers to give them a massage or tell them a story, or simply let them talk while she sits quietly at their bedside. (p.11)

Reflecting on these words, I had massaged Mary and sung her songs while sitting with her. It was no effort once I had given myself permission to respond in this way. Why should doctors be astonished? Is such an approach beyond their realms of possibility? I think so, and even for most nurses at the hospice, although patients like Mary, who present in such a distressing and dramatic way, are singled out for special attention to bound or contain them. Yet, I wonder if the staff are really paying attention to their own sense of horror as Mary invades their boundaries. Rosemary, one of the 'early shift' nurses, says she will not let the nursing student coming tomorrow see Mary. It would not be fair.

Tuesday 13 February 2001

Mary

A week later I share my experience of being with Mary with the students on the post-registered 'Care of the dying' course that I teach at the university. I ask them, 'Did Mary die well? Would people glance back and say that was a good death?' I quote Lawton (2000):

> ...a good death, where I conducted fieldwork, was considered by staff to be one in which the patient 'drifted off peacefully', which in practice meant that the patient died free of pain and any apparent distress. (p.119)

I inform them that syringe drivers pumped diamorphine and midazolam so Mary was pain free and her apparent distress masked. Being masked allowed David to mask his own distress. The students generally feel that perhaps Mary died as well as could be hoped, yet I challenge them – 'What difference did my responses have on the quality of her death?' I invade the silence this question has created by saying I had chanted a Buddhist mantra while giving Therapeutic Touch. The group's reaction was mixed, uncertain. Some doubt – was I imposing my Buddhist beliefs on Mary? Did I know Mary's religious beliefs and should I respect them? I confess I had not known her religious beliefs. They were not disclosed to me, perhaps suggesting that her religious beliefs were not significant within her dying journey. Yet neither had I asked. I am inclined to side with Lawton's (2000) belief that religion does not figure significantly across the landscape of our increasingly secular society, even at death, even within the hospice. I said my response to Mary intuitively felt right at the time; that my response was essentially spiritual which undercut any religious dogma.

More questions: How did I know the Therapeutic Touch had reduced the pungent odour? The word 'stench' is avoided. Indeed, I detect a muted hostile reception to that word as if it offends across a sanitised landscape. The word 'stench' unbounded and needs to be contained. Rather, had I not become acclimatised to the smell? I rather think not. We dwell in Schön's (1987) metaphoric swampy lowlands of professional practice where there are no easy or clear-cut answers. Such is the indeterminate and complex nature of professional practice such as nursing where each situation is unique, never been experienced before. We may have an idea of how best to respond because of past experience or reading some research but, as Schön notes, applying the abstract to the particular situation must always be uncertain and requires careful interpretation. Research can never be more than a source of information – that is if appropriate research exists to begin with. If not then we fall back on some embodied sense of knowing surfaced in our intuition.

I move the students to higher ground to explore using essential oils to neutralise pungent odour. But I have no answers ready at hand. I say I must do some homework.

Davis (1999) considers bergamot the 'most effective deodorising essential oil although lavender, neroli and juniper can be used' (p.97). I check the spiritual profiles of these oils in Worwood's book, *The Fragrant Heavens*, whose work has inspired me to use essential oils with clients on a more subtle or spiritual plane. The descriptions of these oils in the spiritual plane in the context of my being present with Mary are very revealing:

Bergamot

Bergamot works well …the light field…is closest to the body. It lightens the shadows of the mind. We may cry inside, our hearts aching, but bergamot will lighten the heart and dispel self-criticism and blame. (p.194)

Lavender

When deep sadness covers the spirit like a suffocating blanket, lavender gently lifts the weight. When the inner tears fall, lavender wipes them away. And for those with worries that trouble the spirit, lavender lifts the veil of despair. (p.225)

Neroli

Neroli allows the reflection which can throw light on the wounds which tie us to old patterns of relating. As truth is revealed, the self emerges into wholeness and unconditional love, stirring the spirit in ways that can be both unexpected and liberating. Then the spirit can really soar. (p.235)

Juniper

Juniper's message is to complete the task and learn the lessons. Meanwhile it clears obstructions on our pathway to the divine spirit. (p.223)

These descriptions are a revelation; each description a tune to dance to. Appreciating the spiritual potential of these essential oils in working with someone like Mary is awesome. Yet, when I share these descriptions with the group the following week, they are sceptical: 'Do these descriptions have any truth factor?' I sense the creeping insidious hand of reason demands its fill. I ask myself, 'Does Worwood have access to knowledge on a higher plane of consciousness or are the descriptions mere flights of fancy?' Yet whatever the truth, these descriptions create a powerful sense of intention in working with Mary: 'Bergamot lightens the shadows of the mind – Neroli enables the spirit to soar – Lavender gently lifts the weight – Juniper clears obstructions to the divine spirit...'

Have we no faith? Perhaps I should burn juniper in the classroom each day. Reflecting more deeply, I sense the stench was a reflection of Mary's deep fear, a vibration of her distorted energy field. My work was to balance Mary's energy field into a more balanced state by tuning into her wavelength.[3] As essential oils are vibrational they would enhance my effort to help Mary harmonise her energy patterns. As Gerber (1988) notes:

> ...we will eventually discover that consciousness itself is a kind of energy that is integrally related to cellular expression of the physical body. As such, consciousness participates in the continuous creation of either health or illness. (p.44)

I had managed to ease Mary's suffering and ipso facto reduce the stench without the use of these oils. I wonder how much better I could have done it with the aid of different essential oils.

One of the students says that she and her colleagues, at the hospice where she works, were outraged that I had sung a Buddhist mantra. I had courted controversy. Indeed, I had anticipated a reaction so I am prepared. I play 'Deep peace'. She exclaims, 'That's not a Buddhist mantra but a song. In fact it's a song I sing in church!' She felt relieved, if not a little cheated. I had brought the situation back into normal limits. Reading the CD sleeve, the song is a traditional Gaelic song and not written by Donovan. I had assumed he had written the words as a reflection of his Buddhism. I reflect with the group how such words as 'Buddhist' and 'mantra' evoke strong reaction. The dogma of religion lay thick in the air leaving an ugly trace.

I ask the group to consider how they might spend two hours alone with a dying patient. What sort of skill is this? How should one spend the time for

---

3   My thanks to Victoria Cooper-Roberts for developing this insight after presenting this paper at the Royal College of Nursing Complementary Therapies Annual Conference, 2002.

the best? I sense that in the mundane nature of this action lies the sacred key to the meaning of palliative care. Again, we have no answers.

I fantasise: 'Brenda – how shall I spend this time with Mary?'

Brenda: 'Just stay with her.'

Chris: 'How do I do that?'

Brenda: 'The best way you can.'

And, indeed, that is true. But what does 'the best' mean? I had busied myself with doing activity, yet could I not have simply sat with her? Christine Longaker (1998) suggests we can connect with the cognitively impaired person through levels of communication that can reach the deeper awareness of the person through:

- touch
- eye contact
- humour and play
- music or singing
- offering prayers or spiritual practice, for example meditations, essential Phowa and tonglen practices
- sending love and positive thoughts
- resolving our side of any unfinished business.

The idea of reaching the deeper part of Mary was my motivation, which simply sitting there would not have reached. Longaker is a Buddhist, and I am intrigued by Buddhist spiritual practice through meditations, essential Phowa and tonglen practices. These are exciting possibilities to explore, although I sense my concern about appearing foolish and my lack of confidence to follow my heart.

Another student challenges me why *I* had spent this time with Mary? Why not one of the other staff who knew her better? I confess I had not considered the significance of whether a nurse who knew Mary should be with her, rather than myself whom she had not met before. As Mayeroff (1971) says, 'Caring assumes continuity, and it is impossible if the other is continually being replaced' (p.44).

Did my not knowing Mary diminish her sense of being cared for? I had accepted Brenda's request for me to stay with Mary in good faith. Did Brenda 'pick' on me because I was the bank nurse and sitting with unresponsive patients does not seem popular work with nurses, especially trained nurses, at the hospice? Brenda had felt it was important that someone be with Mary, not just to observe for haemorrhage, but also to reassure Mary that she was not alone. I was happy to spend this time with her but maybe someone whom Mary had known, who she knew cared for her, would have been a better option? But would another nurse have responded 'spiritually'? Is spiritual care outside the mainstream of care? Can spiritual care be left to chance? Does it matter? Difficult questions but undoubtedly spiritual care is included with the rubric of holistic care, especially within the hospice setting. I ask the group what they think. They generally felt uncomfortable with responding to their patients' spiritual needs. The usual response was to refer to the appropriate religious person although some would sit and explore the meaning of life and death with patients if they directly asked them. My presence with Mary was caring simply unfolding…simply being with Mary on her journey. I am the ferryman. Mayeroff (1971) says:

> In a narrow sense, being with refers to a phase within the rhythm of caring, a phase of being with the other that is followed by, and may be contrasted with, a phase of relative detachment in which we scrutinize and reflect on experience in order to clarify our understanding and thus be more responsive. (p.56)

Rhythms of life and death unfolding. We who choose to work with the dying must become adept at finding pattern within the unfolding. No room for pity. Barely room for self-doubt. Singing 'Deep peace' set up a rhythm of caring that represented a boundary where Mary and I could meet. Co-creating wavelength where we could both journey and find deep peace. Such caring is amorphous, shape-shifting. How do we learn these things? Reflection opens a space to scrutinise, to scratch away at the surface to reveal the mysteries. As Mayeroff (1971) says:

> Caring enables me to be in-place in the world…My feeling being in-place is not entirely subjective, and it is not merely a feeling, for it expresses my actual involvements with others in the world. Place is not something I have, as if it were a possession. Rather I am in-place because of the way I relate to others. And place must be continually renewed and reaffirmed, it is not assured once and for all, for it is our response to the need of others to grow which gives us place. (p.69)

Florence Nightingale (1860) said that the nursing was concerned with bringing the person to the *right place* whereby nature could work its healing. The nurse is not simply the carrier – she is herself nature, that place, and hence needs to be *in-place*; not a physical place but a sacred place where healing becomes possible in the widest sense of enabling another to find peace. To quote Blackwolf and Gina Jones (1996), 'We must honour our journey to the secret places of self' (p.149).

Writing is self-affirming. I am more in place as a consequence. My being in-place is renewed. I have travelled in the shadow of death. It is not fearful. Indeed, I have grown; wiser, more compassionate, more skilled. For Cixous (1996) writing is reclaiming the (feminine) body, a body confiscated by the masculine, turned into an uncanny stranger on display. Reflection helps me not so much reclaim my feminine body, but to unfold it and integrate it with the masculine. Then I am more balanced and more able to give myself within the unfolding caring moment; with uncertainty but without the need to control, with vulnerability but without a fear of the unknown, with passion but without a narcissistic look for self-fulfilment. I resolve not to censor my breath and speech or be censored. I can wear my regalia with pride. Hear my cry across the sanitised wastelands where nurses perish for loss of caring. I might say I am less contained, which is perhaps an irony in contrast with Mary's experience and my role of contributing to her containment.

Writing Mary's story challenges me to reflect on the way I am writing the narrative. In particular, the work of Cixous (1996) has inspired me to confront the way I express myself in narrative form. Cixous urges me to be more in tune with my intuitive and caring self, to resist the harping voice of reason which threatens to break the rhythm of the caring dance by mocking intuition, by curtailing metaphor, by demanding that assumptions be justified, by denying feelings and perceptions as valid, and even by denying that caring is essentially a mystery story unfolding.

However, the rational form remains the favoured within nursing texts in spite of the emergence of narrative as a valid alternative representation (Wiltshire 1995). For example, one reviewer of this text when first submitted for consideration of publication[4] stated, 'The notion that the author is a light for Mary to see is of concern; there is no foundation for this proposition.' Yet the whole text is the foundation for this proposition. It may be true that certain assumptions are spiritual insights which are beyond reason. Or put another way, if a person treads a spiritual path and lives out their spiritual beliefs in practice, then it is inevitable that spiritual insights will result. Such is the evolutionary pathway towards enlightenment (Wilber 2000). This point raises the issue of validating 'spiritual' truth claims. I am conscious of

4   My story concerning Mary was written as a paper for publication and submitted to *Nursing Inquiry*. The paper was later published in the *International Journal for Human Caring*.

treading a fine line to express myself in acceptable narrative form, I must also be true to myself. Following my Buddhist beliefs, I strongly adhere to the idea of *right or perfect speech* (Sangharakshita 1990). As such, I always endeavour not to embellish or distort my reality, as much as I am vulnerable to self-distortion as anybody else.

Ben Okri's (1997) idea of *narrative as transgression* truly inspires the text. Transgression might be viewed as breaking out of my containment from a normative way of viewing narrative. To illuminate this point, the following text is my response to Okri's words taken from his book *A Way of Being Free* (pp.63–66).

Okri says: 'In storytelling there is always transgression, and in all art. Without transgression, without the red boundary, there is no danger, no risk, no frisson, no experiment, no discovery, no creativity.'

I respond:

> I tear at the boundaries that have contained me
> I experiment with my soul
> I create myself anew
> And in doing so move beyond
> Redrawing the boundary in the sand

Okri says: 'Without extending some hidden or visible frontier of the possible, without disturbing something of the incomplete order of things, there is no challenge.'

I respond:

> Redrawing the boundary in the sand
> My hand quivers with the challenge
> Feathers are ruffled
> Or do I simply imagine that?
> Order is only an illusion to quell the racing pulse

Okri says: 'Quietly, or dramatically, storytellers are reorganisers of accepted reality, dreamers of alternative histories, disturbers of deceitful sleep.'

I respond:

> Broken free from the cave
> The masks are ripped away
> To reveal a new possibility
> To dream another way
> To expose the lies that deceive.

Okri says: 'The transgression may appear to be perfectly innocent and blameless, and even singularly undramatic.'

I respond:

> The truth lies not in the dramatic but in the mundane
> The way we live the habitual,
> The way we are complacent.
> Have I been innocent and blameless or simply blind?
> Or worse, have I caused suffering?

Okri says: 'The transgression could take a more extreme form — that of saying something so true that it is shocking.'

I respond:

> Our masks are comfort zones
> For the reality is indeed sometimes shocking
> Beneath the insulation.

Okri says: 'Giving truth direct narrative expression is to give it a public explosion. The truth — Truth — SHRIEKS: it wakes up all the hidden bullies, the hidden policemen, and the incipient dictators and tyrants of the land.'

I respond:

> I sense the bully that lies in me
> That perhaps I project into others
> The ego pulls me this way and that
> A true tyrant
> The shriek is my cry across the wasteland
> Realisation is painful
> The pulling away of the mask

Okri says: 'The truth could simply be something that everyone sees and knows already, something that we all live with, sleep with, and wake up to, and die as a result of — the truth could be something so obvious and familiar, but which no one has uttered.'

I respond:

> The hospice is a nice place
> Full of nice people
> Nice is so sanitising
> So containing

Okri says: 'And while it lives, uncried out, it devours us, this unacceptable truth that we accept in silence.'

I respond:

> Give me the courage to find my voice
> To speak out
> Not to condemn
> But to take you by the hand
> To the stream of truth
> Where we can bathe our wounds.

Okri says: 'The truth can be our hidden selves turned monstrous (and visible in the mirror to us if only we look with the good eye and not the askew eye); or the truth could be the polluting bacteria of our secret desires (agendas), and all the realities and lies and all the consequences of our strange and unhappy actions that we spend all our time from and avoiding.'

I respond:

> The mirror of reflection…
> Can I bear the image?
> Can I reveal my own soul?
> Yet if I fail I lose myself
> And fail Mary.

Okri says: 'Transgression can also simply reside in creating a beautiful thing. Sometimes the creation of a beautiful thing in a broken age can be an affront to the living, a denial of their suffering.'

I respond:

> Mary, you are broken
> And in your suffering
> You turn your head away
> Let me gently hold you
> And feel such a beautiful flower bloom
> From your withered tree.

Okri says: 'The joy of transgressing beautifully, of taking readers to places they wouldn't willingly go, this joy of seducing or dragging readers in spite of themselves to places deep in them where wonders lurk besides terrors.'

I respond:

> The terror of death is transcended
> In the soft glow of spirit
> Do you feel the glow amidst the suffering?
> If I do transgress
> Then I do so with a smile at your side
> Not as spit in your eye
> I am a small boy
> Led in to a field of forgiveness.

Okri says: 'This delicate art of planting delayed repeated explosions and revelations in the reader's mind, and doing this while enchanting them – this is one of the mysterious joys of all.'

I respond:

> In writing and telling these words I find joy.
> Writing honours Mary and her struggle to die with dignity in the face of such adversity;
> That her dying and her death, just like her life, had meaning.

So, to return to the question: How do you spend time with a dying patient? The answers are tenuous, reflecting the mystery and unpredictability of such work, and the difficulty in justifying assumptions made. Without doubt, reflective writing is deeply subjective. I make assumptions that are not easy to justify because I cannot justify them in any rational sense. As Schön (1987) has suggested, I assume that my assumptions emerge from a tacit understanding, from a deep pool of embodied knowing from which intuition surfaces.

> And in her soft hum
> Her body swayed in rhythm with the dance
> As she gave way and let go
> Deeper inside she went
> Gathering pace
> Until she reached the clearing
> In the soft glow of her soul
> Where she could dance with her shadows and feel
> And weep Joy.

Wednesday 11 April 2001

Gus

Gus is a widower, an engineer by profession who had worked at a local firm for the last 20 years of his working life. Now 88 years old, he has long since retired. He is at the hospice for respite care while his daughter is on holiday. She returns next Wednesday. It has been planned that on her return Gus will be discharged into a nursing home because she feels that she can no longer manage caring for him. When discussed with him, he only agreed to go into sheltered accommodation but 'it is felt' he wouldn't cope.

In the shift report we are told he is 'grumpy' although less so overnight than he has been.

He is quiet, sitting in a corner. Tania, a staff nurse, and myself dispense his medications. He has several which he takes without any fuss; no complaints of any 'symptoms'. Tania goes off to bath another patient. As she departs she says, 'Ask Gus if he wants a bath and raise the issue of the nursing home with him.' She smiles as she says this. I sense a glint of mischief.

Gus has a paper on the bed table in front of him. I casually ask if there was anything interesting in the paper. He looks at me and throws it my way, and spits, 'Don't be sarcastic.' Shocked I recoil, caught off balance. This is more than being grumpy. I defend, 'I wasn't aware I was being sarcastic...I came over to ask you if you would like a bath?' He says, 'Yes...*and* I would like some peace.' The signs are crystal clear. I say, 'I'll leave you alone.' Caught on the hop, I can only retreat.

Shortly afterwards Tania finds me. 'There you are. Time for Gus's bath?' I go and ask him if he's ready. He agrees. He walks to the bathroom. The bath is nearly filled. I ask if he wants the jacuzzi? He snaps, 'That's why I want the bath.' He snaps again as we hoist him into the bath. Tania confronts him: 'I thought you weren't going to be grumpy?' He says he doesn't mean to be, and I can feel he has been put in his place. Tania has a parental nature when she chooses. Gus is reduced to a naughty boy. I feel slightly uncomfortable watching this performance and feel sorry for Gus. My own resistance to him melts.

Gus is safely in the bath. The jacuzzi whips up the water. Tania adds bath foam before she leaves us, a twinkle in her eye. He says that the bubbles do things below that he could barely remember. A wistful humour beneath the gloom. I ask, 'How long do you want?' He says five minutes but after two he's had enough...he's feeling cold. I wrap a towel around his shoulders and use the shower attachment to hose off the bath foam to be met with more complaints that the shower is cold. I had tested the water warmth before but just say, 'Let's get you out.'

Even with the towel wrapped round him he is still cold. I see the sacral sore. He says it's sore. I dress the sore and then struggle to help him get his TED stockings on. He agrees that they're too difficult for him. I note he has just finished his radiotherapy. He says yes, the treatment for the recurrence of his cancer of the oesophagus which was primarily diagnosed and treated seven years ago. He is fed up with the recurrence. He feels cheated it has come back and he has to have the debilitating treatment again. He feels tired and distressed. I suggest that he doesn't like being dependent on others for help to wash and dress? He looks at me wistfully – 'That's right.' I feel a connection and decide to mention the nursing home. 'I hear you are going to a nursing home?' He asks me what I am talking about. I sense his resistance. This is dangerous territory so I back off – 'Just something I thought I heard, maybe I was wrong.' Is this denial, anger or simply forgetting? He doesn't pursue the issue but I doubt myself – was that the right thing to do?

Back at his bed, he thanks me and apologises for being difficult. I resist a tug of pity. I imagine being Gus. Not much fun. Why should he be happy for us when he clearly isn't inside? He is in existential turmoil struggling to find any meaning in his life. The threat to his future, losing his home, being deserted by his daughter. He is not stupid, I suspect he knows well enough the conspiracy against him with the nursing home. But he doesn't want to go into a nursing home. He has dug his heels in and resists. However, his daughter is his main carer and we have to support her decision, as difficult as it is to override his right to be self-determining. Or do we? Given that our role as hospice carers is to help Gus and his daughter find the best solution for his future care, what might be the best decision and how might that decision be ethically justified? A tension or conflict of interests exists between the daughter and Gus. He had refused to countenance a nursing home. She says she cannot care for him any longer in his own home. He is happy to move into sheltered accommodation because he wants his independence. He fears a nursing home will take away his independence. He does not know that – he only assumes it. We could put pressure on the daughter and hope she caves in to her own guilt. But would she be resentful? Such ethical dilemmas are difficult to resolve in everyone's best interests. Gus is dependent on his daughter, which leaves him vulnerable. His voice is weak whereas his daughter's voice is powerful and uncompromising. The daughter's right to be self-determining is stronger than Gus's right. Knowing that Gus will resist and be upset, it has been decided not to tell him

that he will be discharged to the nursing home. It is hoped he will like it and decide to stay.

I put myself in Gus's shoes – I have cancer, I'm dependent, I'm tired, I'm also losing my home and being rejected by my daughter. The losses mount. No wonder Gus feels angry. It highlights the importance of knowing where Gus is coming from. With understanding it's easier to accommodate his anger and talk through these things with him. However, the nursing home issue is a minefield which I tread gingerly around.

Gus shaves himself with the electric razor. I fetch him some tea and he nods off. I tell Tania of my faux pas. She laughs. I like the way she laughs and shrugs it off. At lunch, Gus complains that the pork is wishy-washy and the sweet is too sweet. I say to him that I will sort it out, 'What food would you like?' Something he can mash. He is amenable…we can work together on this matter.

Beneath his grumpy exterior it's easy to forget he's just finished a course of radiotherapy and feels tired. Yet 'grumpy' is a half-affectionate label. I can think of worse. He knows Tania and I are talking about him so I go over and say we were talking about his sore. He says it's sore sitting here on his inflatable. I ask if he would like to lie on his bed? He says he's just got out of his bed but this time with no grumpiness. I say to let me know when he would like another turn on the bed, which he does some 20 minutes later. He's thankful for my help. He has asserted his independence and now he doesn't need to because he knows I respect him and am careful to let him hang on to the remnants of control. I feel for him, this small frail man. I also fear for him just a bit. Will he roll over and give up or will he resist? I can't tell. I like to think the latter even though his daughter struggles. But I suspect the forces will overwhelm and he will capitulate.

So why is Gus labelled grumpy? No matter how benign or half-affectionate such a label is, it does reflect the way we label people in negative terms who make us feel uncomfortable in some way. As Trexler (1996) notes, something about the person offends or transcends normal acceptable behaviour. Labelling is a coping mechanism. The patient is at fault, not ourselves. Gus gets this reputation and so we *naturally* come to see him as if he is grumpy. We are at risk reacting to the surface behaviour rather than explore the deeper issues that make him feel so angry and distressed. Gus is not popular and people tend to treat him like a naughty boy, as Tania did, or avoid him. And yet at such a momentous time of his life, giving up his home and having a reoccurrence of his cancer, he needs understanding and support. Gus offends because he breaks unwritten social rules about the way a 'good patient' should behave; he should be grateful, cooperative, pleasant, but he's not any of these things. And, as I discovered to my discomfort, it is not pleasant getting the sharp end of Gus's tongue.

When I shared this experience at a later date with students on the 'Care of the dying patient' course, I suddenly realised how I might have misread the paper incident. We take two 'popular' newspapers at the hospice, the Mirror and the Express. Gus had the Mirror. So when I asked, 'Is there anything interesting in the paper?' it might seem that this was sarcastic because the paper is so trivial.

His angry outburst prompted my apologetic flight into child mode. I feel sure his anger was not a personal attack but a reflection of his deeper angst. And yet, it created a breakdown in communication between us. Taking it personally I was no longer available to him. Tania's parental response reflected her own personality. She is parental, it is her nature. She does not tolerate fools easily. She responded from her own discomfort whereas I feel she could have stayed in adult mode, respecting Gus as a suffering person, and used a cathartic response to help him express and talk through his feelings. Yet Tania also saw Gus as suffering and so she also responded as a protective mother. Critical or protective mother; either way his adulthood is diminished. As a result he becomes more grumpy because people respond to him in ways that reinforce his dependence when he seeks control of what is happening to him.

On reflection, I could have asked Tania if treating Gus as if he was a naughty boy was okay? Too often health care practitioners expect (albeit unwittingly) that people (and here we might say patient as a 'reduced' person) should fit into the health care pattern. Indeed patients are anxious to fit into the health care pattern in their effort to cooperate and be accepted. All too often patients are labelled 'difficult' when this pattern fit is not accomplished successfully. Even in hospices.

Sometimes we need our colleagues to help us see aspects of ourselves that are uncaring. That is my responsibility to her and I failed because of a greater need to avoid conflict and maintain the illusion of a harmonious team. I am sure that if Tania was irked by something I had done she would tell me.

Transactional Analysis (Stewart and Joines 1987) is a helpful tool to pattern communication within any situation. It is based on the premise that people communicate from ego states; either child, adult or parent. The child ego is fundamentally irresponsible and seeks gratification. The child ego can be split into rebellious or conforming child. The adult ego reflects the age of reason, that people are essentially rational and responsible. The parent ego reflects an increased level of responsibility usually associated with cultural role patterns. Effective communication can take place whenever ego states are reciprocated; adult-adult, parent-child, parent-parent, child-child. When ego states are not reciprocated communication breaks down, for example parent-adult. The ideal communication pattern between nurses and patients and between staff is adult-adult, particularly in an ethical culture that respects patient autonomy and self-determination. However, that has not always been the case. Traditional medical ethics is based on the principles of doing good and avoiding harm whereby the patient surrenders his right to autonomy in return for parental guidance – 'doctor or nurse knows best'. When an 'adult' person becomes anxious they tend to flip into either parental or child ego states as a subconscious reaction to manage their anxiety.

Gus is the naughty boy having a tantrum. His behaviour rouses Tania's anxiety prompting her parental reaction. Gus shifts from being naughty child to hurt child and in response Tania shifts from critical to protective parent. Ideally, Tania would have continued to respond by giving Gus feedback about his behaviour and helping him shift from child to adult, or in other words taking responsibility for himself.

Gus's initial outburst towards me triggered my own hurt child response – with my friendly greeting being met with such hostility. To stay in adult mode no matter what is unfolding requires the ability to pay attention and manage self. In other words, to be mindful. Yet we are all too human and from time to time we lose the plot.

Saturday 14 April 2001

Tom

It is just before 7.30. A candle burns at the nurses' station for Tom who died yesterday. Martha, staff nurse, says it was bad for the daughter; the family and Tom did not anticipate that he would die so quickly. They had no time to make sense of what was happening to him or to prepare for his death. He was ripped away from the family leaving a deep tear. The nurses struggle because they had no time to know them and yet later this morning when the family come in to collect the death certificate we will nurse their despair.

The ritual of burning a candle when someone dies helps me to be aware of and honour that person even when I have not met the patient. It is a public representation of our openness towards death and adds a sacred quality to our work.

Jacqueline

Jacqueline's pale, round and friendly face attracts me. She is open and receptive to my morning greeting, 'Is there is anything you would like?' She says a coffee would be good. I get her coffee but then I need help to position her to drink it easily and safely as she is slightly disorganised and jerky.

Jacqueline has lung cancer with brain metastases. Later Sophie, one of the nurses, offers her a bath. Jacqueline is okay about me helping her but I sense a moment of doubt. I am a male nurse who needs to become a neutral object – simply 'a nurse'. In the bath Jacqueline talks about her own work as a nurse at the local hospital, about her dogs (best of breed at Crufts last year), about her cancer, the spread from slow-growing lung cancer to fast-growing brain cancer. When she came into the hospice she had severe headaches and nausea. We have responded successfully to her headaches using large doses of dexamethasone. As a consequence her face is round and puffy with red cheeks. She has a weakness to her right side that tilts her over. She has recently completed a course of radiotherapy for her brain metastases. I ask if the treatment went well. She says she doesn't know. She didn't ask. I sense her fear with potential bad news; that perhaps it is better to live with not knowing or uncertainty than with certainty and grasp the hope that uncertainty brings. I ask if she would have further radiotherapy. She says,

'No, they said it wasn't possible.' So perhaps she does know she is going to die but pushes that future reality away.

A pause between us before we move on to safer ground. I ask how Andrew, her husband, is coping. Jacqueline says, 'He does not talk about these things…losing the dogs is hard for him…he took them back to the breeder because the dogs on top of looking after me was too much. We've just one Rottweiler left, and she's got arthritis. We had four, three died about two years ago with infections. That was really difficult.'

Sophie returns to help. She says 'bad arm' when trying to manoeuvre Jacqueline's arm into her nightdress. Jacqueline confronts Sophie, 'Not my bad arm…' Perhaps working in a stroke unit has made Jacqueline careful about the use of negative words and their impact on patients. Sophie apologises for being so thoughtless.

Being sensitive to sexuality and body image are fundamental markers of respect. Working day in and day out it can be easy to take people for granted, resulting in insensitive and careless actions. Talking with Jacqueline reminds me just how difficult it is for people to face death with equanimity. They cling to uncertainty as some reprieve from a definite death sentence even as she knows deep within. I want to massage such fear and pull her into the now but we had only just met and we have no time to dwell together.

Gus revisited

Gus is still here, wrapped up in his corner. I cannot help thinking of my daughter's hamster in its cage.

The hamster is also old and temperamental. It does not like its precarious order interrupted, struggling to be comfortable, antagonistic to the kind hand, and being locked into its egocentrism, it cannot easily see the perspective of others. I ask him what time he would like a bath. He responds with some enthusiasm, 'Sooner the better!' I respond with alacrity, 'Okay, let's go now, shall we?' He walks easily to the bathroom. This time I have made sure the water is hotter than last week – 'Too hot?' 'No, it's fine.' We are brisker, more confident – less time to get cold. He spends longer enjoying the jacuzzi, again wrapped in bath foam. His sacral wound looks much better. The TED stockings slip on much easier. Afterwards, he flops onto his bed, tired after the bath. He takes his hairbrush but I sense the effort and offer. He accepts. I brush the few strands left. He says he will shave later. He closes his eyes to dismiss me. I go graciously with a smile on my face. I avoid talk about nursing homes. I trip along his surface but I feel that is enough.

This time, I am more confident with him. Perhaps that's why he responds more positively. Being more confident, I can empathise more with his plight. It is important that we acknowledge his suffering, that he is understood. He shouldn't have to apologise for being grumpy. Why should he? But today he wasn't grumpy – perhaps telling me that he is only grumpy when we get it wrong.

Pauline

Martha, a staff nurse, has prepared a bath for Pauline. But first she checks Pauline's bowels as she is prone to constipation because of her gastrostomy feeding, whereby she is fed directly into her stomach via a feeding (PEG) tube because of her swallowing difficulties due to her motor neurone disease (MND). Pauline is much better than when we first met on Wednesday. An emergency admission when it was feared that her MND might be terminal. She had had a chest infection, and was drowning and choking on her secretions. Her suffering was intense in her effort to breathe. All she could do was writhe across the bed. Diazepam had eased her agitation.

Pauline has an MND-associated dementia. She is 59 years old. Her mouth is often wide open which makes her seem like a child full of wonder. She is very responsive, loves attention, dearly cared for by her son. I am told she loves men, that she responds well to men. Certainly I feel accepted by her. It is a warm feeling, innocent and, as such, vulnerable, an unconditional acceptance and affection which is humbling.

As Martha suspects, Pauline is constipated. She inserts two suppositories while I hold her hand and gaze into her face. Her discomfort is spread across her face, a plaintive look…and then it's over and she is back to her all-embracing smile with her mouth wide open. I observe the dry and caked tongue and mucous at the back of her mouth. Mouth care beckoning after her bath. We leave her for the suppositories to work.

Pauline has her bath and is back at her bed when Philip, her son, arrives. He has a strong presence with short cropped hair, a large earring, very matter-of-fact, thankful. He is very open and deeply caring towards his mother. I suggest I do Pauline's mouth care after preparing a fresh tea-tree solution to help keep her mouth clean and infection-free. My effort is cautious and clumsy. Philip rescues me and suggests he does it. He says (almost protecting me) that his mother does not like this procedure. She has it done at least four times a day which he and the district nurses have done over the past six months. Philip goes deep within the mouth, scooping out the mucous, whispering reassuring words to his mother. I am strongly moved watching this performance. I wonder if I could do that for my mother.

Working with Philip helps me to adjust my role from being the expert nurse to supporting the family. Philip is competent, he knows how to care for his mother. He is the natural carer and continues his caring across the community-hospice boundary. More importantly, he needs to care, to express his love in physical care. I must have humility to accept his guidance. As Mayeroff (1971) says:

> The man who cares is genuinely humble in being ready and willing to learn more about the other and himself, and what caring involves. This includes learning from the one cared for. (p.30)

Maud

After lunch Sophie changes Maud's syringe driver. Maud suffers deeply knowing that she is dying. She does not want to know about it, she wants to be put to sleep away from it all. She says as much to Sophie. Maud has cancer of the head of pancreas. As a consequence she is deeply jaundiced and bloated. She has been single all her life, dedicated to her work as a hospital matron. She is surrounded by friends from her church, especially Judy, the female church minister, who brings Maud great comfort. Maud has a great faith yet she is very frightened. I wonder about this apparent paradox. After Sophie has established the new syringe driver she asks Maud if she would like me to stay with her. I am surprised when she says yes. I have felt clumsy with her, and that she would have felt that, but no. Sophie also suggests to Maud that I could massage her hands. Maud says that would be nice.

I am caught in a trap but also feel the challenge. We who purport to care cannot discriminate and only choose those patients we feel comfortable with. I ask Maud if she likes the smell of lavender – she says she does. I add a single drop of lavender to some grapeseed carrier oil. She says the smell 'is lovely'. I sit with her and massage her right hand in the quiet stillness of the afternoon. I notice Maud's flowers and ask which ones are her favourites – 'the white ones with the golden yellow hearts'. I notice a daily bible reading book on her locker – 'Shall I read today's reading?' She turns her head to look at me – 'Yes, please.'

Today is Easter Saturday – the words are concerned with the silence, the holiness of waiting. I read the words with the passion with which they were originally written, for in these words I sense Maud's own predicament, that now she is waiting and needs to be still. Her fear is to be silenced. I say these things to her and feel her tears well up but she holds onto them. I suggest I massage her left hand and she brings it across to me.

After about 20 more minutes I hear Pauline struggling with her breathing. I must go and help Pauline and yet it is so difficult to move away from Maud in this moment of stillness. Letting go, yet remaining in her heart. Have I planted a seed of love so she knows I am with her on her journey? I like to think so. Being with Maud in such a deliberate spiritual way was a scared moment between us. I felt anxious, but this anxiety melted when I read the first words of the daily reading. In that moment I felt such a stillness, as if in this act my own spirituality was bursting forth. I found in that moment that I had liberated my sacred self I had glimpsed in being with Mary. It was an act of letting go, of surrendering to this deeper self. More than ever before I became aware of the sacredness of our work, of the profound significance of dying and death and the way this realisation has infused my work today.

Jacqueline and Andy

Later Maud is settled. She seems peaceful. Before I leave the hospice I go in to say goodbye to Jacqueline. Andy is in her room sitting by the window. He is of the earth, laughs easily, very easy to connect with. I feel at ease with him immediately yet knowing he wears a mask to hide his deep pain. I can feel the pain there…it ripples within him. I throw open the cue, 'How are you?' He says as I expected him to – 'Getting by' (I feel his sigh). Jacqueline is back on her bed. She asks him to bring her in some decent make-up and take her dirty nightdress home to wash. Some deodorant would be useful.

Smiling at this domestic banter I take my leave. These people are so grateful; they thank us for our attention when I feel it is I who should thank them for giving me the opportunity to care for them. When compassion is the driving force then caring is no effort. The realisation of self is everything. Not as an ego thing of self-gratification but a much deeper level of connection with soul when self merges with the other, becomes one with the other.

Sunday 27 May 2001

Those working in palliative care are strongly motivated to reduce 'suffering', but at the same time realise that our ability to do so is limited because we cannot personally meet the patient's needs. This does not mean that we will not do all in our power to alleviate this complex suffering, but rather acknowledge the limits of professional knowledge and skills, and explore the possibility of relieving distress by means of ordinary human contact informed by our knowledge. (Randall and Downie 1999, p.23)

Ann

I am on night duty for the first time in many years. The night is quiet. In her single room Ann lies dying. She was first diagnosed just five weeks ago with no possibility of curative treatment. She is 68. Although she does not respond to my greeting, I know she is conscious but has turned her head away.

Her eyes are half-opened. She seems to gaze at something far away, an apparent gaze into emptiness.

I sense her mood of melancholy, as if she is shrouded in her suffering, and finding no way to ease her way she submits to it. She does not blink. I sense her retinas are dry and that she may benefit from some eye drops. I squeeze a drop into her eye. She blinks and moves her hand to wipe away the cause.

She did not like that, yet her reaction informed me of her presence within the moment.

I say 'goodnight' and move away. As the night is so quiet I often drift into her room and sit with her.

I like this word 'drifting'. It seems in tune with Ann, that she is drifting in a space between this world and the next. Drifting is flowing with the forces. I need to tune into Ann and drift with her on her journey. I say I need to do this, but do I? 'Need' is such a powerful word. At the hospice we believe it is important that people are not alone when dying. Does Ann need me to do this? It is very difficult to judge her needs although I can read the signs – her head turned away and she does not communicate. Do I imagine that Ann would want me to tune into her when her head is turned away? It feels important that I should know what I intend and be clear that is in Ann's best interests rather than my own.

My intent is just to be with her in harmony.

I am conscious of the way recent past experiences influence the way I am with Ann. In particular, I think of Mary with whom I spent such a moment as this. I had asked myself, 'What is Mary thinking as she lies here?' And now again, 'What does Ann think as she lies here? What does she feel?' These questions ripple across the distance between us.

I was told at shift report that Ann is frightened, that even in her strong Christian faith she feared dying. Just like Maud. I understand this – the fear of descent into the earth. That death is a time of reckoning. She had been given the sentence and now ruminates on the reckoning. Barely time to draw breath. Religion offers no respite. As with Mary, I seek to ease Ann's dying journey. I remind myself of the question, 'How best do I spend this time with you, Ann?' Ann does not answer. Instead she continues to gaze blankly into a distant space. I take her hand and smile. My compassion swells for this suffering woman lying here alone. She is separated from her husband yet she has two daughters who I am told are struggling with their mother's dying. They have gone home to rest and respite in the shadows of their own lives. I can understand their struggle to dwell in the shadow of their mother's dying. Death lurks as a shadow. Yet, even though I understand, I cannot stop a sharp pang of regret at the daughters' abandoning their mother to the night.

Holding Ann's hand I focus my intent to bathe her wounds. I bellow the compassion winds from deep inside me. Cleansing winds to ease Ann's fears. I whisper, 'Dear Ann, rest and melt into the stillness that surrounds us; that flows between us.' Does she hear me? Does she resist me? I cannot tell. Do I intrude? How might I know? Perhaps she does passively resist me. Perhaps holding her hand is as much an irritation to her as giving her the eye drop.

Sensitive to these questions, I dwell with her. She does not move to push me away. This time I do not doubt myself. I sense her response is positive. I hold her hand and feel her years flow through her veins. We both know she will die soon and the life flow will cease. I can feel the changes.

My hands are sensitive, careful, caring – I have always been conscious of my hands after I was told by a client my hands were my prayers. I was giving her a full body massage when she was visited by a Native American who gave her this message to give to me. She had this psychic awareness. Indeed her body massage was intentionally focused to enable her to soar beyond the physical dimensions of the body into cosmic realms. It is also my intention to help Ann soar.

I write Ann a poem.

> I stand before
> I stand in awe
> I pick up my stick and draw a line
> Curved in the sand.
> What is this line?
> Does it mark you from me?
> Or does it mark the point we connect along the curve
> That stretches to the divine sea?
> Reaching that point
> My soul can speak to yours

I sense Ann can see me through the haze. But still I doubt myself. It feels all too easy to delude myself in the nature of this work. I must have unconditional faith. There are no obvious markers. 'Ann, do your eyes pass me by into the empty beyond where the mysteries of death await? Are your eyes transfixed by a distant light that reveals the sacred path through the gathering gloom?'

> Am I a light that helps you see your way along this path?
> Am I the love that helps melt the fear and blocks the light?
> Or am I a boulder that blocks the path that you must find a way to pass?

That I might be a boulder that blocks the path reflects my doubt that I may be in Ann's way. I visualise Ann emerging into a clearing from a dense forest where she had been entangled in hanging branches and held fast in a swamp. The clearing has a soft glow. Perhaps it is the breath of God who wraps Ann in his love. I am simply the guide to hold her hand and transport her to the other side of the clearing.

Then, with my heart in my hands, I do the essential Phowa practice with Ann. I simply say:

> The light above you is shining bright
> Jesus smiles at you
> As you melt into his light

I visualise a radiant light within Ann merging into this light above her head. I am breathless with emotion. Longaker (1997) on the practice of essential Phowa says:

> First sit quietly and settle yourself, bringing all the energies of your mind and body back home. Relax into the deep presence and spacious awareness of your being. Before you begin arouse a strong comp-assionate aspiration. With all your heart, visualise a Buddha or divine being above the head of the other person. Call out on behalf of her, and visualise the presence pouring down rays of light onto her, purifying and transforming her whole being. Then visualise that the other person, now fully purified, dissolves into light and emerges indistinguishably with the enlightened presence. (pp.124–125)

As I write these words, I feel an intense heat in my chest. The realisation of such work renders my soul naked. Such practice is profound. The mind creeps back in. Does Ann mourn her loss? I reflect on the fact that she was only diagnosed her cancer five weeks ago with no possibility of cure. Does she grasp to life as if she is being wrenched from the patterns of her life?

Does she think that her God has deserted her? She has such a strong faith – but what does that really mean? Is she so unprepared to move beyond this worldly realm? Is she too attached to the things of life, unprepared for the moment of body departure? So many questions that have no definitive answers. Such questions dance across my mind as I seek to find a way to move with Ann beyond with ease. Again I reflect on Longaker's (1997) words:

> When you are dying, you are in a powerful transition and you don't have a choice – the ship is already departing from the dock and you're on board. Your task is to let go of all the bonds of responsibility and attachments that may hold you back. (p.119)

I say, 'Ann, you can let go now. God has not deserted you. He is a light above you that you can melt into. Let go of fear and attachment to worldly things.' Longaker says: 'Part of our task in dying is to find a way to make our peace with God' (p.115). These words reflect the words I had whispered to Ann…to feel God's presence and make her peace. To let go of fear, to open herself to receive God's unconditional forgiveness. Perhaps my instincts are grounded in the deeper unconscious of my Buddhist mind. Longaker says: 'Yet letting go is a process, and it takes time' (p.106). And it seems we have so little time. I am at ease with Ann and being at ease I can ease Ann's way from this dimension into the other, and being at ease I am not an obstacle in Ann's way because I flow with her. The boulder is her fear. I am a shoulder against the boulder.

Another poem for Ann:

> I am a clearing
> Where you can emerge into the light
> Where you can reveal and rest in the soft glow deep within your soul.
> And if I fix this image
> In sitting by your side
> Then you can read this sign
> Then we can walk side by side along the curved line
> That joins the shore with the divine sea
> Its gentle waves lap our feet
> In the evening light before the sun drops
> Beneath the horizon of life
> After a life as clear as a bright summer's day.
> Before we melt into the soft moon
> I will return
> And I will let you go.

Ann seems peaceful. She has not responded to my presence even though we have spent much of the night together. The importance to be with the person who is dying, so they are not alone but 'held' on their journey into death's chasm, is reinforced. To be scared is only natural even as death often brings a sweet release.

Did I help Ann? I felt I had but how much of this helping was my need to practise from a spiritual dimension? I do not feel any sense of contradiction – that I had blended Buddhist and Christian doctrine, honouring Ann's Christian faith. Another lesson learnt from Mary. I am letting go more and more of my rational mind into a spiritual awareness. It is a question of faith, letting go not to a deity out there but to a higher consciousness within me, which as yet remains cloaked, yet which guides me.

The journal plots my effort to become more available to people like Ann, to help them find meaning in life and death and respond to their needs. Using the Being available template (see Appendix 1, p.255) I can reflect on the extent I was available to her.

Vision

I have a strong sense of vision to guide Ann on her journey between this world and the next. Although generally acknowledged as significant, the spiritual dimension of palliative care work is not understood well and generally avoided because of the society's secular turn and our ignorance of the spiritual in our own lives. I have only just begun to dance along the edge of the spiritual crater. Slowly I venture closer to the edge to stare into the void. Slowly I shed my fear of the dark as I discover the light deep within. I have read about it and now begin to apply ideas into practice. As if partially sighted, I grope my way in a mist-shrouded semi-darkness guided by a dim glow. No wonder nurses merely dabble or avoid this dimension of practice. Yet I must always ask myself is my vision clouded in delusional beliefs about the nature of spirituality or my own beliefs? As a reflective practitioner I write to challenge myself and be challenged by others.

Concern for Ann

My concern or compassion for Ann is a powerful light within me. Indeed I reflect to dwell in and nurture my compassion. The more compassionate I am, the more available I am. My vision gives compassion its focus.

Knowing Ann

How well did I know Ann? I met her for the first time informed by the words of the nurse at the shift report and her scanty notes. I know she 'has a strong faith' – I know her faith is Christian. I am informed she is frightened. I know she has daughters who struggle with what is happening to their mother. I know she is alone right now. I sense her physical pain is controlled well. I read and interpret the signs on her surface and follow them to her deeper self. But it is dark within her. I do not pretend to know. I give way to my intuitive sense grounded in my flowering spirituality. Perhaps it is only possible to have a spiritual sense of someone like Ann when we dwell comfortably in our own spirituality. But I am a novice in knowing my own. And is my viewing lens clouded by my own confused and uncertain beliefs? However, reflection tunes my empathic ability – to see the other person as both separate from me and yet one with me. A fine balance of connection in order to know the experience of the other through a clear lens.

Reading the signs is essential in order to respond appropriately. Signs ripple on the surface of Ann's being. My skill is to recognise these signs and follow them into the deeper self where much suffering is experienced and meaning found. Kearney (1997) notes:

> Surface is the way to the deep, and surface work is the necessary first step in that direction. For many, this will be enough to create the containment they needed to silently commit themselves to their inner descent; for others, it will only be the beginning. Depth work, on the other hand, might be described as any approach or intervention that brings an individual into an experience of soul. (p.66)

Sometimes, as Kearney (1997) notes in his idea of 'soul pain', connection between the inner suffering and the person's consciousness on the surface is broken leading to intractable suffering where nothing seems to help. Kearney used imagework as a way of working with patients to find meaning and connection at a deep level. In imagework, the therapist guides the patient through an imaginary symbolic journey to help them to connect with their experiences on a deeper level beyond the resistance of the ego. Often, in the imagework, a guide is present. Kearney interpreted the therapeutic significance of this person being present and utilised this understanding in his subsequent imagework story with Baibre. As Kearney says to Baibre, 'Let your guide lead the way. Let the river carry you' (p.102).

Perhaps Ann's head turned away reflected her loss of connection. I chose the image of the guide to take Ann across the clearing to connect with her God. Indeed I planted this image in her mind. The effort is to get onto Ann's wavelength and flow with her pattern through the pitch and roll of her experience.

> I am a chameleon,
> I blend with the shifting horizons
> so I can flow with you
> through the twists and turns of your experience
> like a silvery steam finding its own level,
> yet, even as I shift, I am sure of my footing
> knowing who I am.

In my poems to Ann, I write of a curved line that both separates and joins me from Ann. We are separate bodies but joined in a deeper consciousness. For me this is the essence of my caring practice. Drawing a line is a metaphor for our relationship. It is curved because there are no straight lines in nature.

Knowing and managing self within relationship

To tune into Ann and flow with her I have to manage any resistance I might have in response to her. Put another way, I need to have unconditional compassion for her – that whatever she is experiencing and however she is responding, I have room for it in my heart (Levine 1986). This is always my intention, yet whether I can attain this level of compassion is always a challenge. It is easy to get swept away on the tides of emotions that surround death and dying especially when we don't know the way these tides work. It is like swimming in dangerous water. We may think we are strong swimmers but the tides are even stronger. I may think I know 'who I am' but do I? How do I know this? Given that managing my resistance to Ann is crucial to being with her, then it is imperative I know myself – so that the gusts and storms that blow me this way and that, the prejudices that bind me to repetitive and unhelpful ways of thinking, are under my conscious control.

Practitioners are at risk of absorbing the other's suffering as their own, especially if they feel helpless to ease the other's suffering. The literature warns of this danger of becoming overinvolved and entangled (Carmack 1997; Morse 1991). Jade wrote of wearing a suit of armour to protect her from 'all this shit' (Johns 2000, p.139). What we care about also makes us vulnerable (Benner and Wrubel 1989). Being detached is not an option because I care deeply and detachment is self-alienating. By suppressing or diminishing the emotions, caring itself is diminished. Emotions energise the caring quest (Callahan 1988). Perhaps absorbing the other's suffering is to some extent inevitable. Writing helps me to acknowledge and accept my emotions as valid and reconnects me to the source of caring. Writing is to take a step back from the experience, what Schön (1987) describes as reflection-on-action and what Heidegger (1962) describes as 'the present to hand'. Heidegger describes three interrelated modes of involvement or engagement with practical activity that we have in day-to-day life.

The curved line is a virtual space between the present-to-hand and the ready or unready-to-hand. It is also the space between my prereflective response to Ann and being mindful; a space where I place my feelings and see them for what they are. By visualising my feelings, I can work towards dissipating this 'suffering' energy into positive emotion. I can liberate and harness energy tied up in balancing the anxious self for future action. I concur with Benner and Wrubel's (1989) suggestion that the realisation of caring neutralises any stress that caring brings. I know this because I walk on air after profound moments with patients and families. Sometimes, I feel heavy and tired when the conflicts of the day sap my energy or when caring has been frustrated. Thankfully, working at the hospice, such moments are rare.

Aesthetic response

I ask myself, were my responses appropriate and skilled enough? I am sure readers will have a mixed response. All action is ethical action because it has consequences. The skilful practitioner acts wisely and with compassion, drawing on information gleaned from the unfolding situation, theoretical knowledge, previous experience and most significantly intuition. I have never been taught to respond on a spiritual level. Hence my response *is* intuitive, tentative, intended, creative, courageous and mindful. Being mindful is the ground of wisdom, the weighing up of possibility and consequences. This is in stark contrast with simply applying knowledge of something. When mindful, practice is a constant unfolding learning opportunity. Doing Phowa practice for the first time was a courageous act, putting into practice one of my learning resolves from Mary's experience. Yet I ask, was I adequately prepared for this work? Do I dabble in practices beyond my reach?

Such questions are not easy to answer although I do believe that where genuine compassion flows it is impossible to do harm. I say this rather naively. Kearney (1997) suggests that connecting a person with her or his deep self may result in *soul pain* erupting on the surface whereas before it was contained within. A deep inner emptiness can manifest as physical agitation and despair. Is it better on the surface so we can deal with it or left deep

Table 2.1	
Ready-to-hand	In the ready-to-hand mode of engagement, practical activity functions smoothly and transparently. The person is involved in an absorbed manner so that the equipment is for the most part unnoticed.
Unready-to-hand	In the unready-to-hand mode, some sort of breakdown occurs in the smooth functioning of activity; becoming conspicuous to the user.
Present-to-hand	In the present-to-hand mode, practical everyday activity ceases, and the person stands back and reflects on the situation. Activity is seen as objects with isolable properties and characteristics.
(cited by Plager 1994, pp.71–72)	

within? Either way it is difficult to sit with a person experiencing such pain. Yet it is important not to respond in order to ease our own discomfort through pity.

Creating an environment where being available is possible

Because of the accepting and supportive community within the hospice, I feel increasingly safe to 'come out' as a spiritual practitioner. I sense I belong and do not feel alone. The caring community at the hospice is in many respects a Buddhist Sangha (the spiritual community) – many words come to mind to describe its essence; accepting, encouraging, non-judgemental, caring, moral, disciplined, exquisite.

The right stuff

The Sangha is one of the three jewels of Buddhism. The other two are the Buddha and the Dharma. The Buddha represents my faith. The Dharma is the Buddha's teachings that guide me along the path from the ceaseless turmoil of everyday suffering (samsara) towards enlightenment. Indeed this is my vision in working with all patients approaching death – as a guide along this path.

One Dharma teaching to guide practitioners to realise caring is the noble eight-fold path. This path was revealed to me by Lama Surya Das in his book *Awakening the Buddha Within* and Sangharakshita in his book *Vision and Transformation*. The noble eight-fold path is the fourth of the Four Noble Truths that the Buddha espoused; suffering, the cause of suffering, the cessation of suffering and the way leading to the cessation of suffering. The fact it stems from the Buddha's teaching does not mean it is a religious doctrine. It offers an enlightened way of living your life. Lama Surya Das (LSD) calls each step along the path 'right', whereas Sangharakshita (S) calls each step 'perfect'. However, we needn't concern ourselves with the subtleties of interpretation from the ancient texts.

I have summarised the intention of each step as a reflective lens for readers to contemplate my work with Ann and, more significantly, themselves.

Right view (LSD); perfect vision (S)

The first step of the path is to have a vision of where the path leads. Perfect vision is concerned with cultivating a deep inner sense of the nature of existence, not just of my nursing practice but of life itself. How I practise is a reflection of how I lead my life. I am not two different people. The idea that I can put on a persona when I put on my uniform is an illusion.

A vision guides me in my work and yet such a vision is difficult to articulate because it is beyond thought. Just how do you articulate the sense of wonder and beauty of presence of being with another person on their journey through dying and death? It is the unconditional giving of self in response to whatever the other is experiencing, notably the cessation of suffering. It is also working in harmony with others on a similar path.

Vision is one thing, making it a lived reality is another thing. It is the remaining seven steps that offer a pathway to realisation.

Right intention (LSD); perfect emotion (S)

Right intention or perfect emotion is to use our minds and resolve to free ourselves from ignorance, delusion, negativity and selfishness – to purify our attitudes and thoughts, and in doing so, to develop a working loving-kindness, empathy and compassion to all creatures. In this way we can come to realise that it is our emotions, not reason, that governs much of our responses to the world. Hence with Ann, knowing and managing my emotions were fundamental to my ability to tune into and flow with her. One aspect of perfect emotion is to relinquish negative emotion; by desiring my own interests or gain; by having any sense of ill-will or resistance to others;

and by inflicting any suffering on others – even uwittingly through careless action. The other aspect of perfect emotion is to cultivate positive emotions, what is termed *dana*, the *Brahma viharas* and *saddha* (Sangharakshita, p.43). Dana means giving; my unconditional giving of self to Ann and others. The *Brahma viharas* are fourfold; firstly, *metta* or love extended to all beings. Secondly, *karuna* or compassion which has been a constant focus for reflection; thirdly, *mudita* or sympathetic joy, which is being happy and gracious at the happiness of others; and lastly, *upekkha* or tranquillity, that means being in harmony or balance with the world despite its ups and downs. I interpret *saddha*, or faith, as dwelling in the acceptance of enlightenment or God's presence. Without this spiritual presence, it is difficult to respond in any meaningful way to the other's spiritual needs.

As reflection is most often triggered by the emotions, the eradication of negative emotion and cultivation of positive emotion become a constant process for development.

Right speech (LSD); perfect speech (S)

Right speech is to speak your truth. To tell it as it is. Sangharakshita identifies four levels of perfect speech. The first level is truthfulness – what is really in your heart and mind. However, we have to know what is really in our heart and mind. So we have to learn to discern the way the ego distorts perception. So when I speak with Ann I must tell her the truth and constantly ask myself, 'What is my truth?' Reflection always has this goal of seeking meaning and revealing truth. I say revealing truth rather than seeking truth because the truth is always there, it is just that the ego has a way of distorting it. The second level of perfect speech is always to speak the truth with affectionate awareness of the other person. If we do not know the other person then communication will always be difficult. I did not know Ann very well, but my effort was to become aware of her, to read the signs well. The third level of perfect speech is to speak with someone always in a way that will help expand their level of consciousness; that is to be positive and appreciative rather than negative or destructive even when being critical of another. The fourth level of perfect speech is to speak in such a way as to promote harmony and unity. This is communication at the level of soul and results in a sense of joy. Working with people in a hospice, whether patients, relatives or colleagues, must always be motivated towards creating and sustaining a caring community. Hence the way we speak with each other must always reflect this care.

Right action (LSD); perfect action (S)

Right or perfect action is acting from a sense of integrity, goodness and virtue in the way we treat others and creating harmony in our worlds right now. I must always ask myself the question, 'How do I act for the best?' To answer this question I must know a way of determining what is the best. Certainly my conscience pricks me when I act in careless ways. Virtue is concerned with acting with love, courage and integrity, always to do good and avoid harm. Integrity is always to act from my beliefs even when under pressure to act differently. With Ann I did not feel my integrity was compromised because there was no conflict with the people I worked with.

It is easy to 'take over' responsibility for someone like Ann and act for her when she unable to communicate her own best interests. Benjamin and Curtis (1986) suggest that 'parental' action is justified according to three criteria. Would Ann's sense of autonomy be compromised if I acted for her? Would she come to some harm if I did not act for her? Would she, at a later date if she was able to, ratify my acting for her? If I hadn't acted, she would not have come to any harm in any observable way? Whether she would have come to 'spiritual' harm is beyond my reasoning. She was unable to exercise her autonomy and certainly unable to ratify my actions afterwards.

However, Ann was in emotional turmoil, although again I guess this might be open to controversy. Randall and Downie (1999) in their book on palliative care ethics state:

> It might be said that even if carers have little control over the emotional state of a patient, they can at least try to understand that state. Sometimes this kind of understanding is called 'empathy'. Now, no doubt some carers can sometimes achieve this with some patients, but the belief that we can be trained to empathise is a dangerous illusion. (p.23)

I ask myself, did I understand Ann's emotional state? As Randall and Downie suggest, was I at risk of deluding myself that I can know? Knowing is dangerous because when we think we know then we close our minds to other possibilities. My response was to help her alleviate this turmoil as best I could while respecting her as a person. Randall and Downie continue by stating:

> However, it is possible to give humane treatment without complete emotional understanding. The important point is that we must respect the patient as an individual unique among others. It is this moral

imperative of practical wisdom which qualifies the pursuit of both the intrinsic and the extrinsic aim of palliative care. (p.23)

Randall and Downie challenge me – do I respect Ann as a unique individual among others? Or have I unwittingly clustered her with other similar patients approaching their death, imaging that all such patients will want to melt into the light of God? That indeed all people want relief of suffering? Can I rest in the idea that it is only ignorance that masks people's realisation of their own enlightenment? That my actions help to pull away the veil of ignorance so the light can be revealed to them?

Randall and Downie continue:

> Paradoxically, it is precisely the fact that whole person care implies respect for the patient's own personal goals and values that imposes limits on the scope of professional activity directed towards such care. We must not attempt to inflict unwanted attention or solutions to emotional or social problems of the patient, any more than we would inflict unwanted physical treatment without the patient's informed consent. Recognition of this limitation is an integral part of the concept of whole person care, because included in this concept is the control individuals always have over their own psychological, social and spiritual well-being. Thus we must accept that no treatment or care can be given which the informed and competent patient does not want. (p.23)

Ann has not been informed and is not competent. I am mindful not to impose my spiritual beliefs but simply to use my spiritual presence intentionally to ease her suffering. It is a parental act. If she were competent I would discuss my response with her. I am conscious of a lack of continuity of care; that if I had known Ann when she was fully alert, then we might have discussed the way she viewed her own dying and death. But we have not. Randall and Downie continue:

> It must also be remembered, however, that there can be a pathological side to deeply held personal aims, especially the religious ones. This is the pathology of the 'hidden agenda'…the dying patient is highly vulnerable to those who believe that they have the truth about life and death. (p.27)

Do I know the truth about life and death? As I reflect, I question myself about this truth. It is true that I am deeply influenced by my Buddhist beliefs but this philosophy of death professes not knowing. I like to think I am open and curious about the unfolding moment with Ann…reading the signs and responding in the best way I know yet conscious of my intention to ease Ann's suffering, whether it be physical or spiritual.

Right livelihood (LSD); perfect livelihood (S)

Perfect livelihood is to live out our vision through our work. I am very fortunate to work as a nurse in a hospice and to guide practitioners through reflective practice on the courses I teach at the university. Yet it is not really an issue of good fortune; by acting in tune with my caring beliefs I have worked hard to create these opportunities and resist pressure to work in compromising ways.

Right effort (LSD); perfect effort (S)

Right effort is gently and dynamically striving to realise my caring self. The word 'striving' reflects that this effort is always active rather than a passive waiting for something to happen. Perfect effort is to remain focused on realising perfect vision and in doing so to manage distractions or hindrances that compromise the realisation of perfect vision. Sangharakshita names these hindrances as craving for material things, hatred, restlessness and anxiety, sloth and torpor, doubt and indecision (pp.117–120). I am constantly on guard against seeing my teaching and writing as a need for self-gratification or being anxious that my work will not be acknowledged. Restlessness reflects the way the ego constantly bombards me with thoughts, instilling me with anxiety of this, that and whatever. Rinpoche (1992) says:

> We are fragmented into so many aspects. We don't know who we really are, or what aspects of ourselves we should identify with. So many contradictory voices, dictates and feelings fight for control over our inner lives that we find ourselves scattered everywhere, in all directions, leaving nobody at home. (p.59)

Feeling that I always have to make an effort can feel very tiring. Hence it is easy to relax into a mindset of 'oh, it doesn't matter for once'. Unfortunately, this is often the thin edge of sloth. Lack of decision can reflect a lack of commitment or courage to act in right ways. Commitment, courage, like effort itself, needs to be cultivated and maintained.

Reflection offers a way to pay attention to self and identify any hindrances that distract from right effort. In this way the hindrance can be actively confronted and weakened through understanding. It is helpful to reflect on affirming experiences that reinforce self as caring, and in doing so, reinforce motivation and effort.

Right mindfulness (LDS); perfect awareness (S)

Perfect awareness is being consciously present within each unfolding moment, the dynamic relationship between self and others, things, and a wider spiritual awareness of the meaning of life and death. When I was with Ann I was sensitive to myself being with Ann within each unfolding moment. I was aware of any hindrances that threatened my being with Ann. Perfect awareness is cultivated by reflection on situations. The more I reflect on situations, the more sensitive or aware I become when next in practice, cultivating what Sangharakshita calls 'a witness-like attitude' (p.121).

Right concentration (LDS); perfect samadhi (S)

Right concentration is to focus with spiritual intention and attention towards realising enlightenment. As I sit with Ann and try to ease her approach to death, so I step on my own journey to realise my own enlightenment. This is not to see Ann as a tool to attain something for myself. Indeed that attitude would be self-defeating because it is the antithesis of everything along the eight-fold path. Perhaps perfect samadhi is a shining star deep within that provides the ultimate motivation, that is the door to states of bliss and joy that I sometimes sense when I realise my caring self in being with people like Ann. Then I know I have touched the soul of the other, and touched God.

Wednesday 13 June 2001

Iris

It is some time since I reflected on my relationship with Iris. However, we have continued to meet weekly for reflexology treatments.

Iris is quickly asleep. On waking after the reflexology, she comments as she often does, that she feels totally relaxed, serene and energised. I had added some drops of patchouli to the reflexology base cream for positive thinking. Patchouli is also good for hard skin, anxiety and depression. On the spiritual plane, Worwood (1999) states:

> Patchouli brings with it the sense of the sacredness of life. It is also a fragrance of action, knowing that no ideal will occur unless we take the first steps to make it happen. At the same time, patchouli reminds us that sitting quietly under a tree is good if there is purpose in it – the purpose of knowing and appreciating. Sitting under a tree represents the contemplation of what we can do for ourselves and others in the

way of caring. As the thought of caring for others enters our spirit, so too does the thought of caring for the tree that harbours us, and caring for all else besides. Such is the hope of patchouli's liberation from boundaries. (p.240)

Iris has always been positive in taking action to fight her cancer. My work is to help her relax and contemplate, and guide her to put things into perspective, to let go of her fears or, to use Worwood's imagery, to be a tree for her to sit under. Iris puts everybody else's needs before her own. She is the universal mother. Now she needs to let go and accept being held. At least her liver and bone scans showed stable disease. She expels a deep sigh of relief. Such markers are vital for her. Her fear is palpable.

Thursday 14 June 2001

Winston and Winnie

Kathy is a Macmillan nurse, a palliative care nurse who works in the community to support patients and families. She asks me if I would consider visiting a man in the community who is reluctant to come to the hospice. His name is Winston, a 61-year-old West Indian man who has cancer of the prostate that has spread to the bone. He now has spinal cord compression which has paralysed him from the waist down. He is in despair entering the terminal phase of his illness. Could I help? I suggest I visit him when she visits next Wednesday.

Later, at home I feel strangely anxious about the prospect of visiting Winston, as if I am putting my competence on the line. I am worrying how I can best help him. If he is paralysed, could I do massage? I realise I am concerned for myself, doubting my ability and yet I have yet to meet him! By paying attention to this inner conflict, my anxiety fades as I realise that no matter what I do, if I do it with genuine compassion, then it will benefit him.

Wednesday 20 June 2001

Winston and Winnie

I follow Kathy to Winston's house. His condition had deteriorated since the previous week. On Monday he had a stroke which immobilised his right side and severely affected his speech. He lies on a nimbus bed in the front room, his head slightly raised. I immediately feel a tension in the room that makes me cautious. Winnie, his wife, greets me warmly. Her sister who lives in London is sitting by his bedside.

Kathy asks Winnie how things are and talks to Winston, 'You have taken to your bed?' Winston just looks at Kathy. Winnie intercedes, 'Since Monday when he had the stroke.' Winnie shares her practical concerns about doing the dressings for his deep pressure wounds. She says they smell very badly which Winston does not like and which even she recoils from. They explore the caring support – the district nurses come in several times a day. Winnie distinguishes between them – some of them just come in and do what they need to do to Winston and then go, and some really come and be with Winston as if they really care about him. She says, 'You know what I'm saying?' She says that a lot. Her eyes are full of tears as she speaks. She says she doesn't show her tears but she knows Winston is dying.

I quietly absorb the conversation and the emotions that lie thick within the words, and reflect on the significance of caring. Winnie is sensitive to the caring presence of the carers. Her words reflect her need for the carers to be caring to Winston. Anything less causes her to suffer more when she already suffers so much. I wonder if the nurses realise, as they go about their work, that they exacerbate rather than ease suffering.

As Kathy and Winnie pause in their conversation, I move into the space between their words as an opportunity to approach Winston. I smile at Winston but he does not respond. I take his hand in greeting – it is firm and responsive. I say I have come to help him feel more relaxed. Would he like that? He gazes at me but does not answer. Winnie answers for him, 'Please go ahead.'

I realise it's impossible for Winston to say yes or no. He probably thinks, 'Who is this white man who walks into my house and offers to help me?' I use my eyes to convey my caring and connect with him. But first I must bring myself to a point of stillness, to quell my beating pulse at being closely observed. He closes his eyes. I ask him if he has a great faith? He acknowledges that he has. I know his faith is very meaningful to him. Around us, on the walls of the room, are religious signs. One in particular had taken my eye:

God is master of this house.

Winston had hoped he would recover, that it was too soon for him to die. Now his faith offers little refuge for him. I wonder how he views his death – he appears fearful on the surface but that is natural when confronted with the certainty of one's own death and the uncertainty of what follows mortal death. What does he think or feel lies deeper? I would like to ask him.

How can I best help him? Possibly reflexology or TT. There is no room at the foot of the bed which makes that treatment difficult to execute so I decide TT. Kathy and Winnie ask if they should go? I suggest they remain even though I feel self-conscious.

Placing my hands just above his head I ask Winston to close his eyes. I ask Winston to follow his breath in and follow his breath out. After a few breaths I ask him to imagine that he is breathing in God's light until it fills his body. I then ask him to imagine that he is breathing out the fears that bind him, and to relax into the light and find stillness with his God. Winston is peaceful as I say this. At the same time I focus on stilling my anxiety and harmonising myself with Winston. After about five minutes I am prepared!

I move my hands slowly across his etheric energy field. His head, neck and chest areas are warm. I know his breathing has been difficult for him. For the next 15 minutes I massage his etheric field, visualising a cool blue waterfall cascading over him and drawing out the heat. The heat dissipates. Winston breathes more easily. Once or twice he opens his eyes to see what is going on which makes me smile.

At first I was conscious of my self-consciousness. I could feel the perspiration trickle but that quickly passed as I tuned into Winston's wavelength and flowed with him. Yet part of me still doubted myself whether I could really help Winston. Oh me of little faith! Yet to be fair to myself, it was a profound moment to visit this family under these circumstances. When I finish the TT, Winnie comments that Winston seems comforted and relaxed. Without her realising it, she also comforts me. Intuitively, I know the TT has helped Winston to reach a place of stillness within the chaos of his life.

I ask Winnie how she is coping? She says she is tired, not having slept for two days. As she says this more tears flow from her sad eyes. She says she's also looking after Leo, her grandson, who is only 18 months old. She has cared for him since he was just 12 weeks. Caring for Leo is important for her. She puts out her hands in a gesture of despair – that she cannot choose between them, that she has no choice. She must care for both of them. Yet support is thin on the ground. Kathy suggests we could try and book a Marie Curie nurse for tonight so Winnie can get some sleep. Winston wants to stay in his home and so does she. She must care for Winston whatever the effort. No question of admission to the hospice. I sense Winnie's reluctance to have someone else intrude but she realises she needs help. Caught in a dilemma she turns this way and that. Kathy persuades her to accept the Marie Curie offer.

Although I am busy tomorrow I feel I have to offer something as I listen to Winnie share her despair and Kathy's efforts to find solutions. I say I could visit tomorrow around 15.00 and do some more TT with Winston. They both respond positively, reiterating how much the TT seems to help Winston become peaceful. Winnie asks Winston, who nods affirmatively. I also offer to give Winnie reflexology so she can have an hour out for total relaxation. Encouraged by Kathy she accepts my offer. We joke about cleaning her feet. One of her daughters arrives, so we all laugh. Light relief from the darkness that surrounds us. I feel accepted into this family, especially as Winnie had expressed concern that having so many different carers was intrusive. I understand Winnie's tension of needing help, yet needing to be left alone.

Kathy and I depart. Walking down the steps from Winston's house, Kathy says she was intrigued by my response to Winston, about the heat and taking the heat away. She thought it was good. She feels good about asking me to visit and asks me about being available to other patients. I say I would always try to be. I say that this is good for me as well…my own sharp learning curve.

I am tired after this visit. It is good to sit quietly in the hospice garden and bring myself home before my appointment with Iris this afternoon. Winnie's words that some carers distress her because they do not care for Winston haunts me. Such carers are life-restraining or life-destroying within Sigridûr Halldórsdóttir's (1996) five basic modes of being with another (see Table 2.2). As a therapist and nurse I always intend to be life-giving. Anything less fails the other and fails myself. Being wrapped up in my anxiety threatened my availability to Winston and Winnie. Hence I am tired.

Iris

Iris says her bowels are working well taking movicol. The shoulder pain seems easier. I ask how Robert, her husband, is? She says, 'He ran out of the room when Alma in "Coronation Street" (the TV soap drama) was dying. I was pleased he showed his emotions because he bottles it up … men are not good at showing it, are they? He's smoking more again which makes him snore at night and affects my sleep. I wake at night anyway with thoughts spinning in my head.'

Iris had been sleeping better with the reflexology so I suggest I finally do a Bach flower remedy consultation when we next meet. I have white chestnut in mind. I had given Joan, one patient I had massaged in day care, white chestnut for repetitive thoughts at night. It worked well. Recently, an inpatient for respite care told a nurse who was pessimistic about Bach flower remedies, that when she wakes at night she puts two drops of white chestnut under her tongue and bingo – she's asleep again! I tell Iris this story and she's optimistic. I ask her if Robert might like a consultation or some massage? Iris says that he is not getting any support but would resist my offer, so I don't pursue it. She has kept the Macmillan nurses, who might help Robert talk through his thoughts and feelings at a distance; as she says, 'I don't want this cancer to invade the family.' But it has, it eats away under the cover of silence.

Thursday 21 June 2001

Winston and Winnie

It is 15.00. Winnie opens the front door. Winston is in bed as before. Her sister sits in the same chair. He wears different pyjamas, blue with a white stripe. The colours look cooling. Yesterday he wore dark red-brown pyjamas and he was hot. Interesting comparison – I wonder if there is any therapeutic significance. Winston looks calmer, more settled. The whole room feels calmer. I say this to Winnie. She says she's calmer today.

The Marie Curie nurse had stayed last night. She was very caring. Winnie was greatly relieved; she had slept in fits and starts as she struggled to

Table 2.2: Five basic modes of being with another	
Life-giving (bio-genic) mode of being with another	A mode where one affirms the personhood of the other by connecting with the true centre of the other in a life-giving way. It relieves the vulnerability of the other and makes the other stronger. It enhances growth, restores, reforms, and potentiates learning and healing.
Life-sustaining (bio-active) mode of being with another	A mode where one acknowledges the personhood of the other, supports, encourages and reassures the other. It gives security and comfort. It positively affects life in the other.
Life-neutral (bio-passive) mode of being with another	A mode where one does not affect life in the other.
Life-restraining (bio-static) mode of being with another	A mode where one is insensitive or indifferent to the other and detached from the true centre of the other. It causes discouragement and develops uneasiness in the other. It negatively affects existing life in the other.
Life-destroying (bio-cidic) mode of being with another	A mode where one depersonalises the other, destroys life and increases the other's vulnerability. It causes distress and despair, and hurts and reforms the other. It is transference of negative energy or darkness.

let go of her thoughts and still her emotions. The Marie Curie nurse was a calculated risk that had paid off. As with so many aspects of care, there is no clear-cut answer to these everyday dilemmas. Every decision is an act of judgement; an act of balancing the various tensions within the situation. With hindsight we can say, 'that was a good decision', yet what if the Marie Curie nurse had not been caring? Winnie would have felt guilty and suffered. Kathy would have felt guilty for encouraging Winnie to accept the nurse. We have to live in the present and make the best decisions as we read them. Life is essentially indeterminate.

Winston does not seem to recognise me from yesterday. I take his hand and remind him of my visit yesterday. No recognition. I am confident having connected with him and Winnie yesterday. I hold Winston's head – one hand on the forehead over the brow chakra (see p.232) and one hand over the base of his skull. Holding Winston's head is a powerful act of containment. I hold him as if I were God, saying to him that he can let go of fear and melt into the light. Holding someone in this way evokes such a powerful sense of compassion in me. I work down the front of Winston's body using TT and visualisation. My hands are hot and tingly. As before Winston becomes much cooler. His eyes remain closed but I constantly remind him that he is surrounded in God's love and light, to breathe it in and let it fill his body, to relax in that joy and breathe out his fears and pain, to let go of his resistance.

Afterwards I say to Winnie, 'Now it's your turn.' She says okay and suggests we move into the back room. The back room is a metaphor for going deeper into this family. I am careful to move carefully with the risk of being intrusive even as if I feel Winnie has taken my hand and guided me into the family bosom. Her two daughters are present. One daughter is changing her small baby's nappy. Leo is also there and remembers me from yesterday. They go upstairs leaving me with Winnie and her sister. I ask Winnie if she has any medical conditions – she has diabetes but otherwise she says she is well except losing weight with all this worry.

Winnie is very relaxed with her feet. She surrenders immediately to my touch. Her daughter comments on the nice smell of my stock reflexology cream (mixed with patchouli and frankincense essential oils). The daughter observes me closely. She is protective of her mother at this fragile time. I tell her that the oils will help her mother to relax and gain a sense of balance.

Afterwards Winnie says she fell asleep but does not feel drowsy. She feels good. As she isn't sleeping well, I suggest a drop of lavender on her nightdress or pillow or, if she likes the smell, to put a few drops in her bath to help her relax.

I tell her that if she needs me I can visit again next Tuesday, that it's okay to contact me. She is thankful. I say goodbye to Winston, 'God bless.' He connects with my greeting and smiles.

I feel very good about the visit. It felt no coincidence that Kathy asked me to visit. I was waiting for such a call. Everything about being with Winston and Winnie is sacred. The reflexology created a sacred space within the chaos for Winnie to find a point of stillness and to caress her aching soul. It helped her to gather together the remnants of her energy that had been pulled apart in her suffering for the task ahead of being with Winston as he descends into death. Winston needs to liberate himself from the illusionary boundary that separates himself from his God. This is also my work – to liberate myself from the illusionary ego boundaries that have contained and constrained my ability to realise my spiritual self and use 'this self' in my practice.

The next day, on the train to London, I read Angela Henderson's (2001) paper 'Emotional labour and nursing: an underappreciated aspect of caring work'. She quotes one of her research respondents:

> If you want to be a very good nurse you have to get those feelings in there. Most people don't like the kind of nurses that just go in, do their thing and get out. That's not what people look for most of the time. (p.133)

For Winnie that was certainly the case. It is clearly not good enough for nurses to remain at an emotional distance so that caring is not perceived. Emotional distance is not a neutral thing but a negative thing that is destructive to the soul.

Tuesday 26 June 2001

Yesterday I received Reiki. Today I am full of love. I feel a channel has been cleared through my chakras, clearing away debris, releasing energy and giving me a sense of lightness. The feeling of warmth over my heart chakra (see p. 232) was intense and it continues today. It is important for me to keep in good 'spiritual shape'. Besides receiving Reiki, I meditate each day, in particular to cultivate loving kindness and positive emotion. There is so much conflict in the world that people seem to struggle with. I always seem to be at odds with someone or another over trivial issues. Negative emotion ties up my energy and suffocates compassion. Paramanda (2001) writes:

> It sometimes strikes people as strange that we should consciously have to develop kindness. It seems rather artificial and forced to deliberately

try to cultivate it, but realistically this is the situation that many of us find ourselves in, and it's not going to change unless we are prepared to do something about it. (p.141)

Iris

It's just gone 10.00. Iris rushes from the dentist. She is not so good, not sleeping well and worrying about Robert who is unhappy at work besides his struggle to cope with Iris's illness. As always Iris soaks up everybody else's angst and takes responsibility for easing their pain. She has more pain in her right shoulder and pain in her left shoulder. She also has had two bad migraines. The last migraine started when she was in the car going to the hospital for her chemotherapy yesterday. She felt trapped in the car in the hot weather…the aura commenced and she knew what she was in for! Her head still feels full.

During the treatment Iris drifts in and out of sleep. Afterwards she unusually feels a little drowsy. Normally she feels energised. I suspect this is the after-effect of the migraine attack. She says she feels relaxed – 'I needed that.' She also needs a glass of water. I then do a Bach flower remedy consultation. Between us we select six remedies which I make up into a stock treatment bottle. The remedy descriptions quoted are taken from *The 38 Flower Remedies* based on the original words of Dr Edward Bach (Howard 1995).

AGRIMONY

Iris's predicament is summarised in the description of agrimony.

> People who need agrimony often appear carefree and humorous, but their joi de vivre is a mask for anxieties, worries and even real inner torment which they may be trying to conceal from themselves as well as others. If in pain or discomfort, they are likely to joke about it [dismiss it as nothing], unwilling to express their real fears [link to red chestnut – the overriding concern to protect others]. They try to ignore the dark side of life [death lurking in the shadows] and prefer to make light of things rather than enter into confrontation [with self and others – why she cannot help her husband – note earlier text on his retreat from Alma's death in 'Coronation Street']. They may also suffer from restlessness at night, with churning thoughts [note also white chestnut]. (p.16)

RED CHESTNUT

Red chestnut is for those who have selfless over-concern and fear for the welfare of others. (p.40)

Iris felt she did worry about her husband and her children whatever they did. I felt this was exaggerated because she was also concerned how they would manage life if she died. Iris's face took on a pallor when I suggested that…the truth dawning of that possibility she wished to avoid.

SCLERANTHUS

Scleranthus is for people who suffer indecision. These people lack balance and poise; their grasshopper minds make them jump about in conversation. They are up and down in mood, experiencing extremes of joy/sadness, energy/apathy, optimism/pessimism, laughing/ crying. (p.43)

Iris said she was hopeless at making decisions. She also identified with the description of mood swings: 'Some days I do feel low even though I try not to, and some days I feel okay.'

OLIVE

Olive is for those people who are exhausted in body and mind. (p.38)

Iris feels physically tired towards the end of the day but not emotionally tired 'to the point of tears'.

CRAB APPLE

Crab apple is the cleansing remedy for mind and body. (p.25)

Iris did not have a positive body image. She had lost a breast but felt she had adjusted reasonably well to that. She was self-conscious about her weight. The chemotherapy had brought on an early menopause so she felt her femininity had evaporated. She paid considerable attention to the way she presented herself. She was also house-proud even though it was usually a mess. I also wanted her to have crab apple to help her body rid itself of toxins.

OAK

> Oak people are normally brave, strong and reliable; they need oak when their inner strength wanes and fatigue takes over. They keep going, whatever happens, ignoring their tiredness. Driven by a strong sense of duty, they are helpful to others, conscientious and reliable. The resultant loss of innate strength may lead to depression, frustration and other stress symptoms. These people have a sense of failure when ill but are ceaseless in their efforts to recover. (p.37)

Iris exclaimed, 'That's me!' Just talking through these descriptions was a cathartic release for Iris. The descriptions helped to validate her feelings as normal, that somehow she was not a 'mental case'. I was struck (yet again) by the power of the consultation to reveal deep parts of self in a safe and fun way. Iris took the four drops under her tongue. 'Urghh – the taste of the brandy [used as a preservative]!'

Using Bach flower remedies supplements Iris's reflexology although of dubious proven therapeutic value despite published anecdotes of efficacy with particular cases (Chancellor 1990). My only success had been with Joan using white chestnut. However, its value in enabling Iris to reflect on her psychological and emotional response to her cancer was significant.

Wednesday 27 June 2001

Winston and Winnie

Phone call from Kathy – could I visit tomorrow? 'Winston has become very agitated.' She is contemplating a syringe driver.

I ask, 'Midazolam?'

'Yes, but first – can you do anything?'

'I can arrive after 10.00 but would need to leave by 11.00.'

'Winston's district nurse will be with him until 10.30.'

'Okay – would Winnie also like some therapy?'

Kathy asks Winnie. 'Just for Winston as time is tight.'

I am impressed with Kathy's decision to use complementary therapy rather than midazolam. I always feel nurses reach for pharmacological responses to terminal agitation too quickly without understanding the messages within the agitation. Midazolam will sedate and diminish consciousness. Yet agitation is a distressing symptom for the family to observe especially when they are unable to ease the troubled mind.

Thursday 28 June 2001

Winston and Winnie

It's early – just 6.00. I am reading Thomas Merton's book *No Man Is An Island*. Over breakfast I read his words as if they are a message to me in working with Winston:

> The first step to unselfish love is the recognition that our love may be deluded. We must first of all purify our love by renouncing the pleasure of loving as an end in itself. As long as pleasure is our end, we will be dishonest with ourselves and with those we love. We will not seek their good, but our own pleasure. (p.4)

I ask myself, 'Do I give love in my work?' I feel that I do in the sense of compassion. I ask myself, 'Do I glorify in this love? Do I bathe in pleasure at being so loving?' I can feel the ego goad me. I imagine that if I were to share this story that others would doubt my sincerity, simply because I have doubted it myself as I have become increasingly conscious of my soul. Yet I ask, 'Do I create an illusion of soul as the greatest ego stunt of all?' I read on:

> Charity makes me seek far more than the satisfaction of my own desires, even though they may be aimed at another's good. It must also make me an instrument of God's providence in their lives. I must be convinced and penetrated by the realisation that without my love for them they may perhaps not achieve the things God has willed for them. My will must be the instrument of God's will in helping them create their destiny. My love must be to them the 'sacrament' of the mysterious and infinitely selfless love God has for them. My love must be for them the minister not of my own spirit but of the holy spirit. The words I speak to them must be no other than the words of Christ who deigns to reveals himself to them in me. Only this charity which is as strong and as sure as the spirit of God himself can save us from the lamentable error of pouring out on others a love that leads them into error and urges them to seek happiness where it can never be found. (p.4)

Merton's words both confront me and help me imagine that when I work with Winston it *is* God who works through me. I know Winston has a great faith. I can believe that God will work through me if I am genuine. This is taking me into new dimensions of self. I feel strangely powerful as if I am pure light. I feel it flood through me when I centre myself. I feel a great compassion swell through my consciousness. A few pages further on I read:

> We are not perfectly free until we live in pure hope. For when our hope is pure, it no longer trusts exclusively in human and visible means, nor

rests in any visible end. He who hopes in God trusts God, whom he never sees, to bring him to the possession of things that are beyond imagination. (p.11)

This is the message I am asked to pass on to Winston and Winnie, to let go into the stillness within the love and light of God that surrounds and embraces them. Winston has clung to a false hope that he will not die. Winnie has felt Winston's hope and hoped for him even as she knows he is dying.

Merton's words have prepared me for my visit. Winnie greets me at the door. Maureen, one of the district nurses, is just packing up. I gaze at Winston. He is now on another level of consciousness, unable to communicate, seemingly unaware of people present. His mouth is open and his breathing laboured in a characteristic altered pattern that suggests death is close. Winnie says he has been like that today. Yesterday he was able to communicate, waving his arms, became restless and agitated. Now that has passed. I wonder if he knew he was slipping away and that was his last effort to stem the inevitable tide of death. Winnie says again that Winston knew he wouldn't walk again but would recover, and talked about his fear of dying. The circuit minister had called earlier in the week. The regular minister from their church was away. Winnie was trying to contact him to visit again. Winnie is tired and is hoping for a carer to help tonight but she shrugs her shoulders and says, 'Well, if not then I will be there.' She senses time is short and a final effort has to be made. We can talk about Winston's death. She says, 'I have spent many tears.' I acknowledge how tough this is for her.

Using TT as before cools his energy field but there is no change in his breathing. Winnie asks me if I can come again if she needs me? I say it is difficult tomorrow but I could drive down on Saturday. She looks at me with knowing eyes – 'Will he still be here on Saturday?' I say it's very possible he won't be. It feels almost unreal to be having this conversation with Winnie about something so profound and yet feel so still. I explain to Winnie the way I worked with Winston and suggest she can do Therapeutic Touch with Winston simply by focusing her love in the movements of her hands. I show her how to massage Winston's hand. She says she sits with him and holds his hand. I say how comforting it is to be held, to know we are loved and not alone. Winnie is so grateful. I accept her gift of a cold fruit drink.

As I leave the house, I turn to say goodbye to Winston to wish him well on his journey. I say God is about him and holds him. I say this to Winnie as well, touching her shoulder.

The day is warm. I walk down the steps in a very conscious way, as if each step is profound along the red road. I feel I have been touched by God. I wonder at the way I can talk about God and assume he works through me, as if I have broken through an immense barrier to my practice – to embrace God in a natural and uninhibited way. How have I learnt to do this? Is it truly a reflection of 'who I am'? I have doubted myself because this is so utterly profound. There are no markers – just a sense of light. The fibres of my body tingle.

The words of Thomas Merton were a revelation and prepared me to work with Winston and Winnie. Merton is a Catholic monk whereas I embrace Buddhism. Yet, at a fundamental level, there is no difference. It is no coincidence I chanced to read them this morning for I am constantly amazed at the times I read things in relation to events unfolding in my practice, as if someone had put these words along my path. Why read them this morning? I am learning to trust myself, no longer uncertain or awkward with my beliefs and, most significantly, to fully and unashamedly embrace 'the spiritual' in my own life or, as Blackwolf and Gina Jones (1996) say, 'to wear my regalia with pride'.

Reading the paper by Henderson prompted me to read again a paper by Helen Allan (2001) with the striking title 'A good enough nurse'. Allan suggests that the 'good enough nurse' is a nurse who is emotionally aware of herself and others in ways that are accepted by the patient, and yet is also able to maintain an emotional distance or set boundaries for her level of intimacy within a realistic coping zone. Allan's interpretation seeks to bridge a tension between the ideal nurse and the real world. As Morse suggests (1991), failure to manage the emotional boundary between the nurse and patient can lead to entanglement or overinvolvement when the nurse absorbs the suffering of the patient as her own, leading to a blurring of boundaries that can distort the caring role. Allan is critical of 'ideal' theorists who espouse intimacy, on the grounds that it is not realistic.

However, it is surely not a question of being either idealistic or realistic. It is being able to manage self within relationship or, put another way, to manage the resistance within self is fundamental to developing intimate relationships with patients. Being emotionally aware of self's response to the patient would seem the first step. Being able to understand the patient's own emotional needs would seem the second step. Being able to convey emotional awareness or a genuine concern to the patient is the third step and being able to manage any sense of resistance in order to remain present to the patient is the fourth step.

The idea of emotional detachment intrigues me, a boundary that separates you from me. To be detached would be to see myself as separate from Winston and Winnie, and most significantly from myself, as if there is something I cannot face in myself which I need to project into the other person. In this way I create within myself a boundary, separating a part of myself as I struggle to accept from my real self. It is worth reiterating Wilber's words (1979):

> For a line, whether mental, natural, or logical, doesn't just divide and separate, it also joins and unites. Boundaries on the other hand are pure illusions – they pretend to separate what is not in fact separable. (p.25)

Depending on the way you view it, a line separates or joins. Like the sea meeting the shore it is simply a flowing moment, sometimes gently lapping waves and at other times a mighty roar of crashing waves, much indeed like relationships. Yet when the waves crash, do I fear being swept away? Like a surfer I must become one with the wave.

To surf with Winston and Winnie I needed to tune in to these people. Who are they? What meanings do they give to these dramatic unfolding events in their lives? What are they feeling? I sense the despair that had flooded the room. I felt my own anxiety. Yet even though I was anxious I could manage the anxiety to stay on the surfboard because of my own deep compassion. Caring is a reciprocal thing. By feeling my compassion, Winnie is not only comforted but in return cares for me even in her despair. Indeed, in caring for me she can ease her suffering because we can dance together. I can let go of my resistance and melt any illusionary boundary that appeared to separate us. The curved line joins us. As a healer it is essential I can harness energy in positive ways. If I resist myself I also resist Winnie and Winston and block the flow of my compassionate self. Our dance would be tentative, awkward, out of rhythm.

Carmack (1997) writes of a tension between engagement and detachment. In a similar vein Henderson (2001) writes about being emotionally aware and being emotionally detached. Yet these tensions merely reflect resistance. Knowing myself I can manage this resistance as necessary to flow with Winston and Winnie without fear of being swept away. This does not mean it is easy to surf the wave. Sometimes the wave caught on the storm crashes on the beach. Resistance is simply the boundary beyond which I fear to surf. Resistance is clinging to an ego that whispers fear into my mind. As we strive to be involved with the other person, to respond congruently with emotional awareness (to use Allan's notion), we sometimes feel the need to retreat because we sense a threat to our psychic safety and feel ill-equipped to deal with the consequences of involvement. We take refuge behind a mask of professional detachment, a way of marshalling a plethora of defence mechanisms against anxiety. By using the word 'professional', it is no longer me retreating and viewing from a distance, but the nurse in me. The need to feel comfortable is not a justification for the 'good enough nurse'. From this perspective we limit our potential as carers and healers and justify this position by saying 'good enough'. Emotional awareness suggests not just an awareness of how the other is feeling but how we ourselves as carers are feeling, and the impact of our feelings on the other.

The Buddhist idea of non-attachment simply means that my ego has no investment in what is unfolding. I do what I do for the benefit of Winston and Winnie, not for myself. Put more broadly, I do what I do for the benefit of humanity. It means I must be confident in what I do, not for my own glorification, but with humility. How hard it is to be humble in a world that thrives on competition and material reward where caring can sometimes feel like a rare commodity. So how can you engage in the suffering with others and remain non-attached? As Merton (1955) says, 'It is the surrender of self to a greater force.' Call it God or Buddha, but it is the unifying force in which people find ultimate meaning in their purpose of life. It is the driving force for compassion. Compassion is having room in your heart for another no matter what the other is suffering (Levine 1986). Therefore, to be compassionate is to be mindful and non-attached – so that what the other is suffering does not become my suffering – I become one with the other yet separate from him. To manage resistance requires authenticity and mindfulness. In being 'mindful', I pay constant attention to myself unfolding in space. It is the essence of the reflective practitioner to know and manage my authentic self within the unfolding moment in order to respond most appropriately. So with Winston and Winnie I may feel uncomfortable about my ability to handle their and my own feelings, yet I am mindful of this. I am motivated to resolve the crisis simply because I care deeply, because my compassion is on fire and because I can manage those factors that would otherwise lead me to resist engagement. Mindfulness creates the space where I can contemplate how best to respond within the spaces within the unfolding moment. To respond requires a deep grasp and interpretation of what is unfolding and the ability to choose the most effective response from my basket of available responses. It is the nature of wisdom to weigh things up. So how can I respond for the best to help Winston and Winnie? Can I in fact help them adequately or should I refer them to another therapist? Would my best be good enough?

As therapists and nurses we need to learn to surf the tides of suffering well. Am I an idealist? Yet if people really care and believe they need to work from a holistic perspective, then such ideas are fundamental. We need people who can create the space where we can emotionally and spiritually grow but who do not intrude into our space. When Winnie expressed her concern that people intrude she did not simply mean this on a physical plane but on a spiritual and emotional plane, or in other words that they were not sensitive enough to what was unfolding. Or simply not 'good enough'.

Wednesday 4 July 2001

Iris

Iris says her son, who is nearly nine years old, said to her, 'Mummy, I wish you didn't have cancer.' Iris cries as she shares this. She says it's so hard when the children say such things. I suggest it's good that he is able to say this? Iris agrees despite the pain. 'He doesn't share his feelings very well so it is good he can get this out.' I suggest it must bear heavily on him. I think it's not easy to share feelings in a family; Iris won't because she tries to protect her children and her husband struggles with his own emotions.

Iris says she went to her ten-year-old daughter's sports day. It was a lovely day. Her daughter had kept coming over to her (she wasn't really allowed to) and sitting on Iris's knee. Iris says she felt so sad because she wanted to see her children grow up and she knew she wouldn't make it. More tears. I suggest they were tears of sadness and joy. Iris says that was true…she was trying to take each day as it came, and she said that to her son. I say, 'As if each new day was a gift.' I suggest that Iris move closer to her children because of her fear, the deep fear of losing them. Iris agrees. She says, 'Two years ago when I was told I had the cancer in my liver I didn't expect to live a year. I have now lived two…so you don't know.'

Iris looks at me – 'I hope you don't mind me sharing these things with you. I don't want to load this on to you.' I confront Iris, 'I am your therapist.' Iris again gives me a look as if to realise that she hadn't perceived me from that angle. She smiled, 'Yes, you are.'

Iris says, 'I have difficulty sharing such thoughts at day care on Friday because I don't want to burden others who have so many problems of their own.' She talks about another patient she was close to where feelings were not easily shared. Lawton (2000) writes:

To maintain day care as a safe haven it was therefore necessary for all involved to participate in practices which served to distance patients from their futures and in particular, the physical reality of deterioration and death. (p.67)

There is considerable irony in the idea that the hospice was a safe haven where people could be normal away from the everyday reality of their abnormality within the fabric of society. Hence talk tended to be normal rather than focus on dying. No one wants reminding!

On a more mundane note, Iris says the pain in her shoulder has been better although she suffered another (third) severe migraine, again associated with driving in very hot weather to hospital for her chemotherapy. The migraines are distressing her; she imagines a brain tumour. I imagine it's easy to turn every symptom into a disaster when you have become accustomed to disaster.

Iris and I have moved to another level in our relationship where she is able to reveal her deep fears and emotions, whereas before, as she does with others, she has contained these, not wanting to burden others. She tries hard not to cry, as if that is a weakness when she must be strong. I remind her that is why I prescribed her oak. She laughs and admits she has not been taking the Bach remedies regularly. 'It's so hard to remember and do they do any good?' Clearly they have not had a dramatic effect.

Thursday 9 August 2001

Ralf

Ralf is 65. He has cancer in his bladder which was detected when he had a resection of his prostate gland. Further investigation revealed widespread bone metastases. He was admitted to the hospice for symptom control, in particular back pain that is proving difficult to control. His wife is 53. They have two children. His son is married to a Malaysian woman. They live in London and have a daughter just four months old. I feel the poignancy of his granddaughter's picture pinned to the wall. His daughter is pregnant, and expecting any day. Ralf has been very anxious, finding it difficult to talk about things.

I introduce myself. We sit and Ralf reveals his life to me. He had been working as a courier before retiring in March...and now this. He easily tells me about his illness and his frustration that the treatment has not gone as well as expected. The chemotherapy was stopped because of the side effects.

He is now having radiotherapy to ease his bone pain. He says the pain is much worse when he does any form of stretching.

He accepts my offer of a blanket bath. He says they gave him one yesterday…it had been difficult with movement. Yet he moves quite well in the bed, indeed surprises himself that he can lean forward so I can wash his back when yesterday that had not been possible. His pain control is improving. He asks me to feel the lump on his rib – a hard nodule on the bone. Touching the cancer feels strange. His bowels are okay; he says he had constipation and then diarrhoea, but it's hopefully now okay. He wears a pad just in case but it's smeared with faeces. He is distressed. The loss of dignity more than anything is tough to accept. I give him a clean pad and help him to dress and sit in a chair…the effort into the chair involves two steps. I offer him palladone for breakthrough pain and he settles with his radio and paper. He shaves himself and cleans his teeth. I comb his hair.

Other nurses comment how bright Ralf is today…applause for me but I have done nothing more than tune into Ralf and flow with him. Talking about matter-of-fact things but all the time searching for signs to go deeper, to help him explore his feelings and find meaning in what is happening to him. The signs, if he has read them, are gloomy indeed. Yet he is determined to get well again. That he can beat this. He has so much to lose with his grandchildren – one born and another soon to be born. I have written before that the prospect of losing relationship with young grandchildren seems to be a particularly difficult loss for people to anticipate (Johns 2000).

Saying that he can 'beat this' gives me a cue. I say, 'Have you thought that you might not beat this?' A moment's silence. He wasn't going there. Death was not an option in his frame of things. He is focused on beating this. He needs help to bolster his sense of hope *at this time*. That is his wavelength. It is not for me to cut across his wavelength; it would only topple him from this precarious tightrope.

Such care is mundane yet the essence of palliative care. The key is to be available; clear about purpose, compassionate, knowing him from his perspective, comfortable with self and fully present, skilled in my responses and unhurried.

Saturday 11 August 2001

Angela and Rex

Angela, a staff nurse, 'confesses' her lack of compassion towards Rex yesterday. I observe her closely and wonder about this woman I have not met before. I wonder at her vulnerability and her ability to say this to me. Perhaps it is because we have worked well together with Rex this morning. She says that yesterday she was not getting anything back from him, that she could not understand his whispers, that she felt frustrated. She feels guilty. She wants to purge herself of this feeling and seeks forgiveness. I say how good we have been with Rex, the way we have enabled him to express himself, making him smile, caring for him as if we were administering angels to his broken and emaciated body. We enabled him to enjoy a some ice-filled water – he said how good that was to drink.

Angela smiles. I feel so good that she can open up to share her feelings rather than bottle them up. To be available to our patients we need to be available to each other. Her guilt is a reflection of her compassion. The idea of getting something back is intriguing as if we bargain our services. We need gratification for what we give. Perhaps that is how we sustain our caring.

Today Rex shares his life with me. He is 73. He worked in accounts. He is married and has two children and one granddaughter. In the afternoon, they all visit. The wife is busy over him.

Rex has not been told that he has cancer, he has been told that he has bronchitis. The family are insistent that they don't want Rex told. This fact had been mentioned in the shift report a couple of days previous. Later that morning Rex was withdrawn, and hence Angela's frustration.

We have drawn him out of the shadow but despite such cues as 'this must be tough for you', he does not pursue the cause of his illness. Other nurses said, 'He must know what is going on with him, mustn't he?'

I look deep within his eyes and see no signs. Others say he is anxious, and without doubt his breathlessness makes him anxious. He is very cachexic…not an ounce of energy except to hold his beaker. Like a broken bird he can no longer fly. If he were to ask me if he was dying I would have no hesitation to tell him the truth. But for now I flow with the family's demand, being available to help them move within and cope with the shadow of the death.

Gayle

Gayle has cancer of the pancreas and liver metastases with massive ascites and lower limb oedema. She is 43, and is separated from Luke although she was getting it back together with him when the cancer was discovered. Her big event is being confirmed and christened into the Catholic faith on Sunday.

Just before lunch I go and speak with Gayle. I say hello to her two children and her brother and ask her whether she might like some reflexology after lunch? She says she would. However, she is too tired, which always strikes me as a paradox as reflexology is so relaxing and requires no effort. Perhaps the thought of treatment sounds tiring? Perhaps if she is tired she just wants to be on her own; that the mere presence of someone else is tiring?

Before I leave the unit I look round her door. She is awake and invites me to sit and chat. She talks about her two children; Grant is 10 and Harry is 16. Grant is struggling with her illness while Harry has been fantastic. Gayle finds space at the hospice that comforts her. She is wrapping up her life: planning her funeral and has made her will. Sitting with her I feel a stillness about her. She has found a faith that sustains and gives meaning to her life and death.

Wednesday 15 August 2001

It is 6.45. I love this time of the morning. The day is soft, the rising sun tinges the sparse cloud cover gold. Few cars on the road. As I drive I centre myself to prepare me for work at the hospice. It is as if I am going to a sacred place.

The night staff nurse gives her report. It is customary for the night staff nurse to read a few words for reflection, such as a poem, to honour the sacredness of our work. However, Dolores does not do this. Mandy, a care assistant, moves into this space to say a few words after Dolores has finished. Mandy is a keeper of tradition. She chooses a poem that is very moving. Call me a romantic, but such words remind me why we are gathered here this morning. They inspire me and vibrate through my soul. When it does not happen I feel a void, or a leak where caring imperceptibly slips away.

Meaningful ritual is an important element in sustaining culture.

Gayle

I am working with Sophie, the red team leader this morning. We have two patients, Joyce and Gayle, whom I met last week. Walking into Gayle's room I immediately feel peaceful. She lays there, her skin yellow from the jaundice. Her body is very toxic now. Curtains are pulled round her bed. I say, 'Hello Gayle' – she opens her eyes. She is barely responsive but knows me. She closes her eyes again as I take her hand and focus on communicating my compassion for her. She is hot. I can feel the heat around her head and body. For ten minutes I use Therapeutic Touch to move the heat out of her body, visualising a cool blue waterfall cascading over her. The heat shifts. About her liver area I feel the tumour bulk. It is massive. I try and flood it with light but it is very dense. I can take some heat away from the surface.

Gayle has deteriorated during the past week and will die soon. She was commenced on midazolam 10mg via the syringe driver yesterday because she seemed restless. My memory of Gayle was of a woman who had found stillness in her faith and who was prepared for her death. Perhaps the utter realisation of actual death is a wave that washes away composure and stillness. This utter realisation must be awesome, no matter how well you have prepared.

I wash her with Alison, a care assistant. It is good to work with her. She is so confident in her caring.

Any movement and Gayle is uncomfortable...she just wants to be left alone. But she has been in the same position all night. We also know she has a sacral sore – so we must shift her position. She cannot lie on her right side because of the pressure it would cause on her inflamed liver. I hold her as we turn her...she is moaning. She is incontinent. The smell is not pleasant as I lean over her...breathing through my mouth helps. We pull the wound dressing away...the sore is superficial yet extensive. I apply a new dressing and we make her comfortable. I set up an aroma-stone with lavender and neroli to combat the smell from her wound and faeces. Alison says it is pleasant. Neroli in particular will help to ease Gayle's suffering and contribute to a sense of stillness within the room. Lessons learnt from Mary's reflection (see p.51).

After lunch, we shift Gayle's position again. Harry, her eldest son, leaves the room while we do this. Gayle cries, 'It hurts.' Yet she quickly settles and is peaceful as her visitors arrive. They know Gayle has deteriorated. Anxiety and distress ripple over them. Grant, her younger son, is frightened. Harry is calm on the surface, yet I wonder what emotions vibrate deep within. Harry is trying to be the brave man for his younger brother and for Gayle. Gayle's sister and daughter arrive...her sister is a bundle of strength. Clare, her daughter, cannot contain her crying...she talks at length to me, about the flowers, about her young cousin, about her life. She needs to talk and I am available to her. She needs a hug, to be held so she can feel contained and safe to release her distress and fear. I take her back into the sitting room where her mother and others are gathered. I hover, being there for them ... and then I move away feeling my continual presence may be intrusive into the private grief of this family.

The shift is coming to an end. Gayle's door is closed. The priest and Sister Kathleen are with the family. Should I knock and say goodbye? Or would I be intruding? I am bothered by this dilemma. I want to ask others, but feel I need to make this decision. I want to say goodbye to Gayle and her family as an expression of care. I also want to say goodbye for myself as a moment of closure.

I knock and go in. The room is crowded. A woman I do not know leans over Gayle and embraces her. Gayle is not responsive. A man sits close to Gayle. This must be Luke, her estranged husband. He looks at me with deep sadness but I do not know him and cannot easily respond except with sympathetic eyes. I touch Sister Kathleen's arm and say I just want to say goodbye. I say goodbye to Harry…he waves and I feel his care. I pause momentarily – whether to overtly say goodbye to Gayle but the room is too crowded. Across the solemn distance between us I send her my love and best wishes for her forthcoming journey and leave the room.

Outside I feel intense emotion. Sophie catches my eye; she reads me well and says, 'Gayle?' I nod and depart. She knows. It is so important that we are sensitive to each other and care for each other, to help each other release the suffering we unwittingly absorb. I feel as if I walk on a cloud. I feel incredibly light as if I have trodden with angels, and yet I feel my tears, not of sadness but of intense poignancy.

Gayle has taught me to have faith and that with faith any challenge is possible. I feel the truth of something Rinpoche (1992) says 'Every dying person is a teacher, giving all those who help them a chance to transform themselves through developing their compassion' (p.206).

Joyce

Joyce will be 60 in two weeks time. I speak with her daughter on the phone. I inform her that Joyce is on the commode and that if she rings back in about ten minutes she can speak to her mum. I ask her if she wants to talk to me? Her daughter expresses her anxiety – whether the radiotherapy Joyce had three weeks ago had worked? She knows her mum needs another scan to see if the brain tumours had shrunk. I acknowledge her anxiety, suggesting that these are uncertain times and we do not know the impact of the radiotherapy. She agrees and thanks me. She asks again what my name is. I say 'Chris' and she says, 'Thank you, Chris.' The intimacy is important to her and that she feels cared for.

Joyce says she feels woozy, an abstract sense in her head. She was admitted to the hospice so we could sort out her nausea. She was on a cocktail of five anti-emetics. We have reduced this to three. Her nausea is now better controlled. She has a pot full of dexamethasone to take with her porridge, which she says is delicious.

Joyce is up in her chair after a wash. I kneel by her chair and observe her swollen ankles. She has significant oedema and a granular dressing on top of her right foot. She says it's where the skin has burst and leaked oedema fluid. She has a small, healed wound on top of her left foot where a similar event had happened. I suggest she put her feet up? She agrees. Her feet are very dry with flaky skin so I ask if she would like me to massage her feet with some moisturising oil? She would like that very much. I mix two drops of lavender with some almond oil and work on her feet for about 20 minutes.

As I massage Joyce's feet she tells me her illness story…the brain tumours diagnosed followed by lung tumour. She had a bronchoscopy. She knows she has cancer. She is hopeful the radiotherapy will have zapped the brain tumours (she does not know the widespread extent of the tumours). She is waiting for her scan. She says 'they' will then tackle the lung tumour. I ask her how she feels? She is hopeful. She agrees that these are uncertain and scary times. I ask her what having cancer means to her? She says, 'That's it, isn't it?' I say that these are early days and that she's hopeful it will work out. We touch the edge of doubt. I open a space where she can talk about her fears. She tells me more about her life. She has not worked since the diagnosis three months ago. She has four children, three girls and a boy, and six grandchildren. She is going on holiday in November to Spain but is anxious that she will be fit enough.

I finish the massage. Joyce says it was very relaxing…she really enjoyed it. Massage is a catalyst for opening a space to be with someone – touch is so intimate and trusting, almost beguiling in enabling Joyce to relax and talk through her thoughts.

At lunch Joyce has some soup which she vomits back. She has oral cyclizine for her nausea but she cannot take it, so I arrange for her to have a syringe driver to give her anti-emetics subcutaneously. She is upset that we can't sort out this distressing and persistent symptom. She's again feeling woozy, but her husband tells me she has a history of feeling like this and that investigation has failed to discover its cause.

Wednesday 22 August 2001

I have not slept well. Tiredness stalks me. However, the early morning drive to the hospice is awesome and energising through gold-tinged clouds. It feels very quiet at the hospice. Four patients, with two admissions today and George is going home.

Rachel

I am looking after Rachel this morning until my 10.30 appointment with Iris. Rachel was admitted yesterday but has had a restless and uncomfortable night. She has lower left-sided lung pain that is not well controlled. Her breathing is very laboured. She is also very sad as her husband died just three weeks ago from cancer of the lung. Fate is sometimes hard to fathom.

Rachel has had a mastectomy for breast cancer and with brain metastases. Her face is half white and half red, as if some manifestation of the brain tumour. Perhaps her cranial nerves are affected? We seek explanation to ease our curious minds.

Rachel informs me that she has not slept well … just a couple of hours. She struggles to breathe. I fetch her some tea to help her with her tablets, but she has difficulty swallowing. She says it's painful. Sophie joins me and we decide, with Rachel, for her to have oxygen via a nasal cannulae and to give her ventolin via a nebuliser. Sophie also gives her some diazepam to ease her palpable anxiety. The dexamethasone is left in her pot for her to take later.

She does not want any breakfast and is too tired to wash or be washed. She says that one thing she finds really hard is not being able to use both hands when she goes to the toilet or washes. The loss of dignity and being dependent on others must be very hard to accept.

Rachel has had a stroke due to the brain metastases with little chance of recovering arm function. Earlier I had made a faux pas when I said to her she could look forward to rehabilitation after all this. Well, perhaps she can in her mind. She doesn't mind the pain but gets panicky when her breathing is difficult. I say it must have been difficult to see her husband struggle with his breathing before he died. I give her a number of cues to respond to talk about her husband if she wishes but she never takes these up or she deals with the cues in peremptory fashion. No sense of emotion. He was 62 years old, a mechanical engineer with his own business. He had retired. Like her, he had also smoked.

I massage Rachel's left hand. It is limp in my own. She can slightly move her fingers. I use sweet almond carrier oil with just a drop of lavender essential oil. She loves the smell; very relaxing and comforting. I then massage her right hand…she says she is nearly asleep and then she drifts off. Her anxiety and her breathing have eased. I go into the beautiful gardens and find just a small lavender bush with very bright flowers but no great scent. I pick a few for Rachel so she can have this smell in her room. Lavender will help to balance her anxiety.

Dr Paul sees Rachel as she may have an infection or possibly a pulmonary embolus. Sophie has phoned x-ray and got a report on Rachel's chest x-ray – it shows widespread lung metastases. It's bad news. She is prescribed antibiotics and her analgesia increased. I sit with her and help her take these with an ice-cold fizzy orange drink. Refreshing – she says the ice makes the difference. She takes these and the drugs left on her table from earlier. I leave her to rest.

By 12.00 I am back on the unit after seeing Iris. Rachel is walking with her daughter Kelly. I am surprised but she is sitting outside in the sun having a cigarette. The power of addiction, even when breathing is so difficult. I assume she must be feeling better. Sophie says that Dr Paul has told her the news of her lung scan so perhaps the cigarette in the sun is necessary to calm the potentially devastating news. I leave for a clinical supervision[5] session with one of the staff and return again at 14.30. Rachel is asleep on her bed, drenched in sweat. I express my concern to Sophie…we sense that she has rapidly deteriorated. Having been with her all morning I feel the pang of impending loss. These moments are perhaps the most difficult for myself. One moment we sit and chat through a hand massage, the next moment she is dying. Intimacy also creates a sense of vulnerability. Yet to harden self against impending loss would compromise intimacy – so 'we' have to find a way of being intimate yet not-attached to that intimacy.

Later, writing my journal I ask myself – what was significant about my care with Rachel? Certainly the relaxing impact of a hand massage. I have tended to minimise the impact of this simple massage and yet again the patient's response was very positive. It is a wonderful way to be with someone and sets up a most natural conversation.

Yet again, the anxiety that invariably accompanies breathlessness has been evident. It is not possible to say what had the greatest therapeutic effect; the diazepam, the ventolin, the oxygen, the massage…they all complement each other…the true value of complementary therapy.

---

5   Clinical supervision is a formal contracted developmental relationship between myself and the practitioner. The aim of supervision is to enable the practitioner to develop and sustain effective practice. We meet approximately one hour a month. My role as clinical supervisor is to guide the practitioner to learn through reflection on everyday work experiences towards realising desirable practice, in much the same way I learn through the experiences shared in the narrative.

I wonder about Rachel's apparent lack of emotion about her husband. Does she bottle this up? Was she too focused on her own struggle? Does she try and be strong? I did not challenge her emotional response. It would have been inappropriate to 'force' such issues. It is a dilemma when to push issues or simply to flow with what's unfolding. Responding appropriately is a reflection of empathic knowing – knowing the person from the perspective in contrast with the perspectives I might project. Rachel's life had shattered in pieces. I picked up some pieces and held them up to see where they fit. There was a futility about this, and yet being with Rachel was so utterly profound. It feels as if I pulled a loose thread and the whole fabric of her life unwound as we look on helplessly.

Tuesday 11 September 2001

Iris

Iris reports on her latest liver scan. The liver disease remains stable. Her consultant says that the longest people have kept liver growth at bay has been three years. Iris suspects this is some sort of judgement. She says the doctor has to be realistic. I tend to agree with John Diamond (1998) that doctors tend to paint the best picture. I agree with Iris that false hope is indeed false. However, for now the liver *is* stable. Iris is anxious about her left shoulder pain. The pain has spread along the collar bone. Her consultant is hopeful that this can be treated if necessary with radiotherapy.

I ask: 'How are the children?'

'Charlotte has been playing up – it must be her hormones.'

'Why do women rationalise mood swings and irritability in other women by blaming hormones?'

Iris laughs: 'Yes that's true…we are as bad as men.'

'Maybe Charlotte is picking up your fears and responding?'

Iris thoughtfully responds with an 'umm' and continues: 'Robert has gone bald on one side of his head with worry.'

I suggest the baldness is stress breaking out as physical signs.

'Does he have anyone to speak to?'

'No…he bottles it up…he cannot express how he feels easily.'

I ask how the Bach flower remedy was going (her treatment bottle made up on June 26)?

Iris guilty says: 'I only takes them spasmodically.'

I respond: 'I would say very spasmodically, as the treatment bottle is not yet finished 11 weeks later!' (If taken as prescribed it would last three weeks.)

Iris: 'I'll try harder.'

The Bach flower remedies are ineffectual in helping Iris – yet she is coping better. Her oak is stronger. She no longer wears a mask of coping with me but outside, in her normal life roles, she does. I can understand her need to be seen and responded to as normal rather than as a cancer victim. She feels it is best for her family but, as Robert's baldness illustrates, the stress leaks out from its container.

When I return home a neighbour asks if I have heard the news of the terrorist attack on the Twin Towers in New York. On the television I see the great towers collapse. So much death and suffering in the world puts our efforts at the hospice into perspective. The TV images are mesmerising, deeply shocking, and my heart aches for those who have died. I think of my friend Jane who lives in New York – is she safe? We are all connected, so that even thousands of miles away I feel the suffering vibrate around the world. We live such insulated lives that it takes deep trauma to shatter the containers and wake us up. At such moments I wonder, 'What does it mean to be human?' And, of course, I have no answers.

Friday 14 September 2001

Joan

Joan is 79, a regular attender at day hospice on Mondays. She has fungating cancer of her breasts, extending under both axilla and onto her back. She has become breathless with fluid accumulating on her lung – a pleural effusion. She requires a 'tap' but has been reluctant to accept this treatment. I was struck at the shift report how her refusal was seen as a problem. And with this thought in my mind I began to explore with her what meaning she had about her life and death. I was also told that she was 'religious', which again intrigued me in view of my recent reflections. I was a little uncertain with the MRSA (mecillin resistant staphylococcus aureus) precautions – could I go into her room without dressing up in protective clothing? I could…but I initially kept my distance. Joan is very garrulous. She quickly tells me her dilemma with the lung tap…she is undecided. I sense her indecision about which way to go; to be treated or not to be treated. She puts her life into perspective, talking through the photograph of her grandchildren and their partners on the wall. 'I have had my life. My husband died eight years ago…I nursed him through that illness. When you're alone it's different, I wouldn't want anyone to have to do that for me.'

She is decisive. She knows her daughter would do this for her and she wants to spare her. 'I know someone who had the tap,' she says. 'It just came back.' She is rueful and feels that she doesn't want to get onto this bandwagon of being pulled about uncomfortably – 'for what?!'

I say, 'I am told you have a strong faith.' She affirms, 'I attend the Methodist church but now I'm unable to get there.' She talks about the woman priest whom she was very fond of who has left and the new priest from Ghana. 'He's a bit evangelical,' she says in a soft conspiratory voice. She reflects on how the church used to be full but is now largely empty; changing worlds and the way people view and resist the changing ways. A little sadness – 'The priest can visit me in hospital and administer communion and that would be okay.'

I ask how she feels about death and what lies beyond. She says she doesn't know but if it means being reunited with her husband then she looks forward to that. I ask her if she senses him waiting for her or has any premonition of dying and what lies beyond? She hasn't but she shares a story of someone she knew who had such an experience…of drifting across a field when she met her grandmother. Her grandmother told her to go back, which she did. The woman had such a sense of peace after that. Joan says that this gives her some comfort that death is a moving on into another realm and that she would join her husband.

I suggest that Joan had made her mind up and needed to dispel the lingering doubt (fear) of dying (that having the 'tap' would delay that) or whether she wanted to hold on to life as long as possible. Joan simply smiles. I feel very comfortable dwelling with her in this conversation. I sense the sacred about and within us.

Later I give Joan a foot massage. She says it's lovely but then I would expect nothing less than her gratitude. She has such delicate ankles. I note this and say she must have worn high heels and stockings with seams. She laughs and says, 'Yes, I loved high heel shoes. I wore them all the time.' 'And dancing?' Not really, she never got into the big towns for the Palais. Her feet are pale, reflecting her lack of energy. Later she went to the Remembrance service for the New Yorkers; even in a wheelchair she felt exhausted.

Monday 24 September 2001

Iris

At the hospice I meet Iris for her reflexology. She has a dilemma whether to visit her friend Mia at home. They have become very close attending day hospice together. They are of similar age and both experience advanced breast cancer. Mia is now very poorly; she started vomiting while on holiday and now struggles to get out of bed. Iris feels their relationship has been confined to the day hospice…'Would Mia want me to visit?'

I ask Iris: 'What would you want from Mia if your roles were reversed?'

Iris has no doubt: 'For her to visit.'

'So you have your answer.'

Iris laughs: 'Yes…you make it seem so simple!'

Iris becomes reflective: 'Fridays in day care have not been well attended recently because so many of the group have now died. And now with Mia deteriorating…'

Iris breaks off her words as her tears swell. I pick up the cue and verbalise Iris's thoughts – 'It makes you think of your own future?' Iris quietly agrees. We have talked before about focusing on the present but it's so hard for her to be positive when these reminders creep up to confront her with her own dying. As we talk Iris shifts her pity to compassion for Mia and moves beyond her gloom.

I spend more time helping Iris to relax. After the treatment she says, 'I could hear the music but I was not asleep…it was as if I was on another plane. I had no thoughts or dreams yet was conscious of myself.'

I say, 'That sounds wonderful.'

Iris gives me one of her radiant smiles – 'It was.' She drinks some water and we check times for next week.

Mia's imminent death had made Iris very introspective and gloomy. Reflexology, including our conversation, had helped to lift the gloom and give Iris a more realistic perspective. Iris and Mia had shared their diseased-lives and now Iris was going to lose her day care confidante and buddy. She felt alone, guilty about her living, and with only the prospect of her own inevitable death.

I pause from writing to step outside into the fresh early night. It is getting dark. The air is very still. Few clouds obscure the sky. The moon is half-full. It is good to step out and linger in this air…tuning into the cosmos empties the mind of chatter and lifts the soul.

Wednesday 3 October 2001

Iris

Mia is dying and has been admitted to the inpatient unit. Iris is in turmoil… What should she do? Should she visit? Would she be intrusive? I listen and remind Iris of what we had talked about last treatment – what would she want from Mia? Iris says, 'I would want her to visit.' Iris then prevaricates when she should visit. Lena, the day care lead nurse, says, 'One of us could come with you if you wish. Would that be better?' Iris struggles to find answers. She says, 'We mustn't take up all of Chris's time.' As we walk towards the treatment room we meet Mia's niece in the courtyard. They embrace…the niece's tears flow. I suggest to Iris that perhaps she should visit now as it is so much in her head. She agrees so I sit and wait. Fifteen minutes later Iris returns. She says the room was full of Mia's relatives but Mia was not responsive – 'I don't think she knew I was there.' I suggest that she probably did, gently confronting Iris's negative perception, shifting it round to help her perceive the experience as more positive.

Iris is visibly disturbed by her visit to Mia. She puts her fears and distress into words – 'Mia was my only friend left in day care…now there will be no one left.' Iris fears being left alone. Mia was the only person Iris could really talk to, the only person who really knew how she felt.

As we walk Iris expresses her grief through her tears. Although I do not seek to reassure her I do share my thoughts that death released Mia from her suffering; that was a positive side to her death.

We eventually reach the treatment room. Iris informs me that her last bone scan had revealed a new 'hot spot' in the humerus bone on her left upper arm. Not surprisingly, she is unhappy with this development. She does not understand why she has this pain in her shoulder and collar pain – 'Is it referred up the arm? The consultant said that there's no new tumour growth there. He's prescribed radiotherapy for the new tumour…I'm having that next week…just one shot. I told him about these nodules (she shows me along the top of her left chest wall).' Her mastectomy scar is visible. I think of the cancer's continual presence in its different guises. Iris continues, 'He says there's nothing to worry about.' She rubs the nodules along the top of her scar line as she worries about them. 'He said if it's anything it's just a local reoccurrence as if that's nothing to really worry about. He said he was pleased with me.'

Words for Iris to reflect on – 'pleased with me'. What does *that* mean in light of Mia's death? That her own death is postponed for a while longer? She is caught on an emotional roller coaster with Mia's death and her own bad news. I must simply flow with her, being there yet not absorbing her suffering despite its intensity.

Iris says the reflexology was just what she needed. She had relaxed very deeply.

On the way out we again meet Lena and the conversation returns to Mia. Iris asks, 'Should I visit again? Would I be intrusive? Do the family want me in there?' Iris's anxiety bubbles over. Lena acts to reassure her – 'I'm sure they would welcome you.' But Iris is uncertain. I say, 'You said your goodbyes to her earlier?' Iris says, 'I did…not aloud but to myself…I'm thinking of Mia's daughter, Jasmine…she's just ten years old…I was wondering if I should bring my daughter and Jasmine together?'

Iris is entangled with her emotions; she wants to take Jasmine's pain away, to take responsibility, feeling compelled to move into the void that Mia's death will bring to this family. Iris wants to take the pain away as if taking her own pain away. These are deeply poignant moments.

Later, I walk past Mia's door. The corridor is full of her relatives in different places. They are quiet and seek out my eyes. I acknowledge them with a sad smile…the respectful posture. I do not know these people so I do not pause to offer myself. I only knew Mia very slightly from visiting day care.

Friday 16 November 2001

Rose

The morning is very still. The chill north wind has calmed. Cloud cover has kept the temperature above freezing. I know this through experiencing many such mornings. It is dark with just a hint of the new day, the first fingers of daylight pulling away the indigo screen. As I drive the screen is continually pulled back exposing a uniform cloudy sky. Leaves line the country lanes, beneath trees of shifting colours in the dull morning light. Such moments of stillness and solitude dwelling in nature connect me with my deeper self beyond mind. Such moments help me to focus myself as caring within each breath I breathe in and breathe out. My compassion is stirred and surfaces as a deep sense of joy. Forty-five minutes later I am at the hospice present within the unfolding day. My heart vibrates yet my head is still. Jill, the night care assistant, offers me tea. I melt into her warm welcome. Her warmth and consideration exemplify the essence of a caring community.

> We gather together in common purpose
> We gather ourselves to be most available
> We gather each other in caring embrace

Four nurses on this morning, all qualified, and just three patients and one admission expected. I feel very comfortable in the company of these three women. I wonder what we will do today to fill the time. Yet, time is an opportunity. I am working with Christine in the green team. We have two patients, Rose and Kit. Both women have cancer of the lung. Both are breathless. Christine offers, 'Which one would you like?' I choose Rose. I am intrigued by Christine's description of this 'young' 80-year-old who has such spirit. I had waved to her earlier when I had briefly walked round before the shift report. I was struck by her nasal cannulae.

Before I visit her, Christine and I dispense her medication. We note the struggle to manage her nausea has been complicated with the introduction of oromorph 2.5mg as a trial to help her breathing.

Rose is clutching a vomit bowl. I inform her I am Chris and am caring for her this morning. She says 'Chris' – even as she retches and struggles for her breath. Rose asks if she can sit up better. I help to lift Rose, bringing the back of the bed higher for Rose to lean against and a table for her lean on. It helps her although she is still vomiting. I offer to massage her hands if she would like that. Rose tries a smile and says she loves the smell of lavender. I hold her hands. They are large, as large as my own as I place mine over hers. They are soft, creative. I ask if she was an artist or sculptor? 'Oh, no.' 'Maybe a gardener?' 'Yes.' 'A decorator?' 'Yes.' Such banter is intimate and relaxing.

Two hours have passed and I am still with her, constantly tuning into her wavelength, finding the pattern of her rhythm and flowing with her. Her rhythm is staccato, the flow punctured by her continued vomiting and desperate effort for breath that takes all her energy. Yet there is a rhythm to her purse lip breathing. I find myself purse lip breathing with her. It is hard to be with someone as they struggle for breath. Rose has managed to take some diazepam to help her balance the anxiety that breathlessness brings but we have to resort to an injection of metoclopramide to help her vomiting. We talk of the need to set up a syringe driver, which Rose accepts and Christine sets up.

I have prepared a massage mix with lavender to massage Rose's hands. She is drinking a lot of water. Her mouth and lips are dry. I get her some ice-cold water – she says it is refreshing. Small comforts are extraordinarily significant. At home she plays Radio 4 and signs for me to put it on. However, after a few minutes it is clear that she struggles to concentrate. Christine suggests some classical music. Rose agrees. The sound drifts along the corridor. Rose says it helps to relax her. The nausea has diminished. As Rose seems more comfortable, we leave her.

About 15 minutes later I pop in to see how she is. She asks for a commode. Christine helps. Rose uses the commode but suddenly 'goes off' – her complexion becomes ashen grey. We get her back onto her bed...she is breathless and barely conscious. Slowly she recovers her colour and her consciousness. However, it marks a dramatic deterioration. Christine and I look at each other knowingly across Rose's limp body. The moment of her death draws near. Again we struggle to get Rose into the best position so she can breathe most easily, but she can no longer lean forward onto the bed table. I abandon the idea of a hand massage even as I stroke her hands, my effort to communicate through her suffering and fading consciousness that she is not alone, that she is loved, that she can rest in our presence. Rose recovers her awareness and settles despite her laboured breathing. She is tired and slides into an uneasy sleep. Christine goes to call Emma, Rose's granddaughter, to come to the hospice. It will take her some time as she lives in London.

Kit's call bell buzzes so I respond and rescue her from the toilet. Reams of toilet paper strewn about the floor. 'Have I been?' I reassure her she has and help her settle back into her chair. She is both apologetic and thankful. I sense her embarrassment at making a mess. It wounds her dignity. Dying well is like climbing an unknown and treacherous mountain in a fog.

John

Across the corridor I check that John is okay. I had met him and his son on his arrival at the hospice earlier in the day. His son has gone to 'get some things'. John has moved from the chair into bed, partly undressed. I ask him if he wants to change into his pyjamas? He declines – he is okay like this. I ask him if he would like a newspaper. Do we have the Daily Mirror? Indeed we do. I fetch it for him and also a television. Immediately he feels more comfortable as he begins to transform the room into his home. I was struck by Sophie's comment earlier when he arrived – to treat the hospice as his home while he is here. I thought, 'That's easier said than done, especially in a hospice with its connotations.' Yet he really does seem settled.

I had noticed the tattoo along his fingers when I had first met him – 'True Love' – a letter on each finger. He laughed, 'The things you do when you're young and in the army.' He had many tattoos and showed me the ones in Chinese he had done in Hong Kong. He had travelled widely during his national service. He is 64. The swelling of the tongue tumour in his neck is very evident. He has refused radical surgery. He has three sons who live locally. He was divorced 20 years ago, yet remains in contact with his wife. Neither remarried. The banter of strangers, yet my intention is to know him. The tumour prevents him from eating. Now he has a PEG tube in situ to feed him directly into his stomach. He seems relaxed about this. I ask him if he knows Helen, the Clinical Nurse Specialist for nutrition. He cannot place her. I am struck with the way we make connections by seeking common experiences. I leave him knowing that the 'formal' admission process is yet to come. Meeting people under the shadow of death is always a mystery. As I sit and talk with John I ask myself, what does he feel and think about his life? How does he view his forthcoming death? Perhaps the hardest question I ask myself is, how do I feel about him? I feel non-attached sitting here, and yet a strong sense of compassion grips me. Like the surfer riding the edge of the wave, we can learn to flow with suffering without drowning. Every wave, like every patient, is unique. We may have technique but the unfolding moment always needs grasping and interpreting for the appropriate and skilled response.

Rose

I need to get back to Rose. She is dribbling from her mouth and dripping from her nose. I wipe this away and she stirs. I assume she is sleeping but her consciousness has deepened. I need to replenish the lavender in the aroma-stone. I had left the mix bottle in the sitting room after I had grabbed a cup of coffee earlier. Now two women occupy the room. One woman is crying while the other comforts her. I enter and apologise for being intrusive. The woman crying asks me if I have come to see her? I ask, 'Who are you visiting?' She says, 'Rose.' I say, 'Are you Emma?' She is, and I tell her who I am and that I have been looking after Rose. I say something like, 'She's not doing so well this morning.' Christine comes in. I say to Emma, 'Have you spoken with your grandmother?' Christine says, 'Rose was unable to respond.'

They must have arrived when I was talking to John. Clutching my empty bottle I make my apologies and return to Rose and sit with her gently holding her hand. Rose's breathing has become more compromised. Each breath is a struggle to inhale. She is past being aware of me sitting here. She is slipping away. Maybe I should have stayed with her rather than speak with John? I hadn't anticipated the rapid deterioration. A slight feeling of guilt ripples through me. I say 'sorry' to Rose.

After a while, Emma and her friend come in. I offer to move and give Emma my chair. Emma strongly says, 'No, stay there.' She squeezes in behind me and holds me tight. It feels strange to feel her sobbing body and her tight hold as we sit and watch Rose's breathing pattern shift. At first it is irregular and then it becomes less forceful and less frequent. The natural flow of her breathing rhythm is punctuated by gasps and pauses. Staccato rhythm. Percussion in slow motion. Observing Rose's breathing I again find myself breathing with Rose, to help her find balance breathing in and breathing out, the rhythmic letting go in order to flow and the holding in to ensure we are not simply swept away. We follow the curved line in the sand that guides us towards the divine sea.

I am conscious of a heaviness in my chest; the chaos of emotions rippling through me. What do I feel? I can hardly say. But we settle into this chaotic rhythm as we dance this final dance with Rose. And yet we merge into the background as if Rose has to dance the final dance alone. We are in suspense as we watch her intently. A lightness descends, my feet are so light on the floor. Emma has moulded with my body. I am her mother. I am a womb of sanctuary. There is no resistance as I flow along Rose and Emma's wavelengths. 'To offer no resistance to life is to be in a state of grace, ease and lightness' (Tolle 1999, p.155). I sense this state in dancers who dance well, the way they surrender to the unfolding rhythm.

Rose's neighbour comes in, a retired doctor. Emma leaps up and hugs him. He takes her outside. I stay with Rose and Christine as we wait until her breathing stops and we share her death. It is an intensely moving moment to be with someone through the descent into another dimension. The rhythm shifts and we can rest with Rose in the stillness of this moment. I close my eyes and concentrate on the essential Phowa ritual; of helping Rose's spirit melt into the light. Christine asks if I am okay. I tell her what I am doing. She says that is beautiful. I am releasing my love for action.

> Then, close your eyes and sit in your own darkness, becoming aware of the light emanating from within you. This inner light is love, an emotional prism reflecting all your facets. It isn't abstract; you can see it, feel it, smell it, taste it, be it. Love is energy; don't hold it back, it's the catalyst for your enlightenment. (Roth 1999, p.70)

I stand up yet transfixed. Rose lies here, her life force is departing. Her dying has been hard work for her. Imagine what it is like to die of lack of breath. Now she lies peacefully. Sweet release. She was not alone as she had feared she would be at home. I wonder what she senses in this other world.

Her doctor neighbour comes in and asks mundane practical questions between his tears. How do people respond in the immediate afterglow of someone's death? Simply the best way they can. He confirms that Emma is next of kin. He says Rose's daughter, who is Emma's mother, and Rose were estranged 20 years ago. He smiles and says that Rose had some very fixed ideas. There is a tinge of regret that Rose's daughter is not here, that Rose dies estranged from her own daughter. I wonder what the daughter would feel. I think of my own daughters and my own death.

The need to be practical; Christine asks if Dr Jane is still on the unit so she can confirm the death. I go to find her. I discover she left the hospice five minutes ago. When I return, Emma and her family crowd in the sitting room. Christine is in there. I am outside and feel shut out. I need to release this energy that has swollen inside me. I struggle to name this energy…it is a sense of awe, suspense, unleashed compassion. It is not fear or grief. I need to flow with it but the flow is blocked. Uncertain, I move down the corridor.

Bernard

As I pass his open door, Bernard calls me. He asks if I would help him use the toilet. I help him stand from his bed. He is weak, his legs are swollen but he manages to stand with my help and use the urinal I hold for him. His penis is swollen but he has no sense of self-consciousness. I help him back into his bed. Sophie comes into the room. She has brought him some soup. He says he needs help to drink the soup. I sense Sophie's uncertainty. She does not want to give this time and, as I anticipate, she asks me to help him. I accept, although with a twinge of regret. My mind is full with Rose and Emma.

Bernard is a softly spoken Irishman also with breathing and nausea problems. The tomato and lentil soup is too hot so we wait. I ask about his two children who are 8 and 13. He is 61. My children are 9 and 12. I suggest it must be tough for them to see their daddy so ill. He says it is. There is such a poignancy about losing our connection with our children. A silence between us that I do not rush to fill. I suggest he tries the soup? He has about six spoonfuls before he says enough. He is tired so I leave him and take his tray back to the kitchen.

It is nearly 14.00. I need to leave the unit for an appointment yet I need to close what I have experienced this morning. As I pass the nursing station I see Christine. Emma is alone further down the corridor engaged on her mobile phone. Should I disturb her to say goodbye? What have I learnt from earlier experiences? Emma and I were strangers a moment ago. We danced and now I feel a strong attachment to her. We have flowed together in this dance. I move to where she sits. She looks up and says to the person in the phone, 'There is someone I need to hug.' We embrace and my pent-up energy bursts out. Released I am free, I am light and can float away. I am pleased Emma reached us in time. She has added a richness to my life as I have to hers. The caring dance is always a mutual dance.

Passing the nursing station I pause to ask Christine if she is okay. She smiles and we hug. We have travelled such a road together and are connected in a spiritual union for all time. We have touched the essential nature of our work. We have reached out and touched God. Yet it is only the nature of our work. A patient's death in a hospice is such a normal event. How easy it is to diminish the sacred nature of being with someone as they die. Merely work. Death is such a momentous event for the person that it can never be trivialised or be a normal event. When we accept death as normal, then we lose the plot. We fail. Closure is complete. I tread air as if transformed. Such a feeling of lightness within my body and soul. I have pulled back the curtains of chaos to reveal a beautiful stillness.

Rhythms of dance

The metaphor of dance as caring intrigues me. I wrote a paper, 'The caring dance' (Johns 2001), in which I viewed caring as a dance based on the Native American lore that significant parts of culture are commemorated through dance. I was also inspired by Carol Picard's representation of caring through Gabrielle Roth's five rhythms to illuminate the caring dance she performed at the International Association for Human Caring Conference in Florida 2000. As a consequence (and I must acknowledge a great debt to Carol) I bought Roth's book, *Sweat Your Prayers* (1999).

Now I read the book to see how I might frame my caring dance with Rose, Emma and Christine within the five rhythms. Roth writes with great vitality and I feel myself come alive with the caring dance. The five rhythms, *flowing, staccato, chaos, lyrical* and *stillness*, and the way the pattern of these rhythms unfold within the caring dance help me reflect deeper on my experience with Rose and Emma.

Roth says *flowing* is the feminine, the rhythm of the earth, being able to tune into natural rhythms and flow with them, the path of least resistance. This is the essence of my nursing practice – to flow with my patients, families and my colleagues, finding the rhythm of the caring dance, letting go to the intuitive self, yet grounded in the practice, in the knowing of who I am, and the connection to all things. This is the plot that weaves through my stories, the realisation of this sense of self within a greater whole. I reflect on those forces that cut me off from this flow – self-doubt, guilt. Roth calls these *flow freezers*. 'Different things cut us off – panic, over-exertion, self-consciousness, laziness, worry, and stress are all flow freezers' (p.53).

It is easy to doubt myself as if some false humility. I know I have not resisted the flow of energy. Roth suggests that three archetypes are associated with feminine rhythm of *flowing – mother, mistress* and *madonna*.

> Flowing is more than a rhythm; it's a specific energy field in which the feminine aspect of the soul is revealed in all its awesome beauty, fierce power, and animal magnetism. Deep within each of us is a mother longing to nurture, a mistress impatient to flirt, and a madonna serene in her wisdom. And they all bop out when the beat kicks in. (p.54)

I can see that being with Emma is the union of mother, mistress and madonna; the reflection of my feminine self. Such a powerful image to grasp. My *mother* reached out to her – to protect her from the blast of suffering that was threatening to overwhelm her. As a mother I offered my body to shelter her. As a *mistress* I felt our emotions swirl in the unfolding moment and dance in the wind. And my *madonna* was guiding me within the unfolding moment to respond most appropriately. 'Madonna is the part of soul that receives data, spins it into patterns, weaves them into the web of our higher intelligence, and inspires the necessary actions' (Roth 1999, p.72). The *madonna* taps the sacred part of me, enabling my spirit to soar. It fuels my sense of awe at the nature of hospice practice, transforming mundane events into things of exquisite beauty. The habitual, the taken-for-grantedness of much of practice, is a constantly unfolding playground. Indeed, through reflection the mundane becomes sacred.

> We need reminders, rituals to feed our sacred hunger, ways to devote ourselves to the divine spirit within us. Whatever our chosen practice, we need to do it simply for the sake of doing it, not for any outside reward. The point is to find a way into the purity of mind that is our Buddha nature. (Roth 1999, p.75)

The *madonna* is reflection-within-the-unfolding-moment. It is being aware of what is unfolding within the flow. The union of *madonna* with *mother* and *mistress* puts this type of energy into perspective with other energies that make up the rhythm of *flowing*.

Yet, *flowing* is just one of five patterns of energy that intermingle within the way the dance unfolds. The feminine *flowing* must be balanced by the masculine *staccato*. Yin and yang. *Staccato* gives the dance its creative form. It is the observable pattern of movement unfolding. Roth identifies three archetypes that characterise *staccato*: *father, son* and *holy spirit*.

> Father knows your limits – he draws boundaries. He's also protective and responsible, your internal father knows best. Son is renegade, a rebel who pushes the envelope, acts on his passion, and lives out his dreams. Holy spirit watches the movie from the back row, a detached witness to your melodramatic tendencies. He's a seeker of truth and student of tantra. (Roth 1999, p.85)

It is my *father* who draws the curved line in the sand. In earlier stories I have been inspired by the work of Ben Okri, who urges the poet to have the courage to transcend the boundaries to reveal the truth. This is the rhythm of my *son*.

> Son lives on the edge of the unpredictable, making us interesting. Embodying the energy of the wild card throws the game in your favour. What is required is a willingness to be passionate and involved, intimate and down to earth, vulnerable and yet bigger than life when it's required. (Roth 1999, p.101)

The creative edge. *Son* is the part of the soul that is emotionally expressive, the part of you that will tell the truth at all costs. Simply engage with and dwell in Roth's words:

> In the feminine mode we are aware of our feelings, tracking them through the body, being receptive to the messages they bear. In the masculine mode, we communicate those feelings, risk offering them, reach out through them, and use them to connect with other people's hearts and minds. This part of us knows it is holy work to bare our souls, speak our minds, and follow our hearts into the wilderness of relationship, where very often we find ourselves dancing in the dark. (p.101)

The sense of holy spirit moves me to practise caring at the hospice with spiritual attitude and to write stories about my experiences. Narrative is a reflection of holy spirit. It is also about being an active part of a community, working with others to create a sense of community where we can rest within each other's souls. Such experiences with Rose are also experiences of being with Christine. Of we who tread the same boards, tuning into each other's soul dance, so we can dance together.

The rhythms of *flowing* and *staccato* collide and create the rhythm of *chaos* (Roth, p.114). In *chaos* I let my intuition free to dive deep inside me. I surrender to the unfolding moment, letting go of the need to impose or control the moment. As such, *chaos* can be an anxious time.

> We try desperately to hold our lives together, to keep everything secure and predictable, but life is none of these things. Chaos teaches us how to hang in the unknown and dig it. (Roth 1999, p.118)

Roth identifies three archetypes within the rhythm of *chaos*: the *artist*, the *lover* and the *seeker*. Each archetype is born from the alchemical wedding of masculine and feminine archetypes.

> The artist is the integration of mother and father. Form without substance is a hollow shell; substance without form is an artist's hell. Lover is the integration of mistress and son. To feel without expressing is to be imprisoned; to express without feeling is performance. Seeker is an integration of madonna and holy spirit. To seek the truth you must be innocent; the moment you stop seeking, you lose your innocence. (Roth 1999, p.120)

The *artist* weaves the story, giving substance and form to the unfolding moment. Without form we would descend into an emotional swamp, where emotions run amok like vapour drifting through the hospice corridors. Uncontained, we risk being overwhelmed in the unbridled feeling. To grasp the unfolding moment and respond with appropriate and effective action is creation. The narrative form is a making sense, an effort to grasp and write down the dance so we can see its shape, and in doing so to shape the dances to come. It is the weaving of the pattern of the caring dance. The steps might be familiar from similar dances but the dance has never been danced before. To dance well is to be creative and passionate. Passionate reflects the *lover*. The unbridled giving of self into the dance, the innocent self. Only with innocence can we give ourselves because when we think we know we are contaminated; our view is obscured and the truth distorted. The difficulty with thinking we know, is that it narrows the lens we use to focus the way we view and interpret the world. Indeed, people seek to justify their knowing reinforcing the narrow viewing lens. The more we think we know, the more at risk we are of becoming attached to such knowledge and the more resistant we can become to seeing the world in other ways. In other words we lose our innocence. To remain innocent we must unburden our mind from, in Krishnamurti's (1996) words:

The accumulation of experience, the ashes of memory, that make the mind old. The mind that dies every day to the memories of yesterday, to all the joys and sorrows of the past – such a mind is fresh, innocent – and without that innocence you will not find God. (10 November 1995)

Hence to be present is to let go of our attachment to knowing, to the accumulation of things past that clog and stifle the mind, in order to be open to the possibilities and to stay tuned to what is unfolding. Reflection feeds and nurtures innocence, the lover within the soul. We learn through experience but are not trapped within it.

The *seeker* finds order in *chaos*. For myself, as a practitioner, I trip along the edge of *chaos*. I stare into the void of unpredictability. I can retreat to a place of safety or I can explore the unpredictability in a state of not-knowing, armed only with my creative and reflective self. The *seeker* is the reflective practitioner, the blend of wisdom, innocence, courage and passion, seeking to find pattern in the chaos, helping to move self and others through expanding levels consciousness. Roth says, 'I'm a dancer, but leaping into the void does not scare me. Inside me, seeker is faith' (p.145). Faith is the integration of vision and commitment. I trip the edge because I care. Caring is my dance and I seek to dance well with each of my partners.

The work of Gabrielle Roth patterns the caring dance. Her work helps me counter any cognitive approach to reflection. Reflection is essentially the tap into and nurturance of wisdom, beyond knowledge. 'Wisdom only comes when we empty our minds, free them from the strictures of knowledge' (Roth 1999, p.145).

I love Roth's words when she says, 'We anxiously paper the walls of our minds with snapshots of how we think our lives are supposed to be' (p.45). It is as if we do not trust ourselves or lack the faith and courage to rest in our wisdom minds. Not-knowing is scary when our education has endeavoured to fill us with knowing. Nursing itself is obsessed with evidence-based practice. Knowledge is useful to inform but it can never predict the dance pattern. It can never give you rhythm.

Pulling back the curtains of *chaos* reveals the *lyrical* rhythm, a deeper dimension of self.

In lyrical we seek truth about both ourselves and our mission here on this planet. No one can do this research for us, it is so highly individualised. Again and again we must reach into the unknown, mysterious part of oneself, eliminating all resistance to the creative process of self-discovery and developing the discipline to be a free sprit.

> To do this, we have to be willing to give up all attachment to specific
> identities based on gender, class, profession, sexual preference,
> nationality, religion, and explore ourselves as fluid fields of energy. To
> do this we have to drop all expectations we may be dragging with us
> from other times, places, and people. We have to strip ourselves bare
> until we unveil our naked soul. (Roth 1999, p.169)

When I told a colleague about Emma's response she was astonished that I let
Emma respond in the way she did. I say I did not so much let Emma but let
myself. People's responses reflect the baggage they drag around. People are
attached to their baggage for fear of losing their identities. Clinging to their
baggage, people are critical of ideas that fall outside the scope of their
understanding and self-knowing. Being open to self we can begin to redraw
the boundaries in the sand that separate you from me. Being in touch with
my soul I am open to all possibilities. This is Roth's archetype of the
shapeshifter; being so fluid that I can shift my shape to fit with whatever is
unfolding. We can see that boundaries are illusions, we are both separate and
joined and that we shed our fears and expectations in order to enter the
dance and dance well. We can be sure that Emma felt held and loved at that
moment, and that in the days to come she will take comfort and rest in such
memory. I am not saying I have mastered this surrender to my soul but it is
something I continuously work towards just as I work towards enlightenment in my meditation practice. Indeed they are the same. The lyrical
reflects the naturalness of the dance. It is no longer an effort. I flow freely,
transcending self in the process, dipping, soaring and floating on the air
currents as I stay effortlessly in tune with what's unfolding.

It is in lyrical rhythm that I know I am a part of a greater whole. It felt if
as we had become one, a fusion of hearts, minds and bodies, and that our
vibrations rippled across the universe to touch the divine. 'In lyrical we
realise we are works-in-progess. Nothing is fixed, particularly our identities.
Its deeper teachings are those of self-realisation' (Roth 1999, p.156).

I reflect always with the intention to dance better and in dancing better
to realise my caring self. Dancing is expanding consciousness. Reflective
writing is my point of stillness, working out the final vibrations of the dance.
The body's expression revealing the patterns that swirled together within
my dance with Rose, Emma and Christine. Christine may seem a minor
figure in the unfolding experience, yet her presence is always there. Perhaps I
sense she is the *mother* who gazes benignly as her wild *son* surfs the waves, the
staggering waves of emotion, and who, at the end comforts me. I can rest in
her stillness, and in doing so find my own.

Stillness is the closure rhythm when the crowds have departed. It is dwelling in my soul between this dance and the next dance, so when I next dance I do so more in tune with the flow of energy, with greater wisdom and passion. The alchemist is Roth's archetype for stillness. It is the alchemy of the dance to take us beyond into new dimensions of self and practice. The alchemist gathers up the fragments of energy and fashions it into positive action towards realising self as caring. It is like the impact of water on rock. Slowly the hardness of the ego gives way to the softness of compassion. And as a carer, compassion is my greatest gift. The expression of my true sense of being. Compassion is the ability to see beyond mere form, to connect with the other's true sense of being. On this level suffering is an illusion. I do not feel sad for Rose or Emma. Sadness and joy have merged beyond form.

> These are the two aspects of compassion. In compassion, the seemingly opposite feelings of sadness and joy merge into one and become transmuted into a deep inner space. It is the peace of God. (Tolle 1999, p.163)

Such is the nature of reflection. I bow to Gabrielle Roth for her astonishing insights. Roth's rhythms of *flowing* (feminine) and *staccato* (masculine) find union in *chaos*. Another image of the union of feminine and masculine found in the Buddhist image of the Bodhisattva. The Bodhisattva is both compassionate and wise, where reason and emotion are one, is both receptive to the ideas of others yet dynamic in taking action, and follows his or her own path to enlightenment while devoting self to easing the suffering of others (Sangharakshita 1999).

Like Roth's rhythms the Bodhisattva ideal offers a powerful image to focus thoughts, feelings and actions as we dance through the day, ever paying attention to the skilfulness of our steps and feeling the rhythm of the music.

Yielding

Rose's story illuminates tuning into and flowing with the other's wavelength within the chaotic caring dance. As I have explored, the practitioner can only dance well when she is able to let go of the ego's grasp. Not easy work when the inevitable death of another person threatens the ego. To safeguard itself from this threat, the ego creates the illusion of separateness between self and other (Tolle 1999). It does this because the other threatens my sense of immortality, threatens my precarious control of the world and threatens the gratification of desire. People normally live with such fear. Working as a hospice nurse has constantly confronted me with these fears.

To tune into the other, I must learn to tune into myself so that I understand and resist the ego's pull and dissolve fear. To be present to self and the other is about being in the now (Tolle 1999). Fear exists only in the future. It is as if the mind projects a threatening future that we then fantasise about. And at its root is the fear of death. That if we do not control the world it will destroy us, even though we know on a deeper level of consciousness that our bodies will die one day. Hence fear is an overidentification with the body. We think we are our bodies when in fact we are really consciousness, that is beyond the body and death. Of course, these words are not easy to understand when we have always been wrapped up in the body and our fears. Indeed the mind, as it interprets these words, will want to resist them because they threaten the ego. These words invite you to move beyond the mind and dwell in your deeper compassionate self. It invites you to let go and stop resisting your true self.

To truly be with Rose I had to let go of my fears and flow with the now. Then my fears dissolved and I experienced such a tremendous sense of joy. Christine also felt it. Letting go of resistance opens up self to experience such moments. I am certain that most readers will have experienced fleeting glimpses of such joy but all too easily the 'real' world slips back into gear and the moment is past. Paradoxically, the real world as we think it is, is an illusion.

When people are subconsciously motivated by fear they tend to expect people to conform to their wavelength. Patients in hospital know this well and will make an effort to 'fit in'. All too easily nurses will label patients and relatives in derogatory ways because they have failed in the task of fitting in or have some 'unacceptable' trait. What nurses do when they do label people in negative ways is to project their own anxiety into the other person. The ego, in its effort to protect itself, says, 'I can't be the problem – it must be the other ego that has the problem.' Hence the need to defend self and attack and subjugate the other's ego. Then the anxiety will diminish. We spend so much of the day locked into ego battles that are never resolved.

Perhaps because palliative care practitioners work under the constant threat of the other's death that it hardens their shells and nurtures resistance. If this is true, it would be ironic in that the nurse's primary role is to care. Hence to care means to surrender or yield to what is unfolding. And to surrender or yield is to let go of resistance. Tolle (1999) puts it like this:

Non-surrender hardens your psychological form, the shell of the ego, and so creates a strong sense of separateness. The world around you and the people in particular come to be perceived as threatening. The unconscious compulsion to destroy others through judgement arises, as does the need to compete and dominate. (p.172)

You might say I yielded to Sophie about Bernard's feeding. I certainly felt a sense of resistance to her request. Yet, in that moment, I could witness my resistance and decide to flow with the request despite my thoughts being with Rose and Emma. I know that Sophie only saw the situation from her perspective. What would have happened if I had asserted, 'No, I need to be with my own patients right now'? Or 'I only responded to his call-bell to help him use his urinal.' Knowing Sophie, I sense she would have accepted my need to be with Emma and the family at this moment. The threat is that we would have locked our ego horns and competed to dominate the situation. The fear of ensuing conflict would have resulted in one of us 'backing down', one of us being a loser with the risk of resentment and erosion of relationship. I ask myself, 'Did I yield or was I motivated to avoid conflict?'

Sophie and I discussed it afterwards and she apologised for putting me in that situation. Reflection after the event creates the space to mop up threads of conflict and raise consciousness of our unconscious (ego) motives and the ways these lead us to act in potentially destructive ways. Reflection creates the space to nurture our compassionate selves yet in ways that issues are tackled rather than avoided. We must always remind ourselves what we truly value and our caring purpose to confront self-interest.

So to yield to the other means yielding to ourselves so we can flow with the other as they journey through the turbulence of their illness and fears. Our role is to create a safe and loving space in which they are able to explore their fears beyond the ego's clinging pull. In this sense, yielding is positive, not passive, action. Blackwolf and Gina Jones (1996) say:

Learn to yield. Yielding is not being passive. It is being sensitive to energy flows and extending wisdom. Allow the winds of change to flow through you rather than against you. Be flexible with what is happening today (now). Yield to the circumstance, yet rooted with who you are. What do you need to yield to? (p.281)

The words of the ancient wisdom keepers are like the sounds of winds in the trees to inform and guide us as we struggle to clear a pathway through ego's debris to realise our true selves as caring. Powerful medicine. And as I keep reiterating, reflection creates the space where I can begin to challenge and shift my level of consciousness to dwell more within the unfolding moment beyond the ego's clinging pull. To be reflective is to be mindful of self within each unfolding moment. In the moment, fear cannot exist and so the true self can emerge in all its compassionate glory. Glimpses of joy become more frequent and constant.

Wednesday 21 November 2001
Iris

I visit Iris at her home because her car is being serviced. As it is her territory, I suggest that she decide which music to play. She chooses the music her healer has prepared for her. We are surrounded by the photographs of her family…the verbal images now have form. This is especially true of the daughter and son. I can anticipate her loss.

I prefer 'my' ground of the hospice for at least two reasons. First, and most importantly, it takes Iris into another place. At home she is constantly reminded of these images that are a weight for her to bear. On 'my' ground she has slipped away and can review her life more objectively. At home she is entangled with these images…indeed, the images are reinforced as they look down on our work. Iris is not so relaxed. Second, the environment is part of the healing place. It is part of the sanctuary I offer. How I set up the environment is therefore significant.

We finish as her father arrives to take her to the hospital for a scan. Busy, busy lives. Can we relax and press the pause button in order to be still for a moment to gather ourselves? Iris likes to be busy, to distract herself from her own shocking reality. This is her pattern. At night, when she is alone with her thoughts, the despair and fear creep in, like unwelcome visitors intent on mischief.

Friday 23 November 2001
Derrick

A pale, baby-faced man smiles as Tania introduces me and asks him if he mind if I join the admission party. His name is Derrick. He arrived at the hospice about half an hour earlier with his wife and son. They have now gone. She had to get back to work. Now Dr Jane is ready to 'admit' him. He moves from his chair to lie on the bed as the three of us spread around him. There is no escape.

Dr Jane takes the lead…she asks him about his illness. He was diagnosed four years ago with cancer of the oesophagus and stomach. Recently he had 'cysts' adhering to his spleen and liver and stomach resulting in infection. I wonder to what extent the word 'cysts' is a euphemism for tumour spread. No giveaway signs on his face or Dr Jane. Derrick talks about the 'cysts' as if they really were cysts. Perhaps they are. We live in a world where the use of the word 'cancer' is still avoided.

Derrick is here for the weekend to enable his wife to attend a family wedding. He is experiencing difficulty managing his 'symptoms'. He was actually offered a week's stay to help sort out his symptom management, which he declined. He talks about his loss of confidence in the local hospital that prompted him to travel a greater distance for surgery at another hospital. Since then he has been admitted to the local hospital, creating all sorts of problems with his medical records. He feels that 'health professionals' have not listened to him, and that one says one thing and another says another. His story is long-winded and now he feels tired. Dr Jane listens to his chest and asks if he is coughing up sputum. Yes, lots of it, thick and yellow. He has a chest infection – he says he has had a temperature of 37.3 degrees for a few days. His pain fluctuates. Some days it's very bad and others no more than discomfort. Sometimes he can never get comfortable. It seems his whole body aches but it emanates from the abdomen. The source of the pain is his lower to left lower back.

He wears three fentanyl patches that total 150umg. He also takes sevredol and paracetamol for breakthrough pain. He has commenced haloperidol 2mg to help his nausea. His sleep has been poor. Tania suggests temazepam. Dr Jane is uncertain. He says his discomfort includes his mind. He is tormented by the illness. The torment spreads through his family. His wife is at breaking point. His son is 21 and has just been made redundant as Christmas approaches. His girlfriend with their baby has left him. Derrick makes light of all this but the pressure has taken its toll.

Afterwards, we professionals sit around and contemplate what's best for Derrick. Dr Jane says he might need an anti-depressant. Tania succeeds in getting the sedation prescribed to use at the nurses' discretion. I suggest he needs 'time out' to explore the meaning of his illness with someone. He may try and cope with it but the strain breaks out in bursts of anger and gloom. He acknowledges this. He has been going to day hospice and has gradually emerged from behind his newspaper to engage some other men. Not so much the nurses or therapists. Of course, talking is not prescribed. It is taken for granted that such work permeates our holistic approach. But I do wonder, as I have suggested with my critical gaze towards midazolam, whether drug responses are grasped at too quickly.

Dr Jane and Tania leave him. I remain for a moment to ensure he has everything he needs and is feeling comfortable. I have listened to his story through the lens of the Burford reflective cues that we use within the hospice's assessment strategy:

- Who is Derrick?
- What meaning does this illness/health event have for him?
- How is he feeling?
- How has this event affected his usual life patterns and roles?
- How do I feel about him?
- How can we help him?
- What is important for Derrick to feel comfortable in hospital?
- What support does Derrick have in life?
- How does he view the future for himself and others?

(Adapted from Johns 2000)

The intention is that the practitioner internalises these cues as a natural way to reflect within each unfolding moment. In this way assessment is a continuous process of knowing and dwelling with the patient or family member. With the Burford cues in mind, I ask Derrick how he feels being here? He smiles and says it's a relief. He is thankful he is listened to. I sense he feels he is in a sanctuary for a few days and feels comfortable here. I ask him if he's still been working. He laughs and says he retired on health grounds four years ago. He never returned to work after the surgery. He worked as a green keeper...cricket pitches, golf courses. He says his pain is more than physical; that he suffers with the idea of dying and death. The question what meaning does this illness have for him is thick within his suffering. As he suffers his wife also suffers. This cue becomes synonymous with the cue 'how does he view the future for himself?' We do not directly touch this question although it lays thick between us, showing its head obliquely from time to time. His hope is a reflection of his fear. The other cues are all in play.

As I tune into his wavelength I begin to flow with him. By flowing we ease his staccato rhythm so he can explore the chaos of his life...the chaotic edge is the creative edge...the point of transformation where he might find meaning and ultimately stillness as he moves towards his inevitable death.

I have begun to help him by simply posing the cues. He would like some help to manage his physical symptoms as best we can in the short time we have with him this time. It's difficult to say beyond this at this time.

I get Derrick some ice-cold water. It was the best remedy to relieve his dry mouth. His mouth ulcers have almost healed. We talk about lunch. His appetite is poor but he will try some soup and fried fish.

I leave him. Half an hour later he is fast asleep on the bed. I wake him apologetically and say his lunch is ready. He sits in the armchair. I ask if he has pain? Only discomfort and he asks for paracetamol.

The cue 'how has this health event affected his usual life pattern and roles' shades in the detail of 'who is this person?' He is a husband and father, yet both relationships are under strain. He has given up work and playing golf. He is sad at these losses because they cut deep into his identity and put strain on his home relationships. The word 'pattern' focuses me to look at the way his life fits together. Cowling (2000) calls 'this pattern manifestation appreciation'. It seems as if his life is crumbling. How can we help him and his family repattern their lives in ways that they can face the future with more equanimity? How can his family find meaning in Derrick's illness so as to grow through the experience of his death? Is that possible or some impossible ideological proposition? There seems no positive side to death. It's all loss and gloom, as if someone is slowly turning out all the hundreds of lights that illuminate life until death turns out the final light and we dwell in the blackness of death. But it needn't be like that. That is the challenge. The support he has in life is fragile and vulnerable. We carers need to help him pull back the dark cloud that has gathered about him to reveal the light.

John

John, who was admitted a week ago on 16 November, has refused radiotherapy. His visit to the hospital for radiotherapy planning was physically very tough for him. The idea of living through the radiotherapy was too much for him. He knows it will not cure him. He has weighed up the choices. Both are grim but he prefers to go out in grace. He seems at peace with himself now he has made his decision. It is brave but then to die well requires bravery as you look fear in the eye.

Thursday 29 November 2001

Iris

After her reflexology, Iris talks about the dark thoughts she has in the mornings – 'I try to push them away but I can't escape from them.' These thoughts are a reflection of her deep fears about death and dying. During the day she finds distraction from her thoughts through ceaseless activity. I suggest she try to accept the thoughts rather than resist them, perhaps to see each day as a gift of life. It is about a year since I reflected on Iris's coping strategies using Benedict *et al.*'s (1994) study about the way women coped with breast cancer (see p.39). The five strategies were:

- diversionary (staying physically busy and mentally occupied)
- spiritual (relinquishing the problem to a higher being)
- interpersonal (seeking reassurance and information through sharing and talking with others)
- hopeful (thinking positive)
- avoidance (blocking the experience from the mind).

The diversionary strategy remains strong with Iris yet is more balanced with a growing spirituality, not in any religious or conventional sense but more a sense of knowing herself, of being more at ease with herself within the unfolding moment. She uses the 'interpersonal' strategy in talking with me and others, yet I am conscious of moving her towards 'spiritual' and 'hopeful' stategies for coping. As before, Iris cannot escape her destiny. She knows she will die, it is just a question of when. Hence she strives to push it away and be positive, believing that her treatments will keep *it* at bay. Iris struggles and I struggle to hold her. My words do not feel right...I wonder if I say them to reassure myself. These fears are like dark clouds coming ever closer across the horizon, threatening to blot out the sky blue. I know it's hard to be positive about the future, to accept the possibility of dying.

I am tempted to suggest making a greater effort with the Bach flower remedies or to meditate but I know she lacks faith in the Bach and that she needs guidance to help her meditate because her thoughts would simply dwell heavily and overwhelm her.

Tuesday 4 December 2001

Iris

As is so often the case, I read something that frames my experience. Tolle (1999) writes:

> To you I would say: 'Don't look for peace. Don't look for any other state than the one you are in now; otherwise, you will set up inner conflict and unconscious resistance. Forgive yourself for not being at peace. The moment you completely accept your non peace, your non peace becomes transmuted into peace. Anything you accept fully will get you there, will take you onto peace. This is the miracle of surrender. (p.161)

Iris – this is your work. To learn to surrender and find peace within; to flow with the chaos without resistance. And how can I best help you? Certainly not by preaching words to you or confronting your resistance. Tolle guides me: 'All you can do is create a space for transformation to happen, for grace and love to enter' (p.131). And that is my work – to create a space of transformation to ease suffering and, as a result, to enable people like Iris to grow through their experience. As I look back over the journal, I can sense this effort. The effort must always be focused on the journey rather than the destination. It is each breath we take now that is significant, not what happens tomorrow or what happened yesterday. Dwelling on the past or projecting self into the future are figments of the mind, a reflection of regret, fear and desire.

Driving to the hospice, the trees are now totally bare of their leaves. Twisted branches against the blue sky look beautiful. The sun is strong. 'Bird feather' clouds float within the sky. I say 'bird feather' because these clouds appear like layers of feathers along a bird's wing. Iris arrives at the same time. She seems to limp. She says she knocked her leg yesterday but it's okay. Perhaps that's it. We joke about arthritis but she reveals that her body scan showed arthritis in her knees which surprised her.

Iris is anxious because Robert, her husband, wants to move house. He's also unhappy at work. He recently changed his job, moving from a job he liked but wanted to move on from. More lumps of his hair have fallen out. Iris says, 'He's a passive man.'

I imagine he turns his angst inwards causing the destruction of his body. Iris soaks up this angst.

Iris says, 'I need to do more exercise, 'I'm getting fat! But what sort of exercise can I do? I mustn't put my shoulders under strain…the surgeon said just gentle exercise. Maybe I could do some aerobics?'

I remind Iris how she fills her day so she is always busy, to distract her from ruminating on her illness. She laughs and agrees. I ask, 'What about going back to work?' She feels she couldn't do this with the demands of her treatment – the weekly visit to hospital for her herseptin and pamidronate injections. Her treatment regimen is her career! She muses, 'Perhaps I could help out at the hospice charity shop.' I say, 'In that way you could give something back?' She likes this idea. And, as she has so often said, 'I feel guilty because so many of the people I have known have died and I'm still alive.'

This guilt often bubbles up to the surface to haunt her. We focus on the word 'guilt'. I confront her, 'Why do you compare herself with others? Focus on your own journey. Perhaps one day you will die but it may help our guilt and fear to focus on *now*…fear exists only in time, in an uncertain future. Yet *now* is where we live our lives.'

I hear Tolle's words vibrate through me and pour forth. Iris responds positively, yet again we sense the gathering of the dark clouds. I say, 'Maybe there are dark clouds in your sky but there's still plenty of blue sky.' Iris likes this picture and she turns her head towards the blue sky.

Despite its apparent morbidity, our conversation flows easily and we can talk about such things with ease. I think there are a number of factors that contribute to this sense of ease despite the fact that Iris's fears have not dissipated:

- Associating talk with a physical therapy such as reflexology that is deeply relaxing which helps pull Iris into another space.

- Visualising a clearing free from the dense jungle of despair where we can dwell together further helps pull Iris into another space.

- The unfolding of an intimate and compassionate relationship that has been sustained over time in which Iris feels loved and contained.

- My deep appreciation of the pattern of Iris's life that has enabled me to develop a strong empathic connection with the way she thinks and feels.

- Simply flowing with what unfolds rather than trying to manipulate the talk into a 'problem and solution' mode (even though I can sense I have responded in this way).

- Becoming increasingly confident in my own spirituality to embrace Iris's suffering and despair without strong attachment.

All of these points are significant parts of the clearing where we can dwell away from the immediacy of the unfolding drama and its trauma. When Iris steps back across the clearing threshold, hopefully she is transformed in some small way so as to face the unfolding tragedy of her life with greater ease.

Wednesday 12 December 2001

Leaving the house just after 6.30 the moon greets me; a bright sliver set within the whole moon against the clear dark blue sky as the first light of dawn spreads across the horizon. As I drive the horizon slowly changes...a crimson tinge lightening to apricot like a kaleidoscopic background to the low-slung moon that seems much lower and closer than usual. The leaves strewn along the road verges have gone. The trees stand bare in the stark beauty of their different forms against the lightening sky.

Percy

Arriving at the hospice, Lucy, the night staff nurse, asks me to help her with Percy. He is restless and agitated. Lucy thinks he may be agitated because he has not passed urine since yesterday. He has refused Lucy's offer of a catheter. Lucy is uncertain what to do. Entering the room Percy lies naked, partially covered by a top sheet. He is restless. I greet him authoritatively, 'Percy, I'm Chris...(he acknowledges me)...are you uncomfortable in the abdomen?' He affirms. I tap his bladder. Not full but not empty. I suggest a catheter may help relieve his discomfort? He agrees.

Lucy goes to set up a trolley. Percy is very hot, burning a fever. I use a cold flannel to cool his brow. He says that feels very nice. He accepts a drink. I try using the cold flannel across his abdomen. I remember the legend that a cold flannel may help to relieve bladder retention. However, to no avail.

Lucy returns. The 12g catheter slides in easily releasing a slow trickle of concentrated urine. Lucy is very grateful. She feels Percy responds to my male voice...a voice of authority. I laugh – 'Do you really think so?' She is certain but I am not convinced. Percy needed someone to take control and be decisive.

However, Percy remains agitated so I stay with him. We suspect he has cerebral irritation. Flick, a student nurse, joins me. She knows Percy from the day unit and has cared for him during the five days since his admission to the inpatient unit. She is shocked at his condition – 'He was so much better yesterday; talking, eating, sitting out of bed!'

The unpredictablity of our work, the way people quickly turn for the worse as if threads of life break within them.

Percy's temperature is 38.0 degrees. Dr Paul will see him at 9.30. Flick asks Percy if he would like the fan to cool him? He had refused the fan in the night but now he agrees. In response to his agitation, the night staff had given him two doses of diazepam (5mg and 2mg) and then an injection of midazolam 10mg, all without easing his agitation. I give him his drugs; sodium valporate to counter the epileptic fits and dexamethasone 12mg to ease the cerebral irritation. Yesterday he took them all at once without water. Now he chokes on the water either by cup lip or by straw. I give them one by one on his tongue which he manages with sips of water.

Percy is 58. In 1996 he was diagnosed with a low grade astrocytoma. This was treated successfully with radiotherapy. In July this year, a scan showed the tumour had grown again. However, this time it did not respond positively to radiotherapy. A biopsy indicated that the original low grade astrocytoma had become a high grade glioma. As a consequence, he was prescribed three cycles of chemotherapy. He is neutropenic from his chemotherapy. His third cycle of chemotherapy was cancelled for this reason. His bone marrow suppressed. The clinical picture is uncertain and he may be transferred to his cancer treatment hospital depending on how his clinical picture is interpreted and negotiated with Sarah, his wife.

Percy continues to be restless. The telltale smell of faecal incontinence drifts. He is a large man – Flick and I roll him and clean the mess. I sense his agitation was related to his bowel and not his bladder. It must be very difficult for anybody to know they are going to pass faeces in the bed and not be able to do anything about it. He couldn't say what was happening to him. He is more relaxed after this. His sacrum is red so we position him carefully to relieve the pressure. He needs a nimbus bed to shift the pressure points, so we decide to change his bed when we next move him.

Dr Paul arrives and we conference. He contacts the treatment hospital and they set out the options. Further chemotherapy is out the question except a second line approach – more to comfort his wife if she wants to pursue active treatment but of little potential benefit to Percy. Indeed it would cause more distress and hence cannot be justified according to the rules of futility (Smith 1995; Taylor 1995). He will be tailed off his steroids. His swallowing difficulties rule out the oral drugs. A midazolam pump will help control his fits.

We phone Sarah. They have been married for six years. No children. It is for both their third marriage. I am told she is very stressed and will probably insist on further treatment. But she doesn't – she accepts that Percy's best option is to stay at the hospice for terminal care. We suggest she visit as his condition is deteriorating.

Percy has his bowels opened again, and again he is very distressed by this. He wears his mother's rings and cross on a gold chain around his neck. He was very close to his mother. His head has been shaved and now a stubble of grey hair sprouts from the middle of his head as it grows back.

He is comforted by my presence as I simply stand and hold his hand. He sleeps, snorting like a pale but sunburnt pig; very drowsy but easily roused. We let him rest rather than wash and shave him.

At 12.00 Brenda, the senior shift nurse, asks me whether she should ring Sarah for the third time and assert that she really should come to the hospice? Brenda is in a dilemma – should she call again and bother her? Perhaps Sarah needs some space to take stock before visiting? How can we tell? Does she really know how poorly he is today when he had been so much better yesterday? With a brain tumour pressing on vital centres anything could happen. Percy is responsive if drowsy and so I suggest a compromise – to phone Sarah again at 13.00. Brenda agrees. It's a tough decision to make. I wish I knew Sarah and then perhaps I would be better placed to make the best decision.

Stephen

Amid the unfolding drama with Percy, across the corridor Stephen dies. His son by his side. Like Percy, he has rapidly deteriorated. Just yesterday the staff were contemplating discharging him to a nursing home. Some staff had sensed that Stephen was much closer to death and defended the decision to keep him here. How right they were. Dying trajectories are sensed yet unpredictable. Some staff can sense these things and others cannot. I believe that staff who have this sense are more tuned into the rhythm of the caring dance and therefore more sensitive to what is unfolding. It is as if they have radar and intuitively pick up the signs.

Flick says that Stephen is the first death she has experienced in her training. She is distressed but brave. It is important within the chaos of the morning that I am available to her, to create a moment where her feelings can be expressed and acknowledged. It is difficult to focus our care when we are wounded. Our concern often turns inwards to lick our wounds. Often people carry on regardless of their wounds until they eventually collapse exhausted. Better some first aid to patch the wound.

Just before Stephen died I had left Percy to grab a cup of coffee. I emerged laughing from the small kitchen to see Stephen's son looking at me. I immediately felt guilty that I should be laughing when he was suffering. I felt I had been insensitive, as if my laughter was a reflection that I didn't care for his inner turmoil.

Should I have been more sensitive to creating an appropriate environment for Stephen's son? Is laughter a release for the emotional strains of this morning's work? Am I simply oversensitive? Is my self-doubt a reflection of a deeper insecurity and uncertainty? Such doubts splinter my confidence and separate me from my deeper self, and in separating from myself I am separated from others. 'To mend our separations from (self and) others we must resolve our own inner turmoil. We must develop inner peace' (Jones and Jones 1996, p.129).

The incident in the kitchen is like a stain on my spirit. Reflection helps to lift the stain and cleanse me. It is impossible for any of us to be perfect. We all have our blemishes. I did not mean to be insensitive, even if I might be judged so. Perhaps it was nothing to Stephen's son. Perhaps the laughter helped him lift his own gloom. I don't know because I did not ask him. I drew the worse conclusion and felt the pang of guilt. Yet I know how important it is to laugh and play during the day. Humour helps to lighten the mood and is a great stress-buster. I must not take responsibility for Stephen's son's feelings. Yet it seems our minds do dwell on these past events and conjure up guilt and fear for what might happen as a consequence. Either way I am pulled into the past (guilt) and the future (fear). To care, I need to be present, in the now. As Tolle (1999) says:

> Unease, anxiety, tension, stress, worry – all forms of fear – are caused by too much future, and not enough presence. Guilt, regret, resentment, grievances, sadness, bitterness, and all forms of non-forgiveness are caused by too much past, and not enough presence. (p.50)

Our caring selves are too valuable to beat up. We have the primary responsibility to care for ourselves. If we neglect this self-care then inevitably we will fail our patients and families, our colleagues and ourselves.

Blackwolf and Gina Jones (1996) suggest I construct a 'war shield' to protect self from the fears that haunt and darken our minds. The war shield is painted with our colours; our inner strengths, compassion, integrity, self-awareness, our purpose, our totem animals and such like. This is not born of arrogance but the deep humility of compassion.

To hold the war shield is to take the warrior pose; prepared to fight for and defend our values and peace. Like the proud warrior we must learn to honour and respect ourselves, to remember that we are beautiful and worthy people and to 'learn from the birds to preen my own beautiful feathers' (p.131). 'Learn to use your shield so you will not tolerate abuse in any form. Like the rattlesnake. Assertively communicate your intolerance for disrespect' (p.107).

Being guilty is a form of self-abuse. Guilt, as with all negative emotions, is dangerous because, in the need to defend ourselves, we may easily project the guilt into others. Visualising the war shield creates a space so I can see and deflect negative emotions appropriately. Sometimes I cannot visualise quickly enough and I am wounded. Yet guilt also draws my attention to potential contradiction between my values and my practice. As such it is a useful sign.

Sunday 16 December 2001

Derrick

Derrick (see p.135) was transferred to the hospice three days ago from the general hospital, where he was treated for a chest infection. He is now considered *terminal*. I wonder if he views himself as such? I greet him. Does he remember me? Yes, he does – 'Hello, Chris.' Sharon, his wife, has slept overnight. She is brushing her hair in Derrick's room. I greet her and sense she is tense. She is going home to sort out some letters and will return in a couple of hours. She can't look into my eyes, and when she does, she bursts into tears. She says Derrick has buried himself under the clothes. He pushed her away when she tried to help him. Evidently he has been helpless for five days and she has done everything for him. Today, feeling better, he pushed her away. She is hurt. She sits by his bed and he emerges from the sheets and asks me to leave. The door is closed. Terminal cancer can be like a hurricane blasting families. It is not easy watching family conflict spill out especially when emotions are raw with suffering.

I feel sorry for Sharon. The door opens. The tension between them has burst. Smiles and wiping away of tears. Sharon goes to make some tea. I follow her and ask how things are. She confirms her hurt at being pushed away...she says that Derrick hadn't realised he had pushed her away, that he hasn't known where he has been for the past five days. She says Derrick will have some breakfast. We pause and in that moment I touch her shoulder. Her relief is palpable. I want to help Sharon understand Derrick's behaviour because I want to take her pain away yet any explanation would have been merely speculative. Anything factual would breach Derrick's right to confidentiality. Better for me to ask Sharon what sense she makes of this. Randall and Downie (1999) state:

> Whilst the obligation to keep information confidential is generally known and acknowledged, and it is clearly described in professional codes of conduct, it is surprising how often information is given to relatives without the patient's consent. (p.69)

It is true. I have often witnessed nurses attempting to relieve the relative's distress or anxiety with explanations about the patient's behaviour, as if they are seeking to relieve their own anxiety. Our own anxiety is no rationale for action. As Randall and Downie state:

> It is easy but not justifiable, when talking to relatives and answering their queries, to give them more information about the illness and its likely progress than the patient possesses. Health care professionals have a natural desire to assist the relatives by answering their questions, and it can be difficult to remember that the patient is the person primarily entitled to information about the illness, and that this information should be passed on only with the competent patient's consent. (p.71)

Sharon goes home for a while. Derrick seems relaxed at having made his peace with her. He has two syringe drivers going; ketorolac in one driver and diamorphine 170mg and nozinan in the other. He has no pain, just feels uncomfortable. I remember these same words when we last met him. He walks out to the bath. It refreshes him. His hair is spikey like mine. We laugh and reminisce about the 1960s. His hair, like mine, had been long. He was a Status Quo fan and I find myself humming 'Rocking all over the world'. The bath rejuvenates him. He says he feels so much better today, that the past few days have been a blur. He is 52. The same age as me. He reminds me of a little boy, boyish in his looks and manner. He was the rebellious child hiding under the covers. Talking about our younger 'rock' days, we are both children finding and flowing with the rhythm. Afterwards he is tired and sleeps until lunchtime, seemingly at peace. He has found, a least temporarily, a rhythm of stillness within the chaos of his unfolding life.

I describe him as a 'little boy' to Tania. Yet am I guilty of labelling him? Do I create an impression for others to view him like this? Labelling is usually negative, a response to our own anxiety. It is true I was irritated by his behaviour towards Sharon. He was a naughty boy having a tantrum under the bedclothes. I am shocked that I witness this now in myself as a negative reaction to him whereas before, I felt tuned into his wavelength. Perhaps I had, but I had also resisted it once I had seen the way his wavelength flowed.

By labelling him as a child I inevitably shift into a parental role. Derrick admits he struggles to express his own suffering. Sometimes he is light, reflected in the twinkle in his eye, and sometimes he is dark, unwittingly projecting his darkness into others, most notably those closest to him.

Without doubt there is something of Derrick that reminds me of myself. Perhaps I recognise my own little boy, the simultaneous need to be loved but also to resist love when it threatens to smother. The constant struggle to find balance between these two forces. Perhaps I unwittingly project this self into Derrick? Such dynamics are fraught with assumption yet need to be understood if we are to realise our caring selves.

Patricia

Patricia sits on the edge of her bed leaning on her bed table. She has just vomited her breakfast. She feels her paracetamol triggers the vomiting. I kneel beside her and ask how she is. She says she has vomited continuously since her last chemotherapy cycle for her cancer of the ovary.

She says she knows she is going to die soon and shares her thoughts about her death, what it might be like. She knows the 'curtain will soon come down'. She pauses and I do not fill the silence. She says she has no fear of death. She is not religious, unlike her family, although she has moved closer to religion in the knowledge she is dying. I ask her what she expects after she dies? She doesn't know – what did I think? I am cautious about imposing my beliefs. I suggest that we have a deeper level of consciousness beyond mind – which is revealed when the body and mind falls away at death. I say this consciousness can merge with the light of God when we die. She likes this image…she thinks it's possible. She talks about Eddie, her husband who died two years ago, about the way they talked about waiting for each other. She feels he's waiting for her. The idea comforts her. She remembers a situation after her son had died. He came and sat on her bed and said everything was okay. He was only 23. She talks about her children and I reflect on the way people talk through their lives, finding meaning and putting things into perspective.

I tell Pat her green-blue eyes sparkle. 'Really?' she says. She has some eye shadow to enhance the colour. She is pleased I notice, flattered to be admired. Such things are important boosts for people's self-esteem flattened in the remorseless onslaught of advancing cancer.

She looks wistfully at the garden, she says it must be beautiful in the summer. She is astonished that the garden is maintained by volunteers – 'I must come to one of the garden fêtes if I'm still alive next summer.' We talk of garden smells and she says she loves lavender. She smiles, 'I hope when I die it will be on a nice day.' I bask in this conversation, intrigued to talk with someone contemplating her own death in such an open and curious way.

In talking, Patricia tests out and develops her thoughts about her death. She confronts and works through her fears. It is a mutual process as I reflect on my own views and feelings about death.

She gladly accepts my offer of a jacuzzi bath and a foot massage in about half an hour. In the meantime I fetch her the Daily Express to read and set up an aroma-stone with lavender.

Her nausea has ceased. We have struggled to bring this unpleasant symptom under control. I am rather perplexed we have not reviewed her nausea medication since her admission for one week's respite care. Tania laments we no longer keep people long enough in the hospice to respond adequately to symptom management. Patricia is planned to go home on Sunday so how can we adequately adjust her medication?

Pat loves her jacuzzi bath. As she dresses afterwards, she says she used to be 16 stone. Now she is less than 10 stone. The ravages of cancer. She walks back to her room and talks with Tania. She likes to talk. As a therapeutic approach I feel talking and listening is undervalued and neglected, even in a hospice.

As I massage Pat's feet with lavender mixed in grapeseed oil, I suggest she close her eyes and relax. I guide her to focus on her breathing – following her breath in and following her breath out. To breathe in love and light and to breathe out her fears, simply to flow with her breath. She is very still as I work on her feet and lower legs for about 20 minutes. I hear Tania ask staff to be quiet outside the room as Pat is having a massage. I smile. Tania cares so much it can make her intolerant of what might be construed as carelessness in others. She is passionately loyal to her patients even at the risk of upsetting other staff. Yet they recognise her passion and accommodate her attitude with labels such as 'that's Tania for you'.

Tania has a 'reputation' at the hospital for speaking her mind. My respect for her is grudging because she is fiercely loyal to her patients and her sense of what is right even at the risk of rubbing staff up the wrong way. She does not play games with misplaced loyalty, although, as I noted with Gus (see p.68), Tania has this parental trait that can make others feel like naughty children.

Pat is enthused by her massage – 'It was wonderful.' I leave her to enjoy her lunch – fish and chips followed by bread and butter pudding, and no nausea!

At shift report Mandy, another staff nurse, says it's been quite a week with so many deaths. The chaplain had said yesterday that all the patients he had met the previous week had now died. We spend a few minutes talking about Percy's death – he had died at 20.30 last night very peacefully. How right we didn't send him back to the treatment hospital for further chemotherapy. It is *so* important that we spend some minutes reflecting on these deaths and releasing our feelings. These people have become part of us and have touched our hearts. We have held them and cried with them, easing them towards as peaceful a death as possible. As we sit we can honour our patients, their families and ourselves, not in a smug way, but in a way that nurtures and strengthens our purpose and fans our passion. Caring may make us vulnerable yet it also nourishes and sustains us. A fine balance.

Tuesday 18 December 2001
Iris

10.35. Iris and I arrive at the same time. It is a family gathering as her mother, who has terminal breast cancer, now attends day care. Her father is also there having brought her mother. He tells me his hip replacement operation is arranged for next February. The hospice has offered her two weeks respite care that has eased his fears. He is pleased although anxious because she is so dependent on him.

Iris had another panic attack at the chemotherapy unit last Friday. They sedated her and, as a consequence, she missed her pamidronate infusion.

I ask: 'Did you sense it?'

'I did have a premonition because I asked Robert (her husband) to accompany me.'

Iris cannot explain why she panicked. Perhaps a deep fear had broken free from her psychological defence system and surfaced as a panic attack. People can lack conscious connection between the conscious mind and the deeper self (Kearney 1977).

Through the journal I have described the conversations between Iris and myself. These conversations are 'surface' conversations, dealing with thoughts and feelings that Iris is conscious of. Perhaps some of these thoughts and feelings are pushed up from deeper within her; sensed as vague fears that cannot be understood or resolved. Iris can only push these away or escape from them through relaxation or distraction. Perhaps Iris might benefit from 'deeper' work to connect with her deeper fears.

Part of Iris wants to contain the fears, to push them away, to bury them deep inside. Another part of her wants to resolve them because they ache. We tread this fine line of prodding yet without bursting. The panic attack was a bursting, as if the container was full and had overflowed.

As usual reflexology is deeply relaxing and comforts her. Iris is certainly under additional strain with her mother also being terminally ill and her dad's forthcoming operation. And I know that Iris always puts other peoples' needs before her own, especially her family's.

Tuesday 8 January 2002

Iris

Another new year – one that Iris had felt she would not live to see. Iris tells me about her drama. Her 'hickman' line became infected so it was removed on Christmas Eve requiring 24-hour hospital admission for intravenous antibiotics. She has also hurt her right shoulder when her daughter jumped down on the settee next to her and knocked it. Iris thinks it's dislocated but she has to wait to see an orthopaedic surgeon. Her arm is perched in a sling. She takes it out of the sling to drive and no doubt to do all the housework things. A question of priority despite the discomfort. Iris's roller coaster ride with cancer; a ceaseless procession of difficulties to overcome that gather momentum.

Tuesday 15 January 2002

Jean

Jean is 49. She has an unknown primary cancer that has spread to her liver and lungs. Lesley, her Macmillan nurse, wrote in Jean's referral to the hospice:

Jean has been remarkably composed about her illness/prognosis up until when she was told further spread was evident (December 2001). Now becoming fearful of duration and how things will be at the end. Many practical arrangements of her death have been made but now finding it difficult to live day to day.

The nurse who assessed Jean on arrival at the hospice wrote:

> Jean wishes to die in the hospice. She lives with her daughter Clare, 20, at home. Also [has an] older son who is married and has a child. Palliative chemotherapy offered and declined. She wants quality rather than quantity of life. Admitted for one week for assessment and symptom control and emotional support. Nausea, vomiting, breathlessness, fatigue, loss of appetite. Lady wants to be in control of her situation and her rapid deterioration is very hard to handle. Concerned for her daughter [who] can't handle her dying.

The words paint a dramatic picture of struggle. Jean is struggling to hold together what is falling apart. I say, 'Hello – I'm Chris. You must be Jean?' She responds with openness and says, 'Hello, Chris.' A thin smile moves across her face. I say I am looking after her this morning. Another smile. There is nothing she wants just now except for me to pull the curtains to reveal the day. I feel a chill wind through the open fanlight window. She says she likes the coolness. The day is dark and threatening rain. How easy and yet significant to engage in weather banter as a way of engaging with someone you have not met before. Rituals of engagement. Perhaps one reason I sometimes open my journal with a reflection on the day is the connection between nature and caring, especially caring in the context of dying. Perhaps people who are dying or those who work with people who are dying have a stronger affinity with nature. Perhaps it is no more than simply not taking anything for granted anymore. The weather may also reflect moods – 'cancer is dark and threatening...'

I like patients to return my name because it expresses their willingness to connect with me. It fosters intimacy. Intimacy creates a warm, safe, healing place for the patient to dwell. Intimacy can never be imposed because it is a mutual process. Patients may shy away from intimacy preferring to be detached or suffer in silence. Meeting a new patient like Jean I must first tune in to who she is and radiate my compassion as an invitation for intimacy. Practitioners may also shy away from intimacy because it is always unconditional, and the consequences may exceed personal boundaries. Boundaries simply create conditions that keep others out or keep the self in. Either way, wrapped in ourselves we are not available. If so, they risk being uncaring, what Jameton (1992 cited by Corley and Goren 1998) describe, so powerfully and appropriately, as 'the dark side of nursing'. It's cold on the dark side of the hill. The practitioner wraps herself up in herself to keep her warm. Her focus is inwards, not outwards warming others.

Jean is nauseous. A vomit bowl is within reach. She declines breakfast and confirms her loss of appetite but is concerned that she should eat. I ask if her mouth is dry? It is. She has a diflan spray on the table but she says it doesn't help. I suggest an ice-lolly? They do help, but the dry throat is persistent and even lollies bring only temporary relief. She knows she needs to eat to have strength. I tell her I am a complementary therapist and would she like a treatment later this morning? She says a foot massage would be wonderful. Perhaps after her wash? She bathed yesterday and thinks a wash will suffice today.

10.00. Jean has moved into her chair. She hasn't washed but has accepted Heather's offer of a bath later. I look at the photos arranged on her bed locker – 'Your children and grandchild?' She affirms. I say, 'Dressed in blue – he must be a boy?' 'Yes.' I sense the loss that she anticipates. Words are thick between us but left unsaid. Photographs of a patient's family are always poignant. Deeper emotions surface when talking about loved ones and the impending loss of relationship. Her grandson is just one year old. I smile – 'Does he call you Gandma?' Jean laughs, 'He calls me nanna.' I say, 'You live with your daughter Clare?'

'Yes.'

'Does she have a boyfriend?'

'She's in-between boyfriends.'

'How is Clare coping with what's going on?'

Jean pauses…she says she tries to protect Clare by containing her own distress. Now, as we talk, there is no hint of distress in Jean's talk. Her feelings are contained. Now is not the time to pursue her feelings. I have sent a cathartic probe. Whenever I sense feelings lay on or just below the surface of experience, as they do with Jean, it is important to acknowledge and validate these feelings as possible. Otherwise the feelings are like a barrier that hinder our ability to dance well together. By acknowledging her feelings, I inform Jean that I care about her and her daughter. It is not idle curiosity or a corkscrew to release her feelings. The probe is gentle because it is vulnerable ground. I do not want to intrude but I do want to communicate I care about her, that I understand her predicament and am available to her should she want to talk.

I ask if she would like her foot massage now? 'Yes, please!' She is enthusiastic and expectant.

She loves the smell of the patchouli and frankincense essential oils I mix with the reflexology base cream. The music 'Chaco Canyon' by Rusty Crutcher vibrates on the level of the soul. Jean says she likes it. She calls it floaty music. Jean loves the massage. Periodically, she murmurs, 'That's wonderful.' I laugh – 'You need this every day.' She laughs – 'I need it all the time.' I am mindful that each stroke of my massage is infused with my concern for Jean, and the way each stroke feeds my concern. As my massage strokes get deeper so does my concern for this woman. My hands and Jean's legs become one…we flow in a caring dance until we reach a point of stillness.

I ask her how long she is staying at the hospice? She doesn't know exactly, but will stay at least until Friday. I sense this is difficult ground…that perhaps Jean does not want to go home. I do not push it. I inform her that I am not in again before Friday but will ask Lindsey, one of the care assistants, if she might massage Jean's legs and feet.

At lunchtime Jean is laying out on her reclining chair in bright yellow and red pyjamas. She is the Queen of Sheba, resplendent in her robes. She laughs. She has had a jacuzzi bath which was good. Her swollen legs spread out before her elevated on the reclining chair. She says the massage has not reduced the swelling in her legs. In fact, her legs feel very heavy…she struggles to move from bed to chair or walk. She feels frustrated and distressed by her loss of mobility. She thought the massage would help the oedema. She says the water tablets (spironolactone) are useless, she has been on them before and even though the dose has increased it won't make any difference. I note that she was allergic to dexamethesasone? Yes – they made her lightheaded. I say I will review her medication with my colleagues. She says she feels better and might try some lunch.

After lunch Jean clutches a vomit bowl. In front of her is an empty soup bowl. Tomato by the colour. The nausea persists, perhaps it is worse after eating because it is related to her enlarged liver and the way her liver has squashed all her abdominal organs.

I mention Jean's despair about her legs to Martha, one of the senior nurses. We agree that she really needs steroids. Brenda, the late shift leader, says she will talk to Jean about this. A balance needs to be found between tolerating the steroids and reducing the swelling. What is most important for the quality of Jean's life? Symptom management can be so difficult to balance. We note the pattern of symptoms and the way the emphasis has

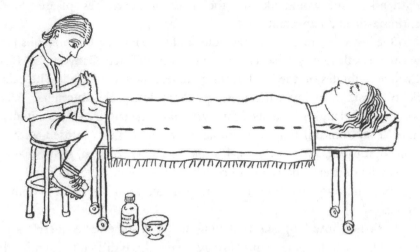

shifted through abdominal discomfort, nausea, dry throat and now her legs, which were barely mentioned on admission. Are these symptoms expression of her grief bubbling up to the surface? As Schön (1987) describes, practice is indeed like a swampy lowland, complex and indeterminate.

Just before I finish the shift, I pop in to say goodbye. A woman is sitting facing Jean. I inadvertently say, 'Is this your daughter?' She laughs – 'No, this is my friend.' Just then her son comes in. He looks very different from the photograph taken ten years previously. I say who I am and he says, 'Another nurse, how many nurses are there?' The comment feels hostile and I find myself explaining that we are between shifts. I accept his anger. Nurses are in the firing line. It is important to accept that relatives need to vent their despair and anger and that such expressions are not personal. It cannot be easy to come into a hospice to visit your dying mother, especially when we seem unable to deal with her symptoms successfully.

Doris

The first smell that struck me this morning was the faecal odour drifting in the corridor, seeping from Doris's room. She has a loop colostomy but has magically passed formed faeces after being given a phosphate enema last evening. She had been experiencing some faecal leakage and it was felt she might be constipated in her colostomy loop. We expected the stool to come out the colostomy, not her rectum. The faecal odour is a result of the pad she wears at night. The smell is worse in the morning. I introduce myself and ask her if the odour is bothersome? She seems surprised and says she is not aware there was an odour. I suggest I might use an essential oil to give the room a pleasant smell?

There are no spare aroma-stones, so I put four drops of neroli on a gauze eye-pad and place it on the radiator. Doris says she likes the smell. I inform her that neroli is an oil pressed from orange blossom and helps create a sense of calm besides its exquisite smell.

I kneel by her bed and we talk. Doris expects to go home tomorrow. She lives alone. She has a daughter and son who live close by and another daughter who lives on the North Yorkshire Moors, married to a sheep farmer. They were spared the foot and mouth epidemic. We talk about Government compensation. Without prompting, she shares her diagnostic story. She was having difficulty passing stools and feared something was up. When she started passing blood from her rectum she went to see her doctor. Tests confirmed she had inoperable cancer. She is 87 and her birthday is in May. I ask what day? She says 5 May. I say my daughter's birthday is 7 May, which is also her daughter's birthday. She says everything is five – she was born on the fifth of the fifth, 1915 and got married on the fifth of the fifth, 1940.

She laughs – 'Five is not my lucky number.' She doubts whether she will reach her next birthday.

Doris is genteel, slightly posh, having to suffer the indignity of faecal incontinence and its malodours. I can see why she might mask this from herself, to play it down, rather than admit to this ignominy. I can also see why she might rather die than have to face a deteriorating undignified future. She struggles to contain her dignity but it is coming apart at the seams. Yet, like so many patients, she has a real need to talk through her diagnostic history as if it is a form of sense making, a play on deeply held fear.

Elen

Elen is the senior nurse for adult services at the hospice. She is leaving the hospice after ten years next month. She looks very elegant, dressed in a trouser suit. I comment on her power dressing today – is she preparing for her new role? She says, 'Quite the opposite, I plan to dress more casually.'

I say, 'I must read you something from Ruth Picardie's book *'Before I Say Goodbye'* (1998). I flip the pages until I reach the bit when Ruth attended her first self-help group ('yuk – pass the lemon sponge, will you dear') for women with secondary breast cancer. She says (in an e mail to Jamie, one of her correspondent friends):

Was dreading the whole thing – imagine bunch of old ladies drinking tea. And eating chocolate biscuits (good quality – so much better than prison food). Still reckon I was the youngest there. Only five prisoners in total, plus two warders, including *GHASTLY* breast cancer nurse… in huge floral kaftan and slacks. Nana Miscouri glasses. Fashion victim, moi? Quick to judge, moi? Just like Alison Steadman in 'Abigail's Party'. And her manner – so humourless. Anyway, liked the other women, one of whom had reached Zen-like acceptance. Partly awful visions of the future, too – one woman, aged 50, diagnosed seven years ago, talked about pain relief and hospices, which I am totally not ready for, existentially. (p.22)

I ask Elen, 'I wonder how that breast care nurse must have felt when she read that?'

Elen just laughs but I wonder if the way we present ourselves in palliative care, or indeed anywhere, is significant? How does Jean see me? I wear a white tunic over a white or grey T-shirt. A leather thong can be seen round my neck although the beads are hidden. A small black stud is worn in my left ear lobe. My hair is short and spikey. What does this say to someone dying? Does it matter?

The female nurses have shifted into trousers and tunics. Do uniforms reduce individuality and promote uniformity? Jourard (1971) considers the nurse puts on a 'bedside manner' when she dons her uniform, and that the uniform encourages stereotypical behaviour that diminish the individual.

Many workers in the healing profession assume a 'professional manner' …some nurses always smile, others hum, and still others answer all patients' questions about medication with the automatic phrase, 'this will make you feel better'. The 'bedside manner' appears to be something which the nurse puts on when she dons her uniform…it is acquired as a means of coping with the anxieties engendered by repeated encounters with suffering, demanding patients. (pp.179–80)

Jourard's thesis is that interpersonal behaviour patterns are acquired as a means for satisfying needs and for reducing anxiety. Yet these patterns can become rigid and may limit the patient's expression of need. Instead of easing suffering nurses may actually increase suffering by failing to acknowledge it or by reacting against it. Jourard notes that:

One person's behaviour toward another is a controlling factor in the behaviour of another person. Thus maternal behaviour tends to pull dependent behaviour from the other person. Joking behaviour tends to evoke joking behaviour in return from the other. People seem to function most comfortably with others when the latter limit their reactions to some fixed range. Some people are unable to cope with another's tears, some cannot handle another's anger, some cannot deal with another's sexuality, and still others cannot tolerate spontaneous expressions of despair. Unwittingly they behave in the presence of the others so that the others will find it difficult to express these threatening patterns of behaviour. We may assume then, that one of the latent functions of the bedside manner is to reduce the possibility that patients will behave in ways that are likely to threaten the professional person. (p.181)

Clearly if this was true I could not know the person or respond to the person's needs. Jourard's work confronts me to be mindful of the way I present myself to patients and families. Am I authentic? Do I hide behind a 'professional facade'? Do I risk turning myself into an object – 'a palliative care nurse'? If we perceive ourselves as objects then do we then perceive our patients likewise?

Jourard notes the consequences of 'squelching our real selves because of fear of the consequencs of authentic being'. He says:

Is it possible that the role of the nurse, as this has been learned during training and practice, is one which is detrimental to the physical and mental health of nurses? Is it possible that nurses, by attempting to root out their own spontaneity and replace it with stereotyped modes of interpersonal behaviour, are actually doing violence to their own personalities and bodies? We may propose that another latent function of the bedside manner is to foster increasing self-alienation in nurses, thus jeopardizing their own health and well-being. (p.184)

I suspect that most nurses would cringe from identifying with Jourard's challenge. Yet as Jourard notes, the bedside manner is unwitting, so even acknowledging its possibility would be a form of psychic assault on one's identity.

I remember as a 19-year-old in hospital with a broken leg after a football accident, I was confined to bed for five weeks. One of my lasting images is Tara, the staff nurse, kneeling and revealing her bare thigh above her stocking top. Such moments are momentous in the life of shy boys. I immediately fell in love. I wonder if Tara ever knew how much she had responded to my sexuality. The stuff of dreams.

I also wonder if Jean has any libido with her enlarged liver. Should we ask her? No sign in the notes. No mention of a partner. It reminds me of patient assessments using the Roper, Logan and Tierney model when I first went to work at Burford hospital (Johns 1994). This model was based on a systems mentality that reduced the patient into ten 'activities of living' boxes, such as breathing, communicating, work and play. The 'box' marked sexuality was most often blank or perhaps contained a comment such as 'likes to wear lipstick'.

From the hospice notes I get no sense of Jean as a woman. Yet Jean gives me signs that she is ill at ease with her body, the way she feels about her big legs, that she can't move. More wonderment – should I flirt with her and see how she responds? Perhaps I already have – she said the foot and leg massage was wonderful. Massage is so vital to restore confidence in the body and mind. Touch is very intimate, especially the deliberate strokes of massage. Perhaps the quality of life that Jean desires is foremost being recognised as a sensuous human being, not one riddled with cancer. Yet the literature suggests that body image and loss of sexual identity is a big problem for cancer sufferers (Landmark and Wahl 2002; Woodward and Webb 2001). How would you feel? Perhaps a daily massage is indispensable to begin to help women such as Jean feel less 'broken and torn' (Landmark and Wahl 2002).

Iris

Iris's smile is still as broad as ever although I sense a tiredness in her eyes. Her shoulder is still supported in a badly fitted sling. She says it's dislocated but that seems unlikely. She has a lump on the clavicle. Is this a cancer growth from the bone? Or a callus of healing bone following a fracture? Her bone must be soft from the radiotherapy plus the continuous pamidronate injections. She does not yet have an orthopaedic appointment, although her GP and oncologist are both concerned and chasing it up. Men dancing around her to her tune. She is soon to start another course of radiotherapy to her left-sided chest wall for reoccurrence of chest wall lumps. The never-ending cycle of treatments steps up another gear. The start date for the radiotherapy clashes with her next bone scan. No respite. I wonder how she remains positive or is it just a mask? She is constantly coming apart at the seams and constantly hemming the unwinding thread of her life, yet a mass of loose threads trail about her.

Iris asks if I am into feng shui? I say I am obsessed with keeping the lid down on toilets to stop the positive energy going down the pan. I read it somewhere. Iris laughs till her sides split. As she lies on the couch I sense she is worrying. She says, 'I am a born worrier…I'm worrying about the children...' An unspoken 'will they be okay after I die?' worry. Dark clouds swirl about her.

My response is to encourage Iris to let go of this thought and relax into her breathing and the music.

After the treatment I check out with Iris if the breathing we do at the beginning of the treatment helps her to let go of her concerns and relax. She says she has learnt to relax, which she couldn't do when we started. It makes me think of the cumulative effect of meditation, that at first it seems our thoughts might overwhelm us when we create the meditative space. Slowly, over time, the thoughts are less insistent, and easier to let go, as we unfold into the stillness of the meditation space. No quick fixes, just commitment and purpose. Iris asks, 'Did I snore?' I smile – 'Just a little.'

Wednesday 23 January 2002

I am teaching a group of student nurses foot massage in the belief that every nurse should be confident and competent to do this because of the benefit it brings patients. The first issue is to develop and be mindful of the right attitude – what I call the 'healing attitude' that I bring to each caring encounter. In my view, there are five aspects to the 'healing attitude' as set out in Table 2.3.

These attributes of the healing attitude are similar to the dimensions of the Being available template (see Appendix 1, p.255). The Being available dimensions are in brackets in the left-hand column.

The 'healing attitude' reflects my intellectual effort to grasp what is ineffable. Essentially a 'healing attitude' is simply a skilful approach to ease other people's suffering. The core of the 'healing attitude' is the balance of compassion and wisdom – the Boddhisattva ideal. The compassionate and wise person is by nature intentional, non-attached and equanimous.

Non-attachment is not being attached to self or others. Of course, the ego makes this hard work to achieve. Non-attachment to people is reflected in Sangharakshita's (1999) words:

> [The practitioner is] keenly conscious of the sufferings of others, but she or he don't suffer themselves as others do. If one were literally to experience the suffering of others, it would be completely incapacitating: it would be too much. If one gets too personally caught up in someone else's predicament, one can end up simply joining them in their suffering. One needs a basis within one's own experience which is so positive that even though one is fully aware of other people's

suffering and one is doing what one can to alleviate it, one is not overwhelmed by that suffering. (p.55)

Words that resonate with those of Jourard (see pp.156–157). The students struggle with this concept, and say that they have had little opportunity to reflect on self as caring within their training. There is little emphasis on caring within the curriculum perhaps reflecting a legacy that caring is intrinsic to womanhood and, ipso facto, unskilled and taken for granted (James 1989). Yet my stories illuminate that caring makes such a difference to peoples' lives that it cannot be left to chance or be a lottery.

Friday 25 January 2002

Iris

Iris phones me at home in the evening. She is having radiotherapy to her chest wall lumps each day this week so we are unable to meet. She says it's been okay. The orthopaedic surgeon has looked at her x-rays. The whole shoulder has disintegrated. She says, 'I need a shoulder transplant!' I sense her despair but as usual she makes light of these boulders strewn in her path

Table 2.3 Five aspects of the healing attitude	
Intentionality (vision)	To have a focused vision of caring – my intention is always to ease suffering and grow through their experience towards self-realisation.
Compassion (concern)	To centre my unconditional love so this love is available to the other person as healing energy.
Non-attachment (managing self)	To know that I am both separate from and connected with the other person in order to tune into and flow with the other's journey without resistance and yet without absorbing their suffering as my own.
Wisdom (aesthetic response)	To be mindful of what's unfolding within a stance of 'not knowing' so I can respond with skilful action.
Equanimity (managing self) (creating environment)	To be in harmony with the world, with all things in perspective so I can be present within the unfolding moment.

– 'I shall just have to make do with it.' We make an appointment for her reflexology next Tuesday.

I am pleased Iris is able to phone me. However, it hasn't always been like that. Iris was initially very reticent to contact me at home, not wanting to intrude into my 'personal' life. Again – boundaries that people draw that separate parts of themselves – that I might have two lives, a work life and a personal life. I have just one life. I endeavour to make life fluid and flexible, like a silver birch bending to accommodate the shifting winds. Compassion has no time out. It is not a tap to turn on. The image of the tree bending to the wind reflects the nature of unconditional love. Yet the tree can only bend so far otherwise it will be uprooted. The tree has a natural resistance to ensure its own survival. It is a question of balance, of equanimity. The tree bends in the wind as I flow with Iris. We dance, Iris stumbles with the news of her shoulder. Fear seeps in and throws her off-balance. Staccato! Being a good dancing partner I adjust my steps to accommodate her stumble. I catch her fall and help her regain her dance step. Perhaps we will sit for a while until she recovers her composure. Would I mind if she rang every day? Is there some point along the line when my compassion becomes conditional? How might I respond? I would simply point out to Iris what was happening and review our dancing rhythm. In other words, resistance is simply having something pointed out, and provides the energy for changing the pattern. And, as so often before, I read something that makes utter sense. Pema Chödrön (1997) writes:

> Everything that occurs is not only usable and workable but is actually the path itself. We can use everything that happens to us as the means for waking up. We can use everything that occurs – whether it's our conflicting emotions or thoughts or our seemingly outer situation – to show us where we are asleep and how we can wake up completely, utterly, without reservation. So… [we can] use difficult situations to awaken our genuine caring for other people who, just like us, often find themselves in pain. As one lojong slogan says, 'When the world is filled with evil, all mishaps, all difficulties, should be transformed into the path of enlightenment.' (pp.123–124)

I see how Iris's difficulties inspire and nurture my compassion. But for Iris, she cannot easily transform such difficulties into the path of enlightenment. Yet we talk about such things, and she has changed. She has loosened the tight fist of fear for herself, although her fear for her family remains tight within her. Pema's words reflect the wisdom of reflective practice – the image of waking up to understand the conflict within, to contemplate ways such conflict can be transcended, and to realise the positive emotions and wisdom to transform self.

Wednesday 30 January 2002

Iris

Iris has an appointment with the orthopaedic specialist in two months. Until then she has to live with her disintegrated shoulder. She has had her bone scan but no results as yet.

I ask: 'How are you?'

'Mum is in hospital, she took a bad turn. It's happened before and she has always picked up. I haven't visited her yet. I don't think I can. It's such an awful place and makes me feel unwell. Don't know if I can bear to visit.'

I suggest: 'It reminds you of your own bad experiences there?'

Iris affirms.

I suggest: 'And your uncertainty of your mum's illness, that she might die...makes you confront your fragile hold on life?'

Iris gives me a knowing look behind her barely concealed tears. Yet she cannot let go of the tears.

I gently confront her: 'Would your mum like to see you? If it's so awful there, doesn't she need you to help ease her suffering? You wouldn't feel so guilty either, which you will if you don't visit.'

Iris, resigned: 'I know...I will visit her.'

I laugh: 'You turned that round quickly!'

Iris laughs: 'Yes I did, didn't I.'

I ask: 'How is your healing going?'

Iris says her healer has talked about ectoplasm, but she is confused by what this means. I'm not sure either. She seems less enchanted with the healing – 'I've been really down.'

I sense her worry about her mum on top of all the pressures she carries around with her, burdening her. She sags with the weight. I prop her up so she can blow free in the wind rather than crumple on the ground.

In the reflexology she quickly falls asleep. About halfway through treatment she jumps, and wakes; she laughs – 'The cat just jumped on me...' – and then she is asleep again, a gentle snore. Is the cat symbolic?

Noise permeates into the treatment room. It is lunchtime. I feel a wave of irritation that people can be so insensitive knowing that a treatment is in progress. The day care staff should know better. They are so caught up in lunchtime they do not perceive us behind the closed door. Out of sight, out of mind. Usually the therapists stop before lunch. I remember Tania telling people to be quiet outside the closed door when I was massaging Patricia (see p. 148). Part of me wants to suspend Iris's treatment and ask them to be quiet. But it is the patients' lunchtime – they have a need to socialise over lunch. I let the wave of irritation pass over me and retune with Iris.

I usually finish a reflexology treatment with Reiki but today I do a brief *metta bhavana* meditation for Iris. I hold each foot with my hands and become mindful of my breathing. On successive out breaths I say to myself:

> Iris – may you be free from suffering
> Iris – may you find happiness amongst the gloom
> Iris – may you recover your health or find balance in living with your cancer
> Iris – may you grow from this experience and have ease of being with your family

Metta bhavana is the loving kindness meditation. Doing the meditation practice I am swollen with compassion until it bursts and floods Iris with rainbow colours. Although I do not know for certain, I feel it works in much the same way as Reiki – harnessing and channelling universal energy for healing. I do know the practice energises and balances me.

The smell of lunch seeps into the room.

Iris says: 'Umm…that makes me feel hungry…I haven't eaten for days…my stomach has been too churned up.'

'And now it's easier?'

'Yes, it is, definitely…definitely.'

Iris sips her water. The reflexology has really relaxed her. As she says herself, the reflexology is a 'fix'. It is good to see her released from her tension, at least for the moment. I have used rose essential oil instead of patchouli in the reflexology cream for its feminine and stress-busting properties. Its smell drifts in the room. Iris says it is such a lovely smell. I suggest she could use rose in her bath in the evening to help her relax.

Thursday 31 January 2002

Over breakfast I read an article by Dale Borglum entitled 'The long shadow of good intentions' published in *Tricycle* (Fall 1997). In this article he talks about the 'shadow' side of conscious dying. He sets out a list of the ways the shadow side may distort compassion. I call them 'spiritual traps' (Table 2.4 p.166). Self-doubt creeps in – to what extent do I fall into these traps? My journal is a litany of laying out and exorcising a hungry ghost. Certainly I have been unfulfilled in my life from a spiritual perspective. From a young age I eschewed church because it was thrust down my throat and there was no sense of the spiritual in our home. Church-going had no meaning. I had no sense of God. I could not connect with God or Jesus. On a rational level God did not make sense. And yet, over the past five years I have become reacquainted with the idea of a God. A faith uncovered. Yen Mah (2000) says:

> In our modern world's headlong rush towards speed, profit, efficiency and progress, we tend to lose sight of the details of our true nature. These days, more and more westerners are looking for answers from eastern thought in their search for their inner being. They seem lost and feel a need to find their way. (p.92)

These traps offer a reflective framework to measure the compassionate self. Do I measure up? Could I admit if I didn't? Having just written 'swollen with compassion' I am struck with the notion of spiritual inflation. Borglum (1997) quotes Thomas Merton:

> There is no wilderness so terrible, so beautiful, so arid, and so fruitful as the wilderness of compassion. It is the only desert that shall truly flourish like the lily. (p.69)

Such a stark and beautiful image. Borglum says that 'this desert flourishes because our true nature is compassion'. It is true that compassion is the key to working with people like Iris. Yet is my compassion genuine? What if it is inflated rather than swollen? Am I inflated, floating on a spiritual trip, and drowning in sentimentality? How would I know? I challenge myself in a poem for Iris.

> Sometimes I am a wolf howling at night, as if your suffering haunts me
> Sometimes I feel helpless before your suffering, as if it taunts me
> I howl to ease the suffering but is it yours or mine?
> Whose need is it to touch the divine?

In his description of spiritual inflation, Borglum says, 'We become lost in what we know.' When I do a literature search for spirituality and palliative care I become submerged, or in Borglum's word 'lost', in this ocean of knowledge. I take more and more on board until my boat sinks and I drown. My head becomes full until I can no longer think for myself. The nature of spiritual care is deep within me, not out there in theories. It can be touched through reflection. Theories may be useful to inform the ideas that emerge from reflection. To teach spirituality through theories would be to miss the point entirely.

So how might I tune into my spiritual self? The following questions may give some insight:

- What meaning do I give the word 'sacred?'
- How would I know if I am spiritual?
- How do I view my own life and death?
- What things are important for me to be a good person?
- Am I mindful of myself as compassionate?
- How would others know my spiritual self?
- In what ways do I suffer?
- Can I sense the spiritual in others?
- Am I more concerned for myself than others?
- How do I view the future of my life?

No science, just a bunch of obvious questions. Try them out.

Saturday 2 February 2001

A warm and blustery morning. The roads are deserted. Meditation has brought me stillness despite the bluster outside. I am looking after Megan and Diane this morning with Carol, one of the care assistants.

Megan

Megan is 41 years old. I read her notes. She has been very positive about her cancer of the pancreas, determined to live long enough to go to Dubai and celebrate the birth of her first grandchild. Nick, her son, has just arrived from Dubai. His wife is eight months pregnant. Megan lives with her daughter, Tasmin. She is just 20. Megan has been protecting Tasmin from the brutal reality of her advancing cancer. Echoes of Jean.

Table 2.4 Spiritual traps

Spiritual inflation	We have the impression that we are especially sensitive, open, positive and spiritual, so automatically we must have a gift for working with the dying. Intimacy with death can become intoxicating. We become lost in what we know. We become experts in helping the dying.
Laying a spiritual trap	As caregivers trying to aid a conscious death, we feel there are certain attitudes and practices that one must use. For example, we might implore a dying person, 'Stay positive and hopeful. Transcend your body. Learn to meditate before it's too late. It worked for us so it will work for you.'
Expectation of a good death	There is a moment-to-moment expectation we have of the dying process in terms of what we think one should be doing to achieve a 'good' death.
Fear of drowning	The dying person won't be breathing much longer. What does this imply about our own mortality? Will we drown in the dark waters of this existential abyss?
Unresolved grief	Our unresolved grief compels us to distance ourselves unconsciously from the dying person, forcing him to carry universal illness.
Voyeurism	We want to create good spiritual feelings for ourselves, some kind of 'hit' from being close to the dying experience.
Idiot compassion	Since you are dying and we aren't, we will always try to be nice, soothing and non-confrontational with you. Telling the truth or expressing our own feelings might be too upsetting to you. Idiot compassion is an extreme form of sympathy that doesn't take into account the full range of compassionate action and actually blocks true compassion.
Sentimentality	We become lost in our sweet, romanticised, emotional response to the dying process rather than maintaining a clear awareness of what we are feeling. There are many more examples: wanting the person to live, wanting the person to die, hogging the patient for ourselves, loss of healthy boundaries, burnout, transference and counter-transference.

Now Megan has lost control. The cancer has overwhelmed her and it is likely she will soon die. Nick sits with his mother. He is bent over her gently holding her hand. I do not disturb them. We go to 'freshen' Megan. Every movement disturbs her. Yet she is conscious of our presence. Her lower body is grossly swollen which makes her difficult to move. Two syringe drivers purr their drugs into her. In one driver she has diamorphine for her pain and nozinan for her nausea. In the other driver she has hyoscine for her bubbly chest and midazolam to 'settle her'. Martha, the senior staff nurse, wonders whether Megan is restless and needs more midazolam. I suggest we increase her diamorphine because of the pain she has on movement. Martha agrees, although later in the morning she does increase the midazolam as Megan becomes more restless when she is incontinent. I often observe this pattern – how patients become disturbed when incontinent even as they slip into a deeper consciousness. Midazolam aims to deaden consciousness, so presumably the person and those watching do not have to witness the apparent distress. Nick and Tasmin suffer to see their mother so distressed, although Nick is pleased when Megan becomes more aware as we move her and seems to recognise him. He will treasure that moment, the point of departure if she slips back into her inner world. Such moments are so poignant.

It is also an argument against being too aggressive with sedation. It seems sometimes we overreact to the slightest twitch – interpreting that as agitation. I would probably err on the conservative side and flow with the patient's distress by the bedside using more non-pharmocological approaches; music, gentle hand massage and Therapeutic Touch. It is a fine line to be drawn.

Later in the afternoon, I set up an aroma-stone and burn some neroli. Josie, Megan's mother and her husband John sit with Megan. I notice a large amethyst crystal on the locker. Much of the colour has faded from it. I explain that the crystal has absorbed energy and will need to be buried to recharge its energy and recover its colour. They say how much Megan was involved in crystals and aromatherapy. She would love the neroli burning. They like the smell and feel the peace it brings into the room. Megan lies there as we talk about her but I sense she would approve.

The crystals and oils are connections with Megan. It is hard to put into words the sense of sacredness in the room, but it holds me there. I want to dwell with these people in the unfolding stillness. It is how it should be.

Katie

Lucy, a staff nurse, tells me that Katie is the sort of person who might like a foot massage. She will ask her; the message back is 'Yes please!' Katie is 80 years old, of Anglo-Indian parents. She has a fungating breast cancer. She is a Jehovah's Witness and had refused a blood transfusion at the hospital when her Hb had been 6. It is now 8 after iron therapy. It is alleged she does not communicate well, that she mixes up her history and that she is lonely.

It's a busy morning and it's past lunchtime before I visit Katie. She is expecting me and says she is looking forward to a foot massage. I have time, but first I need to tune myself into this woman – who is she and how does she feel about what is happening to her? She says she has lived in England since 1947 when her husband was killed in the riots in India. She fills me in with her life and health story. She is philosophical about the future. She has a strong faith and family to sustain her. I do not detect any confusion in her talk.

I ask her what fragrance she loves most? She says lavender, so I mix some with sweet almond carrier oil. She smells it and says it is her favourite smell. I also use one drop of frankincense for its spiritual presence.

Frankincense

The sweet protector of the heavens operates far beyond the auric field, in the light realms. It is adaptive – it will adapt to a person's spiritual state of being, like an ever-watchful friend capable of offering support in a wide range of circumstances. But, like a vigilant parent, it will not let us go where we are not ready to go. Holding the wisdom of the ages, it waits for what is asked of it and can do all that may be required. Watching, with infinite sight, if it encounters malevolent energies attached to a person it has the authority and power to assist in their removal. In cases of spiritual shock or loss, when the spirit can step out of the body, even for a brief moment, frankincense can gently ease us back into our earthly home. Frankincense is elevating, spiritual and meditative, and holds some of the wisdom of the universe, that which is manifested in the spiritual self. (Worwood 1999, p.214)

I love the idea of frankincense being a vigilant parent for our spiritual well-being. I often add one drop into most of my mixes for this purpose, especially when I work with people who are dying.

For half an hour Katie is totally relaxed. Foot massage is the perfect relaxant for the body, mind and spirit. It is poetry in motion with the rhythmic flow of my well-rehearsed hands and creates such a sense of stillness within the chaos.

Thursday 14 February 2002

It's Valentine's Day. The early morning air is crisp and cool. The birds are singing and vibrate the air with their shrill.

At the shift report Brenda, the senior nurse, reads a part of the hospice philosophy to focus staff on their purpose and the importance of maintaining our values and quality of practice. She feels values have been slipping recently. A sharp reminder to shake complacency. In the mundane day-to-day practice it is easy to drift into habitual patterns of working that become careless or worse, uncaring.

A shared and valid vision for practice gives meaning to practice and fosters a caring community. Most importantly it focuses caring intent and nurtures compassion. If I am more certain of what I am trying to achieve and value that achievement then I am more likely to actually achieve it. As a consequence I am more available to the patient because I know what I am available for.

Grace

I enter Grace's room and she immediately tells me about her nasal congestion. Beth, the night staff nurse, has given her some eucalyptus and menthol gum that has helped. Grace spits the gum out, but she's still congested. It bothers her. I suggest an inhalation? She thinks that's a good idea. I have no eucalyptus in my 'medicine bag' so I prepare an inhalation with peppermint, rosemary and lavender. I need a Nelson's inhaler but in this modern age, such implements have long been discarded. I compromise with a glass bowl. The inhalation mix smells good.

Grace sits resting with her elbows propped on her bed table and a large towel over her head. I stay with her because of risk of spillage and scalding. Afterwards, she says it helped her even though she continues to complain about the congestion. She rings a friend to bring in some ancient medicine that she has always taken. People are confident in their tried and tested remedies. She has had the problem of nasal congestion since an accident when she was 19. She was thrown when her horse was hit by a bus and landed on her face.

Grace reveals her life. She lives on a farm. Her whole life has been farming. Her husband died four years ago. She woke one morning and he was dead in the bed. Since then she has managed the farm but slowly the work has become too much. She lives with an 88-year-old woman who still does much of the housework and who grows her own vegetables despite her arched back and osteoarthritis. Grace's cousins help her to manage the farm and they will take the farm over when she dies.

She expects to die. She has no illusion. Religion plays no significant role in her life. Her faith has dissolved over the years, yet she enjoyed speaking with Sister Kathleen, the Roman Catholic nun and volunteer, when she visited.

Her congested nose is better but now she complains of earache. Perhaps the inhalation has unblocked a Eustachian tube. She looks at the bouquet of flowers on the window ledge a friend has brought. She says, 'I love the smell of flowers.' I suggest an aroma-stone using a floral fragrance. She goes for neroli. Its smell drifts between us. She says it's very pleasant. Perhaps it's my self-fulfilling nature, but she immediately seems more relaxed. '[Neroli] is always loving and peaceful. [It] brings light into any day' (Worwood 1999, p.235).

It is fascinating to consider that with all her cancer difficulties it was her long-standing nasal congestion problem that most bothered her. On reflection I wonder if a nebuliser may have been a more efficient and safer way of administering the essential oils than a steam inhalation. The risk of scalding or spilling is of concern and probably why such practices ceased under the Health and Safety Act (1994). The advantage of steam over a nebuliser is that the steam evaporates the oil more quickly, resulting in quicker relief.

Betty

Further along the corridor I enter Betty's room. Her granddaughter Maxine greets me. She immediately returns my name – 'Hello, Chris.' Her eyes are open, receptive, love shines from her face. I know from the report just how attached she is to her 'Gran'. I rarely experience such a high level of vibration from another person and tingle inside with expectation.

I explain I am a therapist and can offer Betty and perhaps herself a treatment later. Maxine relays this to Betty. Betty looks to her granddaughter – 'Yes, that would be nice later.'

It is strange communicating to Betty through her granddaughter as if Maxine is her protector. I 'break through' and taking Betty's hand I introduce myself. I have been informed at shift report that Betty is afraid of being alone, so Maxine and her Aunt Trudy are always with her or close by. They have followed her into the hospice because her pain was out of control, and she suffered unpleasant side effects from diclofenac. Now a syringe driver purrs with morphine and haloperidol and another with ketolorac.

Now she is physically comfortable as she eases towards her death. Betty is wrapped in a cocoon of filial love. These two women weave their caring pattern with Betty until they have become one – dedicated to Betty's care.

Later, Maxine is sitting with her partner in the smoking room. She comes out and we talk in the corridor. She easily fills me in with events. I suspect she has said this story before but she needs to talk about the way she is feeling. We eventually sit. Trudy, her aunt, arrives and goes into Betty's room. We finish talking and return to Betty's room.

I give Betty a foot massage adding a drop of lavender and frankincense to some sweet almond oil. Betty enjoys the massage. Trudy and Maxine are pleased. They say later how much Betty has picked up today.

Afterwards, my attention turns to the Maxine and Trudy. Trudy says she has been stressed; her neck and shoulders are tight. Indeed they are. She accepts my offer of an Indian head massage.[6] Trudy confesses she felt excluded earlier this morning when Maxine was talking with me. She thought I was a doctor. She and Maxine had agreed to share caring for Gran/Mum and she thought that Maxine was being told things about her mother. However, they had gone for a glass of wine and resolved their misunderstanding. Perhaps Trudy is oversensitive, tired and stressed, her frayed edges dangling from her hem. Whatever the cause, conflict bubbles up from the surface like a stain that soils the caring between them.

For Trudy's massage I blend one drop of grapefruit and one drop of pettigrain essential oils in five ml of sweet almond carrier oil. The citrous oils are light and fresh. Davis (1999) describes pettigrain as 'having a fresh, flowery light perfume' (p.237) that blends well with the tang of grapefruit. Besides easing her aching muscles, these oils will help Trudy feel relaxed. It is the cause of the tightness, the slow drip feed of unremitting stress I need to help release.

Grapefruit

Rouses the human spirit from slumber, giving it the impetus to pay attention to the guidance being given to mankind. Energising and enlivening, it disallows the egocentricity of just living for the body, without making connection with the spirit. It can thus reconnect mind, body and soul, to help us connect with the angelic realms within us.

Pettigrain

---

6   Indian head massage is a massage of the upper back, neck, shoulders, upper arms, scalp and face.

> Stability is often needed when we are at our most vulnerable, feeling fragile and taking everything a little too personally and emotionally. It's at times such as this that we need a delicate spiritual strength, a gentle outstretched hand to guide us through the days when tears seem ever present. (Worwood 1999, p.242)

Trudy enjoys the massage. Her muscles are certainly relaxed. She shrugs her shoulders and turns her head. She smiles and says it feels much easier. She loved the music – Rusty Crutcher's 'Ocean Eclipse' – especially the sound of water. She says she found it sacred, yet she is uncertain of saying this, trying to find the right word to describe her sense of wonder. The music touches something deep inside, facilitated by the massage and the oils. It helps her to acknowledge the sacredness of Betty's care and forthcoming death, to help her move into a sacred curve. We are in tune and can dance along the sacred curve.

Massaging Trudy I felt my heart would burst. I could hardly breathe at times. Compassion has such astonishing power when unleashed. I now know the awesome healing potential of love. Words cannot adequately express the feeling. It is like floating in a timeless space beyond the physical realm.

As anger breeds anger so love breeds love. This is a significant insight because I am suggesting that if carers communicate love then the patient or relative will absorb this love and become more loving. If love does heal then perhaps carers have a responsibility to nurture and project their loving selves. I am sure every reader will have sensed the difference between a nurse who cares deeply and one who doesn't.

When we return to Betty's room Maxine says they appreciate honesty about Mum's condition. They know the tears will come often, they do not mind that…but most of all they need to rest in our love. Maxine says she feels that and feels deeply comforted knowing that. I say I am not at the hospice again until next Tuesday. As we hold each other's gaze, we are all uncertain of meeting again. Betty is asleep so I do not disturb her.

Besides Betty's foot massage I have had little contact with her. She is cocooned by the two women so I nurse the cocoon, appreciating the family's primary need to care and be in control of caring.

I am conscious of how I position myself within this family group. I try not to compete for control, yet this can be difficult for nurses who need to be in control of situations. In positioning myself I must ask 'what is best?' Clearly Maxine and Trudy have a great need to care for Betty. They are constantly at her bedside because she fears being alone and they have promised her that one of them will always be there. I am mindful that if caring became compromised under this arrangement I would be able to assert my perspective because I have connected with them from their perspective. Working with Maxine, Trudy and Betty illustrates the concept of tuning in and flowing with the family as a whole even though each has a different wavelength.

Doris

Doris is sitting by her bed. She has just arrived at the hospice following a referral by her district nurse for reasons I do not yet know. We have met before (see p.154). She remembers me although calls me Paul. I ask her how she is. She shares her despair with her predicament, her loss of mobility and independence. She says, 'I am surrounded by family and friends but I feel so awful... I can't do anything by myself anymore.'

She tries hard to smile but her face cracks under the strain. I acknowledge her predicament but there is little more I can do at this moment. She says this is a nice room. She has a view across the gardens. Some hospital flowers greet her.

In the corridor, Christine notes Doris's admission. She quips, 'I hope she isn't my team.' Christine's remark reflects the fact that Doris is not a popular patient. To quote James (1989), she is emotionally hard work. Her despair seems to pull the staff down. But even understanding where Christine's negativity is coming from, it still feels shocking to experience such an overtly negative attitude by her towards a patient. Maybe I am falling into the 'nice' trap...a trap because it outlaws negative feelings, when it is better to be honest and express them. I say to Christine, 'Is that how you feel?' and she immediately softens – 'Sometimes people and situations get to us.'

Again I sense the 'dark side of nursing' (Corley and Goren 1998) that reflects those nurse behaviours that diminish caring. Rather than ease suffering, such behaviours add to it. In labelling people in negative ways, the practitioner projects their anxiety into that person. The person becomes the 'problem' rather than the staff's response. The difficult behaviour becomes 'normal' rather than a need for caring. Staff tend to respond by avoiding the person whenever possible and hence the person, whose negative behaviour might be viewed as a cry for help, gets less attention than other patients. We do not dance well with such patients.

I wanted to respond more to Christine to help her ease the anxiety that Doris engenders within her. Yet I know Christine cares deeply. I hope her expression and my quick response will have pricked the bubble and released the negative energy. It must be the responsibility of every nurse to confront uncaring attitudes.

Tuesday 19 February 2002

The early morning sky is folds of grey, like waves in the sea, each wave getting progressively darker. Like a busy mind with wave after wave of thought crowding the clear blue sky.

Audrey

Audrey is 78 years old. She is very open and welcoming. We discuss breakfast and bathing. I inquire about her home. She has lived alone since her husband died 18 months ago. I ask, 'You really miss him?' She talks about Ron; she met him in 1939 when he was 17 and she was 15. They were married three years later. He then went off to the war in India. She didn't see him for four years. 'I met him from the train. It was like meeting a stranger.' She is full of memory. She says that Ron comes to visit her at nights. 'He comes from that door (she points to the bathroom door) bringing me flowers. He never speaks but I speak to him. I used to talk to my mother. She did speak to me, always to say that she was okay.'

Listening to Audrey talk I am conscious of the night staff nurse saying that Audrey is confused, that she speaks to herself at night or imagines she sees her dead husband. On the contrary, Audrey makes complete sense. I have no doubt she sees Ron. Perhaps it is only natural to label another's perceptions that fall outside our own realms of possibility as confused. But it is an insult to Audrey and diminishes her personhood.

Penny has asked me to mention day care as a possibility for Audrey after her discharge. When I drop it into our conversation, Audrey says she attends a Salvation Army day group on Thursdays. She isn't keen on the day care idea but is reluctant to say so. She says the Salvation Army is a lot of fun. I ask if she has a strong faith. No, but she accepts that she will die and that doesn't present any great fears to her. She feels there is an afterlife because Ron comes to her. However, she does fear dying itself...the thought of suffering. She thinks of Ron and the way she nursed him until he died. How he suffered – 'I was phoned from the hospital that he had taken a turn for the worse...and he had died before I could get there.' Not being with him when he died was a great blow for me when we had been so close all our lives.'

I ask: 'How did you feel about coming into the hospice?'

'I was reluctant because I hadn't told anyone I had cancer…not even my two older sisters because I didn't wanted to worry them. I had kept my cancer a secret you see…now the secret's out…they will ask "Why has Audrey gone to the hospice?" Hospice is about cancer and death.'

Audrey reinforces a generally held image of the hospice, which of course holds more than a grain of truth.

I question: 'Perhaps it's good to come out?'

Audrey says: 'Oh, I don't know about that, but going to the day hospice will worry them.'

I sense that Audrey is feeling under pressure.

'I'll talk to Lena, the day care team leader, and explain how you feel. The invitation is open-ended so if you change your mind then your Macmillan nurse can contact us.'

Before coming into the hospice, she had not had a bath for a year. I slowly walk Audrey to the bathroom. When Tracy and I help Audrey to undress, she says, 'I was nursed by a young male nurse at the hospital. I wasn't embarrassed but another woman on the ward said she would refuse.'

She loves the jacuzzi bath, a little whoop of joy as the bubbles vibrate about her. Jacuzzis are fun for everyone! I put a few drops of lavender oil in the bath to help her swollen and tight legs. They have become progressively swollen probably due to her heart failure secondary to chronic bronchitis and emphysema.

After the bath we help her dress and I help her with her knickers. She laughs and says, 'A man doing this, what would my friends say!' Again no hint of embarrassment but I wonder if she is uncomfortable with me helping her and her anxiety spills out in her? Later I ask Tracy, one of the care assistants, her thoughts. Tracy says she felt Audrey seemed really comfortable with me. I wonder if reflection sometimes makes me too sensitive to such issues? It felt okay, but self-doubt creeps in, undermining my confidence, but it is an important issue to address. I know Audrey is sensitive about her body. She says the lumpectomy for her breast cancer improved the shape of her breast. She preferred the shape and wished she could have the other one done. Such black humour!

Betty and Trudy

It is good to see them again. Maxine has gone home to Plymouth to be with her husband and support him when he spreads his father's ashes at sea. Trudy stays close to her mother. Betty seems brighter, more alert, although we have yet to find a solution to her nausea. Betty is eating, but is being sick afterwards.

I suggest a hand massage with peppermint. Trudy says, 'Would you like that, Mum?' Betty says 'Yes' but she doesn't like the smell of the peppermint. She's settled now after her wash so declines my offer of a foot massage. Trudy says she felt very good after her massage last week…her neck and shoulder muscles are much improved. She does not want another massage. She needs to stay close to her mother now that Maxine has gone.

I ask about the future arrangements? Betty is going home. Trudy and her husband are moving in with her. I suggest that Trudy can contact me through the Macmillan nurse if she would like a therapy treatment. Trudy is pleased by my offer. I say that she must look after herself, that it can be hard work being a non-stop carer.

Trudy looks at her mum. 'Can you hear us, Mum?' Betty says she can hear every word. Trudy says, 'We don't mean you are hard work, just that Chris is concerned I can manage.' Betty says she understands but I feel a sharp pang of guilt at using words so carelessly. I try and make light of the tension and say that Trudy is a good daughter. Betty says she is…I say she must have been well brought up. Trudy says that's right. We can relax on the surface, yet I feel the guilt vibrate. One thing I often confront practitioners with is not to give themselves a hard time, and here I am struggling with the same issue. Guilt seems to be deeply embodied within nurses and yet it is understandable if we feel our actions have been uncaring. My sensitivity is heightened because Betty faces death and does not want to be 'hard work'. It is as if I have spoken her worst fears. I know I spoke in good faith yet I am stained.

Derek

Leaving Betty and Trudy I pop in and say hello to Derek and his wife. He sits in the corner chair while his wife crochets. Derek does not remember me. His wife Margaret intercedes and says Derek was confused when admitted. Over time he has become less confused as his drug regime was rationalised.

Margaret recalls Derek's history. The constant sensation of wanting to have his bowels opened. He had been passing mucous but had hidden the fact. Margaret had found some tissues one day and made him go to the doctor. Tests showed a low bowel cancer. He had a bowel resection and a colostomy formed which was late reversed. He was offered chemotherapy post-operatively. The consultant had said chemotherapy would give Derek about a 3 per cent chance of cure. If he was 65 he would encourage Derek to accept chemotherapy. If 85 then he wouldn't recommend it. Being 77, it was in the balance. Derek must decide. Derek refused it. He's comfortable with that decision. He knows he is going to die soon and is okay about that. He spreads his hands – 'Two weeks, five weeks…it doesn't make any difference.' Margaret's face crumples yet she contains her tears. I feel the poignancy of this moment, of sitting with these people who have been married 50 years talk about their life together and face the end of their relationship. I have such admiration for them.

Talking through life situations helps them find meaning in Derek's forthcoming death. It brings them closer. Talking is cathartic, enabling them to express their sadness and their love – sometimes directly but mostly hinted at between the lines. In doing so Margaret makes connections between what is happening now and their past together. She anticipates her grief and begins the healing work now (Marris 1986). I am a catalyst. My presence opens a clearing amid the chaos for such conversations to take place.

Presence is my body radiating compassion. I mindfully project my presence into every care situation so people are wrapped in my compassion. People sense this love and, dwelling in it, can more easily release their suffering.

Connor

In the morning report Dolores, the night staff nurse, had said that Jim, Connor's son, felt guilty because he hadn't given his father a cigarette last night in his room. Later his father 'went off' and became unresponsive. Jim was bereft, feeling he had denied his father a last cigarette.

I introduce myself to Jim and acknowledge his feelings. Jim says he feels so helpless. I acknowledge it must be tough to be with his father like this. Jim has been sitting holding his father's hand. I say, 'Hello, Connor' and Connor responds. Jim is thrilled…it is the first time Connor has responded since he 'went off'.

All morning Jim, his mother and sister sit around Connor. Such a family scene. So much so, that when I do go into the room I feel slightly awkward – Am I am intruding? But the family welcome my presence. Jim asks if there is anything that can be done to relieve Jim's 'death rattle'. They assume it must be distressing for Connor as well as themselves. Connor has a cancer of his bronchus. Dolores had commenced an infusion of hyoscine 0.8 µg. Brenda says she won't mess about and goes for the maximum dose of 2.4 µg over 24 hours. She feels Jim unwittingly makes the rattle worse with his persistent mouth care – soaked sponges that must dribble down Connor's throat. We must confront Jim yet not undermine his effort. As with so much of care it is a question of finding the right balance. But Jim understands. He is so grateful for our help. We move Connor and his breathing is immediately easier. Connor's life is slipping away and we hover around the bed. Four priests have visited. The family's Catholic faith is strong and sustaining. I am moved to see Jim so close to his father. I think of my own father and the alienation between us. Somehow, despite Jim's pain I feel a twinge of envy…that to suffer so much is a reflection of the love between them. I cannot but help think that my father's death would make little impression. This feels like a terrible but important confession.

As I write, I look back on this 'normal' day and feel the way I have brushed against the lives of these people, both relatives and patients who touch death. I have flowed with their rhythms and even if my stillness is disturbed by the pebble of 'hard work' rippling within the still surface of the lake, it is a sense of stillness and awe I experience driving home. Each day I become more open and curious, more compassionate, wiser, more knowing of who I am, more at peace with who I am. The hungry ghosts are well fed.

> Sometimes you may feel as though you are unfolding like a flower, at other times spiritual life may feel more like climbing a mountain… You have a sense of racing forward all the time, moving from stage to stage, climbing that mountain. At the same time, you have to be absolutely still, yet realising more and more deeply where you are now. (Sangharakshita 1999, pp.204–205)

I sense the continuity through this journal, as each experience leads into another. Looking back I can feel my spiritual journey unfolding, and yet each experience is in itself this point of stillness after the dance (Roth 1999), realising self more deeply within the now.

Friday 22 February 2002

Pam

I first saw Pam when she was admitted on Monday but I did not talk with her, wrapped up as I was with my own patients. But today I am caring for her.

Her open face greets me. She is full of warmth and smiles. I ask what her accent is – she says West Yorkshire. She then outlines a brief history to her arrival at the hospice. She had two hip replacements, the last one last year. Then, shortly afterwards, in December she had severe stomach pains. Investigation revealed stomach cancer that had metastasised to her liver. A palliative bypass of her stomach was successful. Now she is at the hospice for symptom management and recovery before going home.

She is happy to be here. She does not like tablets because they make her retch. Even as we talk about her tablets she begins to retch. She says she has nothing to come up. We suggest she should at least take her domperidone. Mandy brings her a cup of tea. She likes it hot and fairly weak. She takes the tablet well. Her appetite has been poor, creating much despair within her family. It must be hard to watch your mother wither away. We commenced her on dexamethasone 4mg daily two days ago hoping to improve her appetite. She declines breakfast because the tea has filled her. I sit with her and we talk for about half an hour. She says she must look funny without her dentures. She talks easily and I slip into her rhythm.

She then feels ready for a small bowl of 'flakes' with hot milk. Eating these, she takes the remainder of her tablets without retching. Triumph. She'll rest now before washing and taking a walk. She is anxious to walk in preparation for going home. We joke about promenading.

Later for lunch Pam eats some greasy fish and chips. She is again triumphant. The dexamethasone is doing its job. She's full – 'Can we save the lemon meringue pie for later? I'm ready now for my foot massage.' I ask her what smells she likes. She says lavender. When I place my hands on the bottom of her feet she exclaims how warm they are. She says my touch is so reassuring.

Afterwards, Pam says how deeply relaxed she feels. I close the curtains, dim the lights and close the door for her to sleep. An hour later I disturb her. She has slept so deeply she is a little disorientated. I get her to drink some water. She asks how much she owes me. I hold her and say nothing. She thanks me for being with her today.

Connor

I sit with Connor while his family have a break. Connor hangs on to life. The family have been with him constantly since Tuesday. Connor's youngest son, Connor junior, has arrived from Indonesia. He slept last night in a chair in Dad's room while Jim had slept in the guest room. We have promised them that Connor will not die alone. Irish music fills the room. I have added some sandalwood essential oil to some grapeseed oil to massage Connor's hand. There is no significant physical aspect of sandalwood that would benefit Connor. However, like so many of her spiritual descriptions of essential oils, Worwood's (1999) description of sandalwood is inspiring:

> A fragrance that stretches out to the universe, into the hallowed space between heaven and earth, to connect with the divine presence. Sandalwood brings our wisdom into a meditative state, quieting us so we can hear and rejoice in the choral singing of the universal soul. It brings us into the great cosmic prayer, the infinite meditation. (p.249)

Such images to conjure. Connor is unconscious. His only reflex is to close his mouth around the mouth swab. I imagine that he inhabits the space between earth and heaven. He is a devout Roman Catholic. The prayer book is on the locker. A crucifix lies on his pillow, a rosary in his hand. A picture of himself with Kathleen taken some years ago is propped up on a Bailey's Irish cream bottle. A card from his granddaughter, Hope, is pinned to the wall – 'I hope you get well, Granddad.'

Again I sit with a dying unconscious patient. Again I pause between the beating of the syringe drivers, between the beating of my pulse to feel Connor's rhythm. His breathing is laboured. He is very hot, a consequence of his chest infection. I use Therapeutic Touch to ease his breathing and cool

him. I visualise a cool ice-blue waterfall cooling him. My words are whispered to ease his journey into another dimension.

The family return. I mention the photograph. Sinead, his daughter, says she has a copy of this photograph. She blacked out the cigarette Connor is holding. Cigarettes – perhaps why Connor is lying here. The symbolism is profound.

Later I meet Mary, Connor's wife, in the corridor. I ask how she is. She says how hard it is to face a future without Connor. The words pour from her, about her life with him, the places they have lived following his work. She says she has a need to talk, as if talking helps her put her life in perspective with him, helps her to grieve for him, helps her to face a future without him as uncertain and hopeless as that feels just now – 'What will I do without him?'

I turn her thoughts into her family, her children and grandchildren, so she can see she is not alone. Perhaps it is the empty house that most frightens her. Last night she went into Connor's bedroom to say goodnight to him. The emptiness of the house is a stark reminder of his death.

Connor has been a hard-working, hard-smoking and hard-drinking man. Yet she talks about what a good man Connor was when he was sober, how generous he was telling her to go into town and buy herself some shoes or a skirt. He wanted her to get some shoes with a chunky heel. She always felt she was sliding back with flat shoes so she's always worn a heel. She talks about his being in the general hospital and how difficult he was as a patient. Looking back she finds it amusing. She says Connor was so happy with his care here that he didn't want to leave. She is so grateful and I sense the vital role hospices play in ensuring memories of loved one's last days are precious even as they suffer.

Mary oscillates between laughs and tears as we talk. I listen and hold her as the tears well up and laugh along with her stories. After about half an hour, she thanks me for listening and returns to the room. Sister Kathleen sits with the family. When I go to say goodbye I feel wrapped in their love. Another poignant moment in a catalogue of poignant moments.

Mary spilt out the suffering she could no longer contain and perhaps couldn't express within her own family. Listening, I had no recipes to fix her suffering…only to flow with its rambling course, enabling her fears and grief to bubble and burst on the surface. The idea of containment is a common theme through the narrative – the way I contain her, to metaphorically hold her through my listening and attention and being a container in which to pour her feelings.

Iris

I go across to the day unit where Iris sits with her two children waiting for lunch. She says, 'This is Chris, my reflexologist.' We hug and I ask her how things are with her mother. Iris's face tells the story – 'They are taking her to hospital to have a scan and drain the haematoma. Dad just accepts that they know best.' Iris knows in her heart that this is not the best. She dreads her mother dying on the operating theatre table. She wants her mother to die with dignity, cared for in the hospice. And so she suffers in her helplessness and fantasies. These fears crash through her efforts to stay in the moment. And if that is not enough, she says her shoulder is very painful yet she can't immobilise it. She is a busy mother.

Indira

Before going home, I replenish Indira's aroma-stone. I have been burning bergamot to counter the persistent stench from her incontinence of faeces. Betty, in the bed next to hers, does not complain, yet she asked for the window to be opened. Betty does not like to complain. Staff say how brilliant the bergamot is in neutralising the odour.

Indira spends the day curled up in bed. Now she sits on the edge of her bed as if she has emerged from her cocoon, surrounded by five Asian women spreading a safety net around her. She is at home with these women yet a stranger to us. These women tend her deeper needs while we clear up the surface mess. I nod and smile and pass a few words about what I am doing. It's very superficial and I do not try to penetrate this community. A cultural divide is not easy to cross and indeed with Indira it isn't necessary.

On my way home I close my eyes and sense my body dissolve until I am simply pure light. I have danced so much today to the rhythms of life and death.

Tuesday 5 March 2002

Iris

Iris is full of smiles, yet she is struggling. Her mother has gone into hospital in London. The outcome is uncertain.

> Iris says: 'I'm so tired with travelling...getting caught up in the London rush hour traffic...'

> She cries: 'Does Mum recognise me? Dad is saying she calls for me...she is alert one moment and then sleepy the next.'

I ask Iris: 'What would I say to you?'

Iris is unsure: 'About being in the moment...?'

Iris is full of fear, anticipating the worst, clinging to some hope. She laughs and says: 'I know but...'

I finish her words: 'it's your mother and you accept responsibility to care for her, like daughters everywhere.'

Iris relaxes in these words.

The soles of Iris's feet are yellow and her toes are sore. She is deeply relaxed but doesn't dream; she questions if she was actually asleep? Yet afterwards she is energised, alert, not at all drowsy. She is very thirsty. I warn her she may be a little 'toxic' tomorrow so drink plenty of water.

Wednesday 6 March 2002

Grey clouds spill across the sky. The mornings are lighter. At the hospice I look at the whiteboard and do not recognise any names. Derek, Doris, Indira and Connor have all died. Patterns repeat themselves. Such is the nature of our relationships; a sense of inevitability that numbs any sense of loss, where the news of someone's death is merely of interest. Am I so cold? Should I feel more?

Beth, the night staff nurse, reads a poem for David and Simon, dedicated to their love.

A Tribute to the Patron Saint of Love

> Where there is love the heart is light
> Where there is love the day is bright
> Where there is love there is a song
> To help when things are going wrong,
> Where there is love there is a smile
> To make all things seem more worthwhile,
> Where there is love there's a quiet peace.
> A tranquil place where turmoils cease –
> Love changes darkness into light
> And makes the heart take 'wingless flight' –
> Oh blest are they that walk in love.
> They also walk with God above –
> For God is love and through love alone
> Man finds the joy that the saints have known.

(Rice 1985, p.56)

Beth's voice fills the room with love as we sit together waiting for the night report. Even though I have not met David and Simon before I feel prepared for when I do. I feel as if my heart has been tuned. I do not know Beth very well and this act of love warms my heart towards her.

David and Simon have been together for 40 years. Beth says how devastated Simon is. He won't leave David's side…has not slept. I remember some words I had written before… 'that the fabric of his life has been torn apart'. The staff ache for them. How can we move easily amid such grief? David 'went off' yesterday. He is just conscious and responsive. He has midazolam in his driver. And yet again I ask myself why?

I move into the room and introduce myself. Simon is small, Japanese, his grief worn across his being. Natasha, a close friend, is also there. Simon is not alone. Strangely (on reflection) I did not say hello to David. Had I assumed he was already socially dead?

Later, when I offer to burn some oil, I rectify this mistake and speak with David. His rosary beads hang loosely from his outstretched hand. He is responsive. Simon is so pleased that David remains with him on a conscious plane. At moments like this I wish I had known him before his condition had deteriorated.

I ask Natasha what smells David might like. She chooses geranium. Later, when the burner is dry, she chooses neroli that I mix with frankincense 'for the soul'. The oils contribute towards creating an atmosphere of stillness and sacredness in which to dwell, perhaps to find some peace or release some tears, to find meaning, perhaps even beauty, and to honour the tragedy of love unfolding that we witness.

David's death needs to be as special as possible to comfort Simon in the dark shadow of grief.

David is not my patient. I drift about like a loving angel trying hard not to be intrusive. I tell Natasha I am available if she or Simon would like some time out for a massage. Paying attention to such small things feels so important at such sensitive moments. It communicates so much about the way we care. I know how important it is as Natasha thanks me for my thoughtfulness.

Later, Sister Kathleen sits with them. She visits from the Roman Catholic convent. I love her company because she has such a large heart. God radiates within her. She tells me about the *Poustinia* at the convent. *Poustinia* is a Russian word meaning desert – a quiet lonely place that people wish to enter to find the God that dwells within. She invites me to visit.

Alice

In her room, the window is open. A strong breeze makes the room feel chilly but not uncomfortably so. Alice says she craves fresh air. She is recovering from a chest infection. I sit on her bed and ask her how she came to be here. She apologises for not having her teeth in. Her hair is long and grey. She spits out some sputum into a tissue. In her rasping and halting voice she tells me that in August last year she had a persistent sore throat. When she eventually went to her doctor he referred her to the ear, nose and throat (ENT) surgeons. The cancer was too deep, too big to remove surgically. So she had radiotherapy and a tracheostomy to let her breathe more easily and speak. She refused chemotherapy. I ask, 'Would you have more radiotherapy if the cancer came back?' She says the cancer is still there. She can feel it like a hard lump. No – she wouldn't have any more radiotherapy.

I ask: 'And the consequences?'

'I don't think about that.'

In her notes it was suggested she was in denial. I don't think so – she has simply pushed the shadow away.

She lives at home with her son. 'My son has been my whole life since my husband died. He suffers from schizophrenia. He chains smokes and is an alcoholic.' Alice is in a dilemma – 'I want to stay at home…my son wants me to stay. Yet I must have fresh air. I choke at home in the cigarette and cigar smoke. I've tried to get him to smoke only in the front room. He accepts this but he often gets up at night between 2.00 and 5.00 when he cannot sleep and then he smokes in the back room. In the morning the air in the room is already thick with fumes. I like this room because I can look over the garden … I think I would be bored in a residential or nursing home.'

But it is more than that. She anticipates losing control. She says she is a lonely type. She does not go into other peoples' homes. She talks of her neighbours who offer help, but she has never been in their house. 'What to do?'

Such thinking burdens her and yet it is a crossroads in her life at 78 years of age with an uncertain but inevitable future. She must have the fresh air…it is life itself.

At last she completes her PEG feeding. It commenced late last evening because she had visitors. She turns it off and disconnects the tube. She then leaps out of bed. She cleans her teeth and says, 'I am still just a girl.' And indeed she is. Determined and independent yet introvert. I bring her the paper and we flip through it together as she gives me a cynical commentary on the woes of the world. An hour has passed. This time being with another is sacred. It unfolds like a silvery stream finding its own level. On one level it is superficial talk and yet on another level it is a search for meaning and connection for both of us.

I am beginning to understand the art of dwelling with people who face death. Such art is non-intrusive and responsive to what is unfolding; it is intimate and tinged with the sense of the sacred. It is being mindful of being available, without an agenda beyond the mantra of easing suffering. It is creating a peaceful and loving clearing within the chaos of dying.

Wednesday 13 March 2002

Iris

Iris says she has been having stomach pains because of worry for her mother. Her mother is still in the London hospital; although not good she is holding her own. Iris is feeling guilty because she can only manage to visit once weekly. Her dad sharpens this guilt by saying, 'Your mother asks for you.' Iris despairingly – 'What can I do?'

I ask if her mother is being transferred back locally? Iris says yes...so that will help. Iris is contemplating anti-depressants to try and lift this sense of doom that has descended about her. I make no comment about the anti-depressants. If she feels she needs them I would support her decision. I know she does not want to take them because it is an admission she cannot cope. The depression is emerging from deep within her, pushing itself against her thin veneer of cheerful coping. I imagine this 'depression' pushing up from within her, dark, cold and menacing. She feels it creeping up and she fears her veneer will crack and that her mask will disintegrate. Then who would support her family? She would fail and reinforce the guilt she already feels.

I suggest she could try the Bach flower remedies again? Iris pulls her old 'stock bottle' out of her bag – dated November 2000.

She says. 'It looks cloudy.'

I laugh: 'I'm not surprised!'

We laugh. She said she hadn't quite believed they could do the job...flowers? She hadn't expressed this doubt before. 'Maybe I could try again?'

I say: 'We could make up another bottle.'

She laughs: 'Will it help me lose weight?'

Through the gloom Iris is concerned, as always, with her body image. Hanging onto her identity and self-esteem. Tears of laughter mix with and lighten the tears of dark gloom.

Iris's feet look much better. The yellow tinge is less marked. As usual I start with my hands flat on her feet and concentrate on my breathing until I sense the boundaries between us melt as we become one within this moment. Concentrating on my breathing, breathing in light and breathing out love through the palms of my hand, through Iris's body. And as I do, I guide Iris to breathe in light until it floods her whole body, and to let go of her fears with each out breath. I guide her to relax every part of her body until she floats like a fluffy cloud in a clear blue sky. She drifts into a sleep or onto another plane of consciousness. My thumbs trip across the soles of her feet, across canyons of her mind, across the desert of her soul. I gaze across her body, so relaxed, her eyes closed, so trusting as she surrenders to my touch. This brave woman I have worked with for the past 18 months. Together we have dwelt in the shadow of her death. It hasn't been a romantic adventure but a testament to a precious and yet precarious grasp on life. If I have seemed to glorify our relationship it is simply a reflection of the wonder that lies side by side with the terror. The words of Ben Okri become realised. When we finish she is surprised – 'I didn't expect to sleep as my head was so full of stuff. I don't know what I would do without this...it keeps me going.'

At home I make up Iris's Bach flower remedy:

- Agrimony to help her sustain the cheerful mask to the world that she feels she must wear. The stoic selfless mother, who feels guilty if she puts her needs first. Yet beneath the mask she suffers. My work with her is to help ease her suffering.

- Olive to help her renew her energy depleted in the constant effort to keep the cheerful face, to be the good mother, to fight each day to keep the cancer at bay. She is so tired; mentally, emotionally and physically.

- White chestnut for the worrying thoughts that churn and plague her in the stillness of the night and interfere with her sleep.

- Sweet chestnut for the despair she works hard to keep at bay but lurks like a deep dark blanket threatening to obliterate the light.

- Oak to help her sustain her strength in her effort to struggle on as her inner strength wanes against the unremitting storm.

- Star of Bethlehem to help her combat the never-ending sense of shock that she is dying of cancer and the persistent sense of grief that so often threatens to overwhelm her, reflected in the poignant remarks of her children and the suffering of her husband. And, if that was not enough, anticipating the imminent death of her mother.

The Bach flower remedy descriptions reveal the magnitude and complexity of Iris's suffering. Yet, as always, her smile remains broad as she rests on the life raft.

Saturday 23 March 2002

In the notes to his CD 'Pray', Douglas Spotted Eagle states the purpose of his music is to take the listeners to a place of vision and clarity, which he believes lives within us all, and where life's rhythm synchronises with a higher consciousness. And it seems that the purpose of this text is to take you there, where, deep within you may realise spiritual freedom through your caring, so you and your patients can dwell in a higher consciousness.

Wednesday 27 March 2002

Iris

Iris has been to see the specialist orthopaedic surgeon in London. He found four new hot spots. The most significant is in her left femur, which requires radiotherapy. He also found hot spots in her ribs and humorous. As for her right shoulder, the surgeon said he would need to remove the shoulder joint and leave the bones as they were just held together with the tendons and ligaments. Her arm would be useless. Iris also has new lumps in her neck which also require radiotherapy. The merry-go-round spins. Yet Iris is caught on it. She cannot get off as she clings on to life. Yet she rejects the radical surgery. Her mother is holding her own, although is immobile. They are planning to discharge her home. Iris exclaims – 'How will she manage?' She has asked for her mother to be discharged to the hospice as we know her well and can help her (literally) get on her feet again.

Iris relaxes deeply with the reflexology. I mix a drop each of grapefruit, vetiver and frankincense with sweet almond carrier oil to use instead of my reflexology base cream. The earthy scent of vetiver lingers in the air. It is called the 'oil of tranquillity'. 'Vetiver is deeply relaxing, so valuable in massage and baths for anybody experiencing stress, anxiety, insomnia and depression' (Davis 1999, p.308). 'Gently, and without disturbing the creative forces, vetiver steadies and calms any inner disquiet – and in that calmness may come the answers we seek' (Worwood 1999, p.254). Vetiver is exactly what Iris requires to help her find some stillness among the carnage of her life. Grapefruit and frankincense enhance the mood. I play the CD 'Walk in harmony' by Brian Carter. Afterwards, she says the music was beautiful.

Easter holidays, so it is difficult for Iris to make an appointment for the next two weeks. She sighs. Her disappointment is tangible. The interminable struggle continues. It feels we go round and round, like the Buddhist image of samsara that characterises conditioned existence – the effort to avoid pain and seek pleasure. Within this image my effort is to guide Iris to find some meaning within her in contrast to clutching at hope to things outside her. Only then might she let go enough to find some stillness and control. Because she loves so much, she needs love in return to nurture her along her journey. Not pity but a deep compassion. So I wrap her in my compassion that nurtures us and gives rhythm to our caring dance.

> When love awakens in your life, in the night of your heart, it is like the dawn breaking within you. When before there was anonymity, now there is intimacy; where before there was fear, now there is courage; where before in your life there was awkwardness, now there is a rhythm of grace and gracefulness; where before you were jagged, now you are elegant and in rhythm with yourself. When love awakens in your life, it is like a rebirth, a new beginning. (O'Donohue 1997, p.26)

Each encounter is a new dawn, a new beginning. We turn away from the dark night ahead and rest within the stillness of now.

Monday 8 April 2002

I am working an early shift. As I arrive Josie dies so staff are pulled away. John gives me a report on the patients. As he talks about Humphrey, he flips through the patient's notes. With some surprise he exclaims – 'Humphrey is a Methodist… I hadn't realised that.' I ask him whether he thinks religion plays a significant part in the hospice's care. John considers this and says it probably doesn't. He can tell that some nurses are more 'religious' than others but it's not pushed. He isn't religious himself – 'more of the humanist school' – and doesn't think that religion should be emphasised. John is very caring, reflecting his humanist beliefs, yet his comments reflect the predominantly secular world we live in. Will knowing that Humphrey is a Methodist make any difference to the way people see and respond to him? Is 'Methodist' just a label with no real meaning except perhaps to another 'serious' Methodist or someone who is committed to their own faith? Humphrey has advanced cancer and will die soon. Does being a Methodist have any meaning for him and the way he now wants to live and die? We don't know because we have not addressed the issue. Perhaps the minister will pop in and say hello and Humphrey's religious or spiritual needs will be met, or at least we may believe so. Are we, as people who care for the dying, less caring because of this lack of attention? Walter (1994) notes:

> Flourishing religions today come in two varieties. Fundamentalism, which provides an external authority by which believers may live…[and secondly] there is the replacement of religion by *spirituality*. If religion puts you in touch with a God out there and with meaning and mores external to the self, spirituality puts you in touch with your inner self and with the God inside. (p.28)

> Spirituality can be viewed as the soul or spirit, the essence of persons, which transcend immediate awareness of self. It gives life purpose, provides a motivating force, and relates to unconditional love without knowing the source. It leads people to strive towards living life according to values … through the spiritual dimension persons attempt to make meaning through a sense of relatedness that transcends the self in such a way that empowers, not devalues, the individual. (Cohen, Headley and Sherwood 2000)

These authors continue by citing Reed (1992):

> This relatedness may be experienced intrapersonally (as connectedness with oneself), interpersonally (in the context of others and the natural environment), and transpersonally (referring to a sense of relatedness to the unseen, God, or power greater than the self). There is an expansion of boundaries inward, outward, upward. (p.350)

For most patients I meet at the hospice, neither religion or spirituality *appears* to be significant. I say appears because it does not ripple on the surface of people's being. Perhaps, as Engebretson (1996) suggests, patients expect spiritual aspects of care to be ignored within the dominant biomedical culture.

Walter (1994) notes:

> Physical pain and symptoms are generally what brings a patient to the attention of a palliative care team in the first place, so if these are dealt with, all parties are happy. Emotional and spiritual care is an added extra, which may easily be forgotten. (p.92)

However, I shall assume that the spiritual is significant for people who face the inevitability of their own death or the death of loved ones, even though it may not be directly expressed. Indeed it may be difficult to express and need coaxing. And if coaxed then nurses must be able to respond skilfully. If spiritual need is surfaced then the nurse may see her role is to refer the patient or relative to a chaplain rather then engage herself on a spiritual level. Those nurses with definite religious or spiritual views are more likely to engage with patients on a religious or spiritual level. Yet, is responding to the spiritual needs of patients outside the remit of nursing and the domain of the chaplain? Is the chaplain part of the caring team? Perhaps, but peripheral. At the hospice, the clergy do visit although their religious cloak is evident except perhaps for one volunteer nun.

Kuuppelomäki (2001, p.608) in her survey of spiritual attitudes of nurses working in health centres in Finland concluded that:

> Almost half of the nurses felt poorly equipped in terms of both knowledge and skills to provide spiritual support to terminally ill patients. Over one-third were unwilling to provide such support

although Kuuppelomäki was unable to determine within the confines of the study reasons for this. She notes that: 'Half of the nurses felt that terminally ill frequently express spiritual needs but the other half said that patients express these needs rarely' (p.668).

The study was able to differentiate that nurses who had attended seminars on terminal care provided more spiritual support than those who had not. Over half the nurses said they talked with patients about the meaning of life. The most common forms of spiritual support were: to take the patient to spiritual events arranged on the ward; to organise holy communion; to participate in discussions about the meaning of life; and to invite the chaplain to see the patient. However, Finland has a strong Christian society in contrast with the UK, where formal religion has been in a constant decline. Do patients and families actually want spiritual attention? Walter (1994) quotes one hospice chaplain:

> A nurse walks into a four-bedded room to attend a patient and the other three want her too. I walk into a room to see a patient and the other three hide under the covers. (p.98)

Perhaps the chaplain by his or her presence evokes the relationship between spirituality with religion, a relationship that is redundant. Perhaps the nurse is best placed to respond to spiritual need in its 'meaning of life' secular guise, as part of the 'whole relationship' rather than fragmenting 'whole care'?

Josie

I do not know Josie. She has been constantly restless all night, despite the diazepam and midazolam the night staff have given her. Only a few minutes before she died had she been able to settle. Perhaps she had realised the game was up? Evidently, she had been restless for the few days she had been at the hospice. The care assistant went into her room to find her dead. Caught in the moment Josie died alone. Do drugs take the edge off restlessness or are they just a blanket to stifle the anguished cry? Was her restlessness the expression of her existential crisis as she approached death? Could we not have journeyed with her in her path of restlessness? Do we know how? Questions with no certain answers bombard and haunt.

I walk down the corridor. Josie's door is open. She lies there, very petite with high cheek bones. Her large beautiful eyes are wide open. Her lips are slightly parted. Some spit has congealed on her teeth. I imagine her as a young girl, so free and beautiful. I am told she was a free spirit, a hippie child. I whisper, 'I have never met you Josie, yet I am so connected in you.'

I sit with Josie for a while holding her cold limp hand and practise the essential Phowa. I feel she should not be alone even after she has died. Am I compensating for her last breath being alone? Am I acting out some collective responsibility that she should not have been alone at that moment when her breathing ceased? Maybe I am, but it is deeper than that…much deeper. I haven't realised before how much I have absorbed a responsibility to help people reach the light. Perhaps it is the Bodhisattva ideal soaking into my very spirit. Whatever, it moves me greatly.

> I shall never forget the stillness in your blue eyes
> Reflected in the tear I shed upon your bed
> And felt within the ache that burns deep within my chest
> And radiates within the light I shine
> To guide you to embrace the light divine

Later, I reflect on Josie's death with Lindsey, one of the care assistants. In particular we reflect on the failed effort to sedate her in the belief that she was agitated. Was her restlessness a sign of suffering or was it her way of dealing with her knowing that she was dying? Lindsey tells me about an Indian woman, who was close to death when admitted. She was 43. She spoke English as did her husband although they spoke different native languages. They had a son who was about 28. Her son said she didn't want anything to cloud her consciousness even if she experienced some pain. And what did Brenda do? She immediately gave her a sub-cut dose of midazolam and put up a syringe driver with double dosage! The patient's talk was viewed as 'confusion' and her wanting to get out of bed was viewed as agitation. Lindsey felt the patient simply wanted to rest in a chair rather than in bed. The relatives were overwhelmed. Being *just* a care assistant she felt couldn't interfere but it bothered her. The patient died quite quickly.

Who sets the parameters of a good death? From Lindsey's perspective the drug response reflected an insensitive and hasty response to a symptom rather than seeing and responding to the whole person. Perhaps a better response would have been to stay with this woman and her family and help them all live through death in a more conscious way as they desired.

Some practitioners reach for the midazolam quicker than others. Our response should not be a lottery but a careful decision. Lindsey should also be able to voice her concerns without fear rather than whisper in corridors. She is clearly distressed and angry remembering this situation. It weighs heavily as she carries it around with her in her proverbial emotional rucksack. It gnaws and weakens her spirit.

Iris

Iris is full of fear waiting for radiotherapy planning to zap her 'hot spots', specially her shoulder that gives her considerable pain. She's anxious about her backache and wonders whether she should have radiotherapy to her spine? I shrug and say I am unable to give an opinion and suggest she talk to her oncologist about this.

'Yes…' Her words trail off. I sense she is tired with this effort. It is ceaseless, remorseless, a struggle against what seems mounting odds. I mention her oak is straining. In response she exclaims, 'I'm taking the Bach flowers!'

'Do they make a difference?' I inquire slightly mockingly.

'I don't know… I think they do.' Iris's lack of confidence in the Bach flower remedies is palpable. I don't push it.

After the reflexology Iris is so relaxed. As she so often says, she has been transported beyond her suffering to dwell in a soft light that has comforted her. And, as always, I am humbled.

Later Sarah, the bereavement support nurse, stops me. She had just met Iris in the entrance who told her how valuable her reflexology is for her.

More humbling, but I feel proud that my work is known and valued. I am reminded of and challenged by the Buddhist path of perfect action:

> Unskilful actions are defined as those which are rooted in craving or selfish desire; in hatred or aversion; and in mental confusion. Skilful actions are those which are free from craving, free from hatred, free from mental confusion; positively speaking they are motivated instead by generosity, or the impulse to share and to give, by love and compassion, and by understanding. This very simple distinction at once places the whole question of morality in a very different light. The moral life becomes a question of acting from what is best within us; acting from our deepest understanding and insight, our widest and most comprehensive love and compassion. (Sangharakshita 1990, p.83)

The tension between arrogance and humility is always a challenge. I sense a part of me craves recognition like a hungry ghost that can't get enough to fill itself. Working at the hospice and the words of the Dharma are like an antidote for this craving, enabling me to become more secure in 'who I am', more accepting of my weaknesses and my strengths. Humility can be a false pride, a self-deprecating stance, so I am ever-mindful of any descent into self-gratification.

Sarah's words remind me of the need to value others for what they do. It is a form of giving, or *dana*, that flows from compassion, equanimity and sense of community; words that leave me feeling warm to her, thankful for her feedback, and warm towards myself, thankful I have helped Iris.

Tuesday 16 April 2002

Lena informs me that Iris is reluctant to phone me. Iris does not want to be a burden; not wanting to burden me with any demand, or hint of expectation. Iris does not like the cancer invading her home and so she does not want to invade my home despite my 'open invitation'. Iris, like many people, sets boundaries which she is reluctant to transgress.

So I must be active and assault her boundaries. I phone her but she is not at home so I leave a message on her answer phone. I understand why she feels unable to phone me even though I thought we had resolved this difficulty.

Success! She phones several days later and we arrange an appointment.

Tuesday 30 April 2002

A candle burns at the nurses' station for Sylvia who died yesterday. She had been at the general hospital for treatment for her heart failure since my last shift on 8 April. Last Friday the hospital accepted the futility of further curative effort and sent her back to the hospice to die. The small candles are always red. They flicker as if the spirit of the dead person dances. When I share a story of a patient who has died with students or at a conference, I light a candle to honour that person and to symbolise the campfire where we gather to share and listen to our stories. It is a sacred ritual that sometimes makes people feel uncomfortable because they do not embrace the sacred within their own lives.

Mary

I knock and enter Mary's room and greet her. She is 63 years old. Grey-haired but young-looking. I immediately pick up her discomfort with lower back pain that compromises her breathing. She affirms. I pull back the curtains to reveal the grey sky. Sensing her need I ask her if she would like the window opened for some fresh air? 'Please.' The cold draught sweeps across her brow and she thanks me. I rearrange her pillows to ensure she feels more comfortable. She has been having heat packs during the night but declines another one just now.

Mary is a diabetic and requires insulin prior to breakfast. Her nausea is proving difficult to control so we are giving her nozinan half an hour before eating – which she says helps. I watch her inject her insulin amid the telltale bruises of past injections across her abdomen.

On the window ledge stand two vases of flowers. I say how pretty they are. She looks at me and smiles. 'The ones on the left are mine. I don't know where the other ones came from.'

The flowers that Mary identified as her own are orange-yellow chrysanthemums – such is the intensity of their colour that they seem to glow in the grey morning light, cascading colour around the room.

The other vase contains delphiniums – rich blue yet without odour.

I ask if the flowers are from her garden. They are, although she's quick to assert that her husband is the gardener. She smiles – 'I just enjoy the fruits of his labour.'

John brings her breakfast tray. There are no flowers on the tray. I don't say anything to him but go to the kitchen and fetch her a small vase of flowers for her breakfast tray with a flourish as it is Mary's birthday. Putting flowers on the tray is another hospice ritual – even for a cup of tea. John is new, and as with so many 'small touches', these caring rituals are slipping. I sense the loss of ritual is linked to the loss of the spiritual tradition of this hospice. Volunteer women make up the small vases of flowers cut from the gardens. We always make a point of putting flowers into someone's room. It is a caring gesture that acknowledges the way flowers, as nature, touch the spirit.

This situation brings to mind Rosie, a student on the 'Care of the dying' course, who shared her thoughts on the insidious erosion of her hospice's 'spiritual tradition'. The hospice was once called the Hospice of Our Lady of St Mary – but now it is called after the village in which it is situated. The student group had speculated why should that be? Is it a reflection of the secular or is it more than that, a positive discrimination against religious influence? Perhaps it is a reflection of a multicultural society – so the hospice must not be seen to be overtly Christian? Rosie noted the loss of tradition in other ways; for example, that she didn't attend funerals as often as she had, a trend she also noted with her colleagues. Now I have never attended a funeral for a hospice patient, but then I have never been invited. I do not hear funeral talk at the hospice – is this again a reflection of loss of spirit? I must investigate.[7]

While Mary eats her breakfast and takes the remainder of her medication, I read her notes. She had a mastectomy last year for breast cancer. Liver and bone metastases were then diagnosed in December. She has a 'massive liver' that is squashing her abdomen and which makes her nausea difficult to manage. Curative options have been ruled out and we are on the long trajectory towards death. She feels its relentless pull. I am told she is anxious. Yet in my mind she bears her tragedy with equanimity. Perhaps she masks the suffering.

I pop back into her room and plan her morning care. One of the care assistants will assist her to wash after Mary has a rest while I go to day care to give Iris a reflexology treatment.

Iris

I have arranged to fit Iris into the morning's work pattern. She is sitting in day care waiting for me with Lena and Felicity, the care assistant. Iris immediately shows me her swollen abdomen. Slightly shocked but not

7   I discovered that funerals are put into a book for staff to note.

wanting to overdramatise I say, 'Where did that come from?' She laughs and pulls out her heat pack – 'Fooled you!' She splits her sides with laughter – 'Oh I needed that…'

Iris's current cycle of radiotherapy to her neck has finished. She complains of pain to her hips – 'I must tell him [her oncologist] when I next see him – perhaps I need some more radiotherapy.' She asks if I can reheat her pack to ease her hip pain. Two minutes to 'cook' in the microwave.

After the treatment, Iris says, 'I hope I didn't snore?' I say only a little. 'Oh, you!' She says the treatment was deeply relaxing. Within the turmoil of her life the reflexology is the only space when she can let go of her fears…and the fears loom large just now. I reiterate she can call me at any time, anxious to counter her reluctance to call me, not wanting to invade my personal life.

Tom

Back on the inpatient unit I visit Tom. He has a rare degenerative illness of his nervous system that he has lived with for 11 years. I am told that the longest known survivor lived for 11 years. Tom knows this. His illness has increasingly become a destructive force within his family. His marriage is crumbling; his wife becomes more frustrated with him but also guilty that she feels that way. It is easy to be judgemental and criticise her for her attitude but I can imagine the strain on both a physical and emotional level. I ask him how things are at home and his angst spills out – so much in fact I wish I hadn't asked! Yet he needs to offload. He is enthusiastic about a modified reflexology in the half hour we have before he is being taken for a swim in the new pool.

His left foot is rigid in comparison with his right foot – yet the massage loosens and relaxes him. He is happy with the massage. He used to have regular reflexology as a day care patient but as his condition deteriorated he was no longer able to attend day care because he could not sit in a chair.

Feedback from others later was that Tom felt the massage had eased the pain in his legs. Later I explore with Penny, one of the senior nurses, the loss of ritual – that Dolores did not read a poem at the morning hand-over and no flowers were placed upon Mary's breakfast tray. Penny feels that these two rituals are quintessential symbols of caring at the hospice. She had visited another hospice where such rituals did not take place and she was struck by just how significant they were – sending out messages about caring. It is the little touches that mark the difference and say so much.

I also challenge Martha, another senior nurse, are staff prepared well enough to use their 'spiritual self'? Or is the spiritual just a lottery?

These two women are gatekeepers to quality at the hospice; I confront them with their responsibilities and, in doing so, ease my own concern. We cannot bleat like lost lambs; we must take action and shepherd the flock if it is astray, if our values have any meaning.

Sunday 5 May 2002

As I pull back the blind that covers the small window overlooking our courtyard garden at home, the early morning sun floods me in its glory. I stand with my eyes closed and feel my body shiver with the penetrating warmth. Chakra colours (see p.232) flicker through the glass prism that hangs in the window. Such radiant colours blister my soul.

I move into my study that is also my shrine room. As I meditate, I am flooded several times with light and warmth. I open my eyes to see if this sensation is a reflection of the sun moving in and out of cloud, but no, the sensations are within me. A sense of bliss engulfs me. However, meditation is not always like this. Often it is a struggle as I wrestle with distracting thoughts or a sense of urgency that other things need doing. The discipline is being patient with self, as it is within clinical practice, that issues of the spirit cannot be rushed or seen merely as some task to accomplish within the mindset of a functional day.

I compose a new poem in my series 'In the stillness of the desert'[8] as a reflection of this moment and decide to include it in my journal as a reflection of my spiritual emergence.

In the stillness of the desert/6

> Between this breath and the next
> I feel the warm wind
> Against my neck
> My eyes are closed
> And I feel your presence near
> Warm wind
> Like soft words

[8]   'In the stillness of the desert' is a series of poems inspired by the idea of *Poustinia* and my relationship with the divine and 'soul' friends.

Whisper love
And I can only smile
Do you feel my smile across the distance
As if the first rays of the morning sun
Penetrate the cold dawn?

The desert is the stillness; the silence of solitude; an embrace with the divine. I live on the edge of the desert, never having the courage to dwell within the desert itself. I suppose I am like many people who feel an ache within and edge closer but are entangled in the trappings of everyday life. The desert becomes an image to yearn, and yet I am conscious of not grasping. In my meditation I sit within the desert and give way to the solitude and those moments of light and warmth that envelop me. It is the same with my spiritual practice – I shift imperceptibly into the desert, becoming less afraid of losing my way.

Saturday 11 May 2002

6.40. The sky is a colour wash of uniform grey. A soft breeze flicks the edges of the trees. As I near the hospice, the grey breaks up, revealing patches of blue as if the thoughts that cloud the mind disperse.

Emmy gives us the night report. Clifford has been very restless. The night staff has given him two doses of midazolam to sedate him and now finally he is exhausted. Once during the night he managed to get out of the bottom of the bed. The staff found him and offered him a urinal which he filled. After that he settled for a while until, as the first fingers of light pulled back the night's curtain, he too arose to dispel the quietness of the morning. I go into his room and say hello – no recognition – he twitches and moves his arm, as he picks the air with his outstretched fingers. However, he is not my patient[9] so I do not dwell with him. I'm helping Lucy care for Maud and Alice.

9   As may have been gathered earlier in the journal, I am allocated to care for particular patients each shift I work. The patients are allocated to one of two teams. Staff are allocated to one of the teams and generally care for their own 'team' patients.

Alice

Alice and I have met before (see p.185). She lives at home with her son who drinks and smokes heavily. He has schizophrenia. She has a tracheostomy as a consequence of the laryngectomy for cancer of her throat. She remembers me and immediately fires off her anxiety at me about her sputum being bloodstained. At the general hospital she was told not to worry…but she does. She sits and worries. Why do health staff who work with people suffering cancer offer such glib reassurance – 'don't worry'? Do they merely try and reassure themselves or get the patient off their back? Perhaps a bit of both, but either way it is unskilful because it does the opposite, it feeds rather than melts anxiety. A wave of irritation like a dark cloud passes through my mind.

I remember Alice's dilemma from her previous admission – whether to move into a nursing home. She was caught between her need for fresh air and supporting her son at home living within a cigarette smoke haze. Lucy had visited them at home; she reported that she could cut the smoke with a knife it was so thick. Yet Alice's son is her life; she has always protected him. Perhaps she feels guilty that she was somehow responsible for his illness. She cannot desert him now, at least until her death. Then he will be on his own.

I stand a few feet from her and contemplate her anxiety. It would be easy to pity her from where I stand. I try to reassure her by saying I will contact the doctor and ask him to speak with her. I sense that only the doctor can take Alice forward at this moment. I move closer and kneel by her chair holding her hand and accepting her anxiety. She is quiet and relaxes as I massage her hand.

Maud

Maud looks up from her bed and smiling says, 'A new face.' She is lying on her side to ease her lower back pain which she attributes to osteoarthritis. I ask if she would like a heat pad but she declines for the moment. I go round the bed to the window side she faces. She pulls herself up and easily engages in conversation.

Maud was admitted yesterday for symptom management. Nausea and vomiting have been the major problem for her but she is pleased to have managed a cup of tea this morning. She's thirsty and asks if she might have another cup of tea? Small gains seem so immensely significant. She is a diabetic, induced by steroids given to help reduce brain swelling. She says her diabetes is under control and will have just a quarter spoon of sugar with her tea to make it palatable.

While she eats her breakfast I read her notes. Maud is 68 years old. She had a right mastectomy ten years ago. Then in December 2000 she was diagnosed with bone metastases and now she has newly diagnosed brain metastases.

The remains of her breakfast lay across her tray. She is complete. I ask if she would like a bath this morning? She declines the jacuzzi and suggests that the small bath in the en-suite bathroom would be fine. I ask if she might like a foot and leg massage later? She has had a foot massage before and found it most beneficial. However, she is uncertain today, so I don't push it. It is her second day at the hospice and she is finding her feet. We sit and pursue our conversation, talking about our respective families. She hasn't had a good chatter for many days.

Shortly after I leave her Lucy informs me that Maud will have a jacuzzi! As Maud tells me later, this is typical of her. Lucy also says that Maud is happy for me to help her bath – that she has 'taken' to me.

The bath is luxurious for her partly because she is unable to manage to bath at home. She eagerly accepts the offer of a hair wash. It hasn't been washed for seven days. Her hair thinned after the chemotherapy and never really became thick again. However, she did not completely lose her hair. She is going to have radiotherapy for her brain cancer, which means shaving her head. But she's okay about that.

In the bath I cannot help but notice the neatness of her mastectomy scar. A thin pink line beside her remaining defiant breast. A thin pink line of mutilation to stem the cancer's grip. Yet the cancer concealed had already gone about its deadly business, spreading inexorably in its own time into distant places. The treatment effort caught in its slipstream.

Back in her room after the bath we pick up our conversation. 'When I was first diagnosed with cancer I went to pieces for a few days believing I was about to die. However, as the operation was planned for the following week I realised it wasn't true otherwise they would have operated sooner. I saw recovery as a series of steps to be made…focusing on the now rather than the uncertain future. I said to myself, "one step at a time", to set myself targets. It [death] could be two years away or I could get nine years which is what I've had. For the last two years the signs have been there. I was off work for seven months and could go back part time until I was 60 because of accumulated annual leave.'

I ask: 'What was your work?'

Maud: 'I was a civil servant working in employment benefits. They asked me what I wanted to do at 60 – to retire, to stay full time or go part time. I chose part time – three days a week – and then two-and-a-half years later I packed it in. I was a workaholic before the illness…but it made me re-evaluate my life. This time my feet have become really swollen. I couldn't feel my feet, even yesterday, but today the swelling has gone down dramatically. I can feel my feet again on the floor.'

I again mention the possibility of foot massage, picking up our earlier bathroom conversation about different oils. But just then her son arrives and our conversation is cut short. I had been moving our conversation towards exploring with Maud her thoughts about her death. On reflection it is fascinating to see the pattern of conversation emerge from social chat, through illness story, and now faced with the inevitable dying and death despite the radiotherapy. I leave them. Robert stays for the day and I can only pop my head around the door to say goodbye. Maud has told Robert all about me and our conversation.

There is nothing remarkable about my conversation with Maud. Such conversations are hopefully commonplace within hospices. My intention was to tune into her wavelength and flow with her along her life trajectory, being mindful, reading the signs correctly and responding appropriately in the effort to ease her suffering and help her grow through the illness experience.

If I ask myself what is significant about this process, it is about listening, empathising, enabling the expression of feelings, flowing at her pace, and helping her to feel she is understood. Maud has certainly told her story many times but she had a need to tell it again, releasing tension and working things out in her mind. Being listened to is to feel cared for and being understood is to feel in control at a scary time.

Wednesday 15 May 2002

Iris

Iris is very distressed because of her shoulder pain. In desperation she says, 'I will have to have the operation.' But she is uncertain about this. Lena has arranged for her to see Dr Brown, the hospice medical director, after her reflexology, to explore ways of managing her pain better. She has commenced on oxycodone elixir for breakthrough pain but she feels it isn't as effective as sevredol – 'I must go back to that.'

I suggest it's possible to increase her fentanyl patch but I suspect that the pain adjunct drugs will be more helpful. I listen and sympathise. Iris is tearful. I tenderly say, 'I have never seen you cry before.' She smiles. 'I know, I try so hard not to cry but they're always there under the surface. Today they just burst out... I'm sorry.' I say, 'No, no...the tears need to flow, you can only contain so much.'

Iris can no longer contain her tears, they spill over the lip of her container. I muse, why is it that someone like Iris should apologise? Is it a reflection of our culture whereby tears and distress should be contained, not for public display, as if a quality of being good is to be brave? I know Iris does not want to burden others and feels embarrassed to lose emotional control. She says her son has been upset. I ask, 'Because of you?' She thinks so...and as a consequence she becomes more upset and more determined to put on a brave face to spare her children.

It is an emotional moment and I ache deeply for her, unable to resist absorbing her suffering.

Tuesday 28 May 2002

Iris

Iris's hip is still painful, so I give her reflexology sitting in a reclining chair. I kneel on the floor uneasily shifting my position to manoeuvre her feet. She looks tired – 'My pain regime is making me drowsy.' She is now taking gabepentin for nerve pain, besides her diclofenac and oxycodone. As a result she finds her shoulder and hip pain has improved. She does not want to be drowsy because she has a busy life to lead. It seems there is no escaping some pain. She has been put off surgery by horrific tales of getting a flailing arm.

She says they might have to put a steel rod in her left femur to deal with the threat of pathological fracture. She also has a hot spot in her humerus. She is also concerned that her serum bilirubin has markedly increased (from 14 to 45) – she is fearful of what that means. 'Is the herseptin no longer working?' She has a liver scan booked for this Friday. She says, 'If it isn't, they have other options.' I say, 'You mean chemotherapy?' She says, 'Yes... *and* all the side effects they cause!'

In the chair she quickly falls asleep as I go through the mind and body relaxation exercises. I gaze across her body with deep compassion for this suffering woman. We are short of time so I must modify the reflexology. I tread carefully along her skeletal system, sensing the tumours and using visualisation to zap them with her hard-stretched body defences.

Zap zap –
enough now
tumour cells
leave this woman;
she has suffered enough
can you bear her children's cries?

I sense a lump in her liver by her gall bladder – I mention this to Iris afterwards and she says her healer felt she had a gall bladder blockage. Perhaps she has some inflammation causing her raised bilirubin? As a complementary therapist I do not wish to get involved in speculative talk about causation. As always I suggest she explores it with Dr Brown. Immediately I feel uncertain of revealing the swelling on her foot tucked under her diaphragm. Do I just add to her fears? However, her healer has mentioned it – he is focusing his healing on this 'spot'. We joke about the myth of being fair, fat and 40 and having cholecystitis – 'I might be 40 but I'm not fair or fat!' she laughs.

Iris feels relaxed and energised and is now 'fixed' to face the rest of the day. I am humbled and privileged to ease her suffering. What greater gift could I give? Half-term next week means she is unable to make an appointment until the following week.

Tuesday 4 June 2002

Robert, Iris's husband, phones the hospice asking for advice. He was told at the hospital that the cancer has spread to Iris's lungs and that she has only a few weeks to live. Iris was not told this news. He is distressed and in a dilemma of what to do? The burden is too great for him. There was also talk of experimental chemotherapy that he couldn't grasp. Dr Brown says he will visit them at home.

I feel a sense of shock that Iris's death is so close. I sense the dark clouds gather about her. Should she be told this news or should it be kept from her? I feel the hospital doctors had no right to tell Robert. It should have been the other way round. Iris should choose who to tell. It is an act of blatant avoidance, perhaps justified in terms that the news of cancer spread might harm her when she grasps for any scrap of hope. Would it be harmful to pull the mat from under her hope? Certainly, not telling totally disrespects her autonomy. She may have work to do with her children that is being denied. I wonder what Dr Brown will say.

So would the best decision be to tell Iris or not? Consider this question. In Figure 2 I use ethical mapping to challenge the practitioner to understand and balance the dynamics towards making the 'right' decision within the particular circumstance.

In using the ethical map, follow the ethical trail:

1. Consider each perspective in turn commencing with the nurse(s)'s own perspectives.

2. Consider which ethical principles apply in terms of the best (ethically correct) decision.

3. Consider what conflict exists between perspectives/values and how these might be resolved.

4. Consider who had the authority for making the decision/taking action?

5. Consider the power relationships/factors that determined the way the decision/action was actually taken.

Sally

Sally is 46 years old. Ten years ago she had a left radical mastectomy for breast cancer that left her with severe lymphodeama to her left arm. Now the cancer has spread to her bone and her brain. She tells me the story of her recent deterioration; losing mobility, feeling dizzy and a fungating tumour in the deep cleft in her sternum. As if by way of compensation she says she is used to her swollen arm. At her hospital appointment last week, she was told by a female doctor (in place of her usual oncologist) that there was 'nothing more we can do for you, Sally'. And that was that. Sally was left with a deep sense of shock and anger. She felt as if the stuffing had been pulled out of her. Hope squashed. And between the tears she utters, 'I know that I am dying.'

It is a poignant moment as she relives this moment, talking through the event and working out her residual anger. I listen and sympathise, yet in my mind I feel an anger at such carelessness that people who should know better lose sight of the human factor as if people like Sally are merely objects being processed.

Sally lives with her husband and two children aged 9 and 13, the same age as my children. I love these moments of identification. It draws me closer. Her children have been away camping; they returned yesterday and are

Figure 2 Ethical mapping (Johns 1999, 2000)

Patient's/family's perspective	Who had authority to make the decision/act within the situation?	The doctor's perspective
Robert – probably would prefer not to tell Iris because it would distress her and distress him. Prefer a parental response 'for her benefit'. Iris – probably would prefer to be told even though the news is so bleak. She has never been in denial and has always been positive. She would like to prepare her children.	The doctor is a powerful influence and has authority although it might have been preferable to seek a consensus opinion from the nursing staff.	Unknown – although being a palliative care specialist he should be honest.
If there is conflict of perspectives/values, how might these be resolved? There is a potential tension between an interpretation of malevolence and autonomy. It remains to be seen what takes place at Iris's home.	**The situation/dilemma** Should Iris be informed that cancer has spread to her lungs and that her prognosis is now grave?	**What ethical principles inform this situation?** **Beneficence** – would telling Iris lead to some good? **Malevolence** – would telling Iris do her harm? **Autonomy** – does Iris have the right to know? **Virtue** – do professionals have responsibility to be honest with Iris about her death?
The nurse(s)'s perspective As with the doctor I would imagine that nurses would support an honest response that respects Iris's autonomy. However, there is a maternal attitude to protect her. My own view is that Iris has the right to know and that not knowing potentially harms her preparation to organise her death.	**Consider the power relationships/factors that determined the way the decision/action was actually taken** How will Dr Brown respond within the situation? Nurses have been excluded.	**The organisation's perspective** Not known – but would support the professional's decision.

visiting her this afternoon yet she doesn't want them to see her like this...
'How will they manage?'

The question spins in the air, for there is no answer. She says she has a big problem with finances since she has been ill with losing sick pay.

'We have been living the last year off the credit cards... I'm seeing Hilary [the social worker] tomorrow... I hope she's going to help me sort out my life... I'm confident my husband will manage the children and finances.'

I interject: 'But it weighs on your mind?'

'Yes, its dragging me down... I want to die with the sense that everything is sorted...'

A silent pause as the word 'die' hovers between us.

Sally continues: 'I've been told about CHUMS[10] and feel confident that the children will be cared for.'

We talk about honesty with the children. She agrees that she will keep nothing from them but feels the need to protect them as she has always done. I have often felt the hardest part of palliative care is caring for mothers with young children. I say that, but it is also the most privileged part – the sheer intensity, poignancy, intimacy. I feel as if my heart will burst.

Sally shares her grief with the way the cancer has affected her body. 'I was once a fit and trim swimming instructor and gymnast who weighed 8½ stone...now I'm 11½ stone...' Again the words drift in the space between us...as she spills out another loss. She is taking dexamethasone 8mg, which has boosted her appetite but swollen her body. We note the side effects of drugs can be as distressing as the symptoms.

She says she fears going home. Picking up the cue I ask: 'Do you want to stay here?'

She does. She knows that if she goes home then she will try and look after the house as always.

She will feel guilty if she fails as she must inevitably do so. The house is small and it will prove difficult to move her bed downstairs as it fills the living room.

10   CHUMS is a local organisation to support bereaved children.

I confront her guilt: 'You have cared all your life and now you need to be cared for.'

She looks at me and says that's true. Her task now is to let go.

I say: 'It's hard to let go of your tears?'

'I've been crying for much of the weekend.'

As she says this tears leak from her eyes. I hold her hand; it is small and dry ...she says all her skin is dry. I say it feels astonishing that we can sit here and have this type of conversation contemplating her death. She responds well to my words – she says it is good to talk like this.

She says she has trouble holding her neck straight because of pain. I move my hand about her neck as I would with Therapeutic Touch. She does not object so I ask her to close her eyes. As I move my hands from the top of her head down her body I get her to visualise a blue cool waterfall cascading over her. 'Feel the cool blue water...how cooling and refreshing it is taking the heat out of your head and neck.'

She feels the heat of my hand, surprised. Afterwards she feels cooler, relaxed and sleepy. So I leave her to rest.

Later she is much more cheerful. She says she feels good, better than for some time. I offer a foot massage but she declines as she is so comfortable and settled and her family will be here soon.

Later I see the boys running around the hospice, trying to fix the PlayStation. Lindsey and I stay with them for a while, helping them to feel comfortable, encouraging them to play. I pop into Sally's room to say goodbye at the end of my shift and meet her husband. Martha had informed me that they were experiencing marital difficulties but he has stayed with her although he had been distant when Sally had stayed awhile back for a weekend.

Sally was told she was dying whereas Iris was not informed of her cancer spread. Is truth telling such a lottery? Sally had the news of her prognosis broken badly, leaving her angry and distressed but at least she can move on with her life knowing her death will be soon. I imagine Iris is Sally – and know that telling her is undoubtedly the best decision. Of course, every person is different but I know Iris well and intuitively know she needs to know.

Breaking bad news is a big issue in cancer care. Framing Sally's experience within Kaye's (1995) ten steps to breaking bad news, illuminates the poor way she was told:

1.   Prepare carefully.

2.   Inquire what she knows.

3.   Does she want more information?

4.   Give a warning shot to prepare her for what's coming.

5.   Allow her shock and denial response.

6.   Explain in more detail if she requests such information.

7.   Listen to her concerns.

8.   Encourage her to express and talk through (ventilate) her feelings.

9.   Summarise what's been said and plan a way forward.

10.   Offer one's availability.

Kaye's ten steps are essentially about technique. Reflecting on Sally's experience I realise that giving bad news is essentially about being a certain person, not doing a technique. I tease out a number of factors that are significant in giving someone bad news well:

- It needs to be given by someone with whom the patient has a trusting and loving relationship – someone who is able to support the person as a consequence.

- It needs to be done with honesty rather than indirectly, although not bluntly; perhaps a cue – 'the news is not good'.

- It needs to be given by someone who has a good attitude towards their own mortality – in other words someone who is not overly self-concerned.

- It needs to be given under circumstances where it is possible to dwell without being or feeling rushed.

- It needs to be given by someone who has a palliative care attitude – someone who can help the person receiving the bad news put quality of life and quality of death in perspective.

- It needs to be given by someone who is mindful of the impact of the news on the other and who can respond skilfully and flow easily with what unfolds.

Stephen

Further along the corridor I knock and after pausing for a moment, enter Stephen's room. We have not met before. He's buried beneath the bed covers so I decide not to intrude. I am informed that Stephen is a 49-year-old African-Caribbean man, who was transferred from the local general hospital with cancer of the stomach and liver metastases. The cancer is newly diagnosed. His notes display his anger at his GP for not taking his stomach complaints seriously. Since admission he has been withdrawn, cocooned in his bed, shocked by the way his life is being torn from him.

Shortly afterwards, I return to find him on the floor on his knees. I guess rightly that he was attempting to reach the toilet. He is in pain but accepts my offer to help him get there. Just lots of wind. The effort exhausts him so I fetch him a wheelchair. I help him back to bed and fetch his breakfast but he has no appetite. He clutches his stomach complaining of pains. Dr Brown is around and sees him. He prescribes ocreotide for his vomiting. Paracetamol settles his stomach pains, a reminder to think up the pain ladder.[11]

I mention to Kerry, a staff nurse, that I found Stephen on his knees. She surprises me by asking, in her fairly jokey way, if he was he praying? I'm not sure if this was a flippant remark, but he is a member of the Adventist church. A book lies on his bed locker; the title is *Preparing to Meet Jesus*; an ominous title under the circumstances.

He certainly is not well today…a real struggle for him with his pain. His legs and penis are greatly swollen because of the intestinal compression. He says he is drowsy, that he hasn't slept, but that he wants to be alert and is anxious if his tablets will make him drowsy. He is fighting to be awake. I sense his fear, that he is frightened of dying. I pick up his book *Preparing to Meet Jesus* and ask if he has a strong faith. He affirms but I can see that conversation of such nature is not possible, at least until his physical distress is adequately dealt with. Everything in perspective. We have to help him deal with his pain and vomiting, but I wonder if some of his pain is a deeper psychological pain, what Kearney (1997) describes as 'soul pain'. I feel clumsy looking after him, struggling to find his wavelength, but nevertheless, I hang in there.

---

11   The pain ladder [World Health Organisation] is a common sense approach to pain whereby the practitioner progresses up three rungs in responding to the patient's pain: no opioids, weak opioids, strong opioids (+ adjuncts as necessary).

Later I meet his sister, her two daughters and grandson who is just three months old but was two months premature. He stares at me and gives me a big smile. I stand on the threshold of this family. The family notice this and invite me to enter into their world. I make them coffee, chatting about things on a social level. In the background Stephen is restless and groaning – he projects himself into the foreground and the sister recoils – it is hard for them to sit here, listening to his suffering but not being able to communicate with him or ease his suffering. I acknowledge this. She says, 'I feel helpless … I don't know what to do.'

I can't say what she can or cannot do. I also have a sense of helplessness. However, we have broken the ice, we have acknowledged her struggle to stay with her brother. Acknowledging the struggle makes it easier to bear. I simply dwell in the silence between us and communicate my presence to her. My being there is a distraction for her to face up to Stephen's overt distress. She is silent because she does not know what to say. Yet she diverts her attention because she is suffering. I suggest she can give Stephen silent attention, just being here and communicating love.

Saunders (in her foreword to Kearney's book *Mortally Wounded*, 1997), says:

> Sometimes there will be no answers to give to those in apparently desperate situations, and we find ourselves with nothing to offer but silent attention … a feeling of helplessness may urge us to withdraw or escape into a zealous hyperactivity which can well exacerbate the patient's suffering. (p.13)

Using the Being available template (see Appendix 1, p.255), I reflect on the extent I knew Stephen and the way I managed myself within this relationship. The first point of reflection is to consider the extent I knew him. My recent conversations with Maud, Sally, Stephen and Stephen's sister all reinforce the concept of tuning into and flowing with their wavelength. This was easier with Maud, Sally and Stephen's sister than with Stephen. But why? I think it is because I was anxious to move Stephen into a more comfortable place for both of us to dwell because where he was, was tough to dwell. He was suffering mental, physical and possibly spiritual torment. Or was he? Do I make this assumption?

How would I feel if the roles were reversed? How would I want myself to respond to me? Kant's moral imperative (Seedhouse 1988) is always a good tester. First, I would want me to understand where I was coming from. I am whirling uncontrollably round a whirlpool of intense feelings – much more than anger although the doctor's words ring in my ears. I feel there is no escape from this death sentence despite my weak denial – 'this can't be happening to me'. There is little room for bargaining, at least at this moment. Any threads of hope dangle out of reach. I am only 49 years old and this news has been swift and devastating. I feel abandoned by everyone, especially by my God. Indeed, my religion torments me rather than comforts because I cannot accept death's menacing shadow. I feel submerged by waves of depression; my emotions are haywire. Kübler-Ross's stages of dying (1970) merge and swirl about me in dark patterns. I plead, 'Please stay with me on this roller coaster. I do not mean to reject you but it is hard for me to accept you just now. Am I dying?'

To imagine or empathise with Stephen I need to suspend how I imagine I would actually respond within this situation. Yet how would I respond? Would I be accepting or would I too have to run the gauntlet of denial, anger, bargaining and depression? Would my Buddhist belief of impermanence prepare me well enough to face death with equanimity or would I crumple in the utter oblivion of death's inevitability? How do you, the reader, imagine you would respond?

The second point of reflection is to consider how well I managed myself within the relationship. My gut reaction is that I did not manage very well. I was anxious about responding appropriately to Stephen and yet I couldn't fathom the appropriate response. Feeling clumsy is not a pleasant sensation.

Stephen was closed, defensive, angry, rejecting my desire to develop a relationship on my immediate terms. Indeed, I was a target to project his silent anger into. As it was I absorbed his struggle and struggled to find his wavelength. In stark contrast, Maud and Sally were open and welcoming, reciprocating my own stance. A salutary lesson, yet one that is central to wavelength theory and managing self within relationship (Johns 1996). To tune into and flow with the patient the practitioner must be aware of and manage their resistance to the patient; requiring (an almost) unconditional acceptance of whatever the patient is experiencing without *imposing* expectations of how the patient should respond. Of course, human suffering knows no limits and consequently this can be extremely difficult work. The compassion litmus test.

At home I reflect on Sally's words – 'I want to die...' – and the silent pause that followed. Was I momentarily nonplussed by her use of the word 'die'? Sally freely used the word 'die', reflecting her honesty and openness in facing her future. Only by being honest and open can she positively work towards preparing to die as well as she can. Her use of the word 'die' opened a clearing where we could dwell together. As Flaming (2000) notes: 'People will sometimes avoid applying an honest label to a situation if they think negative emotional outcomes will arise' (p.30). I meet so many people who avoid facing the truth because of the emotions that facing the truth surfaces. Flaming further suggests that health professionals often do not use such words as 'dying', reflecting an avoidance or silence. Flaming asserts, drawing from various writers, that the main reason for silence is a universal fear of death. If this was true for myself as a nurse, I could not possibly be available to Sally. And yet I do not know if I am afraid of death simply because I have not had to contemplate its imminent certainty. As a Buddhist, I endeavour to shed fear by melting attachment. My stories illustrate my non-attachment to Sally but attachment to Stephen because I was unable to resist my fear.

Contrasting my response to Sally and Stephen has given me insight into my authenticity, using the definition of authenticity as 'being at one with oneself, despite all suffering' (Janssens, Zylicz and Ten Have 1999). I can sense the vulnerability of my authenticity when faced by Stephen's suffering, which I unwittingly absorbed as my own. I assume that being authentic is central to palliative care because only if I am authentic can I be available to the patient. Yet, given the vulnerability of being human in the face of the other person's suffering and death, being *truly* authentic is not always easy. I emphasise 'truly' because the practitioner may deceive themselves.

Monday 10 June 2002

Returning home from a conference in Holland, my thoughts turn towards Iris. I phone her to confirm our appointment for Wednesday but it is engaged. Later, her phone is connected to the answer machine. Her mobile phone is turned off. I phone her landline again to leave a message when Robert answers. Iris comes to the phone. Her voice is tired. 'It's not so good, Chris. The liver shows signs of progression. They stopped the herspetin and are going to try me on a new chemotherapy drug...'

She falters but continues, 'I am feeling a bit nauseous even though they have put me on metoclopramide three times a day...do you think I should have more?'

As I usually do when confronted with such questions, I suggest she phones Dr Brown. She hesitates, so I say Dr Brown would want her to do that. She doesn't mention her lung involvement although she says we will talk more when we meet.

I reflect on her words, 'not so good'. She knows she is looking down the barrel. I shout 'fuck it' in response to the tension inside me. I want to treat her now so she can relax into my care, to help ease her suffering, but I can't.

Wednesday 12 June 2002

While waiting for Iris to arrive I listen to George, the music therapist, play beautiful music on the piano. His music opens a creating where people who live with the strife of terminal cancer can dwell, be still and reflective. He is so engaged in his playing...like watching poetry. Soul music to enable the spirit to break free and soar. He finishes to a ripple of applause. I play music that resonates with the soul with each treatment to create a similar sense of the sacred.

Jill Jarvis (2002), in her reflection on the environment, says:

> Music has been demonstrated to decrease pain, reduce anxiety and promote relaxation (McCaffrey 2002). Given the effectiveness of this non-invasive pleasure *it should be offered to hospital patients in all situations that are known to be stressful* (Evans 2002, p.9). Music improves the mood of patients and may reduce the need for sedatives (Evans 2002).

Music also helps the carer feel relaxed and more tuned into the caring task. Yet creating a therapeutic environment is almost certainly a neglected area of clinical practice. Florence Nightingale's emphasis on the nurse's responsibility to provide a healing environment has become diminished.

Are we, who purport to care, mindful enough of creating healing environments?

Iris

Iris arrives. Her feet and hands are covered in cuts where she has scratched herself. She dabs at the blood with a tissue. She says it's because of her liver disease causing toxins to build up in her body that make her itch.

We move into the treatment room. She tells me that the liver scan was not good news. It showed disease progression. *They* have given her months to live. However, she is adamant she will fight this...no sense of giving up. She shows me the yellow of her eyes. It's strange to see her jaundiced eyes, as if they are someone else's. We have contained the cancer these past 20 months and now it breaks free from its moorings. No longer contained, it is on an orgy of destruction. She has cancelled her planned holiday because of the threat of deterioration or 'who knows what might happen'. Such a euphemistic expression for death. She is going away next week to be spoilt in a posh hotel.

Certain phrases spring to mind – 'going out in style', 'enjoy life while you can'. She says, 'I bought some new clothes last week but feel it was a waste of money... I'm anxious about leaving money behind so the family can manage...'

Signs that mark the way the reality of her death has crept up on us. We cannot so easily turn our face from its starkness. Yet she does not say the 'die' word.

Iris reclines in the chair and I work from the floor. My right knee hurts for some reason. We go through our relaxation ritual and Iris is quickly asleep. Working with her today I am conscious that I am more tuned into her ...each thumb movement reflecting my concern. I feel her left shoulder bulging but the liver feels strangely subdued. The heels of her feet are dark red-purple, informing me that she is saturated with her emotions. I know she struggles to express how she feels, even with me...playing down her dark fear of death yet it is etched in her face and congested in her feet.

Sixty minutes later we have finished. I rub calamine aqueous cream over her tortured legs and even then she is scratching again. She thinks she may not be able to drive much longer, so is thinking of giving the car back and using taxis. More signs. She is seeing her healer twice a week now. She continues with her dairy-free diet. As the odds stack against her she makes even greater effort to balance the forces. I sense the way she grasps at things to combat her growing anxiety as if grasping at hope itself.

I mention Bach flowers, but Iris has never had any faith that they work for her. We make an appointment for next Wednesday, the day before she goes on holiday. I will cancel a meeting to accommodate her. Reordering of priorities to be available to her.

She has not mentioned her lungs. I assume she was not told simply because she has not mentioned it. Yet she cannot escape the visible signs of her deterioration. In particular the jaundiced eyes are a giveaway that her liver is in free-fall decline. The toxins are rampant.

At home in the evening I play the track 'The bluest eyes in Texas are haunting me tonight' by 'A Camp'. This is such a beautiful song. I muse over the tune and change the words – 'The yellow eyes of Iris are haunting me tonight'. I tell Susan, my partner, about being with Iris today. Susan feels I have absorbed some of Iris's suffering.

Thursday 13 June 2002

The sky is dark, threatening rain. Where is flaming June? Yet the morning is still. Stephen has died. His struggle continued without finding acceptance. He simply had no time or space to fathom the meaning of what was happening to him. The cancer had crept up on him and struck with venom, ruthlessly.

Sally

Sally is still at the hospice. It feels good to have this continuity with at least one patient, especially someone like Sally with whom I feel a strong connection. She greets me warmly. Physically she does not look any different from when I last saw her nine days ago. I ask her how she feels about going home today. She is more positive although anxious about getting to the toilet... 'I can't move myself at all now.'

I suggest a commode will have been planned and she is immediately reassured. 'Yes, that's right.' I say I have heard she is baking a cake with her son when she gets home. She says, 'I've always loved baking but keeping this promise is going to be tricky!'

She takes her handful of medications in one mouthful. I had imagined she would struggle with her tablets – how easy to underestimate someone. She tells me that when I gave her the Therapeutic Touch last time she had seen this gold band circle her shoulders and then spiral up through her head – 'I had such a feeling of contentment at that moment. I tried to tell my mother about it and she said, "yes, dear" as if only half-believing.'

It may not be easy for others to understand Sally's experience. It defies the rational mind. But I do not say this, but offer more TT. Sally purrs her approval. She closes her eyes as I work with her for about 20 minutes. Longer than before, more confident as I know she now appreciates how this brought her contentment within the unfolding chaos. She comments on the warmth of my hands as I hold her – with one hand over her brow chakra and the other hand over the alta mater chakra at the base of her skull to form a triangle with her root chakra (see p.232). This is a brilliant position to centre myself and visualise the healing energy radiating through my hands into her body. Holding her is much more than a physical event – I hold her whole being beyond the dimensions of the physical, and connecting her with the universal energy. Feel it flood through me and experience such stillness working. Words have limitations to describe such experience.

Now she is ready for breakfast...the dexamethasone has given her quite an appetite but today she just wants some toast and marmalade. In the blink of an eye someone else has brought her breakfast. Again, no flowers on the tray and her last morning with us at that! I fetch her some red carnations with gypsophelia. She thanks me for the flowers – 'They're lovely.' She tells me that the gypsophelia is called 'baby's breath'. There is something profound about 'baby's breath' as she nears the end of her life. We smile. I leave her buttering her toast, saying she will manage fine. I wonder how does she really feel about her forthcoming death? The fear I had met last time has melted away, or at least seemingly so. Has she found some contentment even within the prospect of going home? I wonder about the gold band – what it meant to her, whether it was an angel who has come to care for her on a spiritual plane. Her sensation of this force was real, powerful and so peaceful. And seeing Sally, she does seem to glow. Perhaps the deliberate placing of my hands on another is the most profound act I do during a day. Even as I write this I feel my hands tingle as the chi' stirs in anticipation for this action. Yet I wonder if the significance of touch in easing suffering is really understood. I wonder if touch is ever really considered beyond its habitual nature. Paramanda (2001) writes:

> We associate healing with hands – as in the ancient tradition of the laying on of hands. We speak of people having green fingers, of being in safe hands. For the deaf, hands can be taught to speak, having a language of their own… The hands seem to represent our being in the world, our ability to relate to life. It is with hands that humankind has fashioned the world, and it is through the hands that the arts are born. When we first attempt complicated activities with our hands, such as playing the piano or typing, we say we are all fingers and thumbs, but once we have mastered the task it is as though the hands have themselves learned. (p.30)

I have become very conscious of my hands and the way I touch people. I am more mindful of the way they connect me with the other, communicating what is in my mind and in my heart.

Wednesday 19 June 2002
Iris

Iris does not arrived for her reflexology appointment. Like a mother hen I scurry around, asking people if she's left a message. No reply from her landline. The answering service voice greets me on her mobile. Perhaps she has forgotten but I feel uncertain and anxious if something has happened. I know she is going on holiday tomorrow. Perhaps she is busy getting ready, last minute shopping. But it's not like her to miss her reflexology.

Sunday 30 June 2002

Iris

Iris missing her reflexology continues to bug me as if the smooth flow of our relationship has been fractured. And yet for Iris, what is smooth flow? Wrapped up in the prospect of her imminent death, what turmoil must she be experiencing? Smooth flow is an illusion, a grasp at some order. I must flow with the staccato rhythm; or better, help Iris create the rhythm.

I pick up the phone and dial her number. She answers – 'Hi Iris, it's Chris.' She's pleased to hear from me. She says she has had a good restful holiday – 'Plenty of food and lolling about...'

I laugh: 'You'll get anxious about putting on weight.'

'I lost so much weight before we went away and then they put me on the steroids. *They* are going to stop them, what do you think?'

'I can't answer that...the steroids will certainly boost your appetite'

We pause and I say: 'You started on a new chemotherapy drug, how is that going?'

Iris: 'It's okay. I haven't really noticed any drastic side effects. My legs are such a mess though. I keep scratching and bleeding. I wake up in the middle of the night...it's those toxins.'

'No better?'

'No... Can you fit me in this week?'

'I could see you around one o'clock on Wednesday?'

'That's exactly the time a bunch of girlfriends have arranged a big lunch get-together at the pub... Is there another time?'

We agree 12.30 on Wednesday. Iris will put her girlfriends off for half an hour. 'I've got to have my reflexology. I'll see if I can also get an appointment to see the doctor to talk about the steroids.'

I'm pleased I phoned her because Iris doesn't like phoning and burdening me. She needs things in her life that give her hope as the yarn unwinds...life rafts to hang onto as the storm gathers force. I do not believe in abetting a false hope that somehow Iris can find a cure. Yet hope is a big word in cancer because cancer exposes people to the fact that they are not immortal. And people, especially younger people, are afraid of death and dying because they have become attached to the permanence of existence.

Joko Beck (1989) says:

So what I want to talk about today is having no hope. Sounds terrible doesn't it? Actually it is not terrible at all. A life lived with no hope is a peaceful, joyous, and compassionate life. (p.63)

Hope is a reflection of desire for something or fear of something. Hope is about living in the future when the person, especially the dying person, needs to live in the now. To live in an uncertain and fearful future is not to live at all because there is only the present. The future does not exist except as a mental illusion. Blackwolf and Gina Jones (1996) say we should live 90 per cent in the present and only 5 per cent in the past and the future. Yet when fear grips it pulls the person into an uncertain future. How can people let go of fear? Blackwolf and Gina Jones say we need to find a way home into our heart, what they describe as Ain-dah-ing:

> Ain-dah-ing, your home within your heart, is accessible through the awareness of your breath. Slow down to life and experience the calm of Ain-dah-ing. As you experience Ain-dah-ing, the place of peace, you will understand that even death cannot touch you. Once you have experienced this freedom on a personal level, you will be able to extend this love out beyond self…this inner strength or Mash-ka-wisen neutralises life's fears. (pp.239–240)

So when I focus Iris on her breathing I help her reach Ain-dah-ing where she will find inner strength or Mash-ka-wisen to help let go of fear. Over time she has found this place of sanctuary although it is short-lived when thrown back into the everyday world where her fears once again control her life. Perhaps if she were guided to breathe every day she could better let go of fear and dwell in the love of Ain-dah-ing, or deeper level of consciousness beyond the grasping ego. Kabat-Zinn (1990) has shown the impact of guided breathing in reducing stress for people recovering from heart disease.

It is also significant for caregivers to access Ain-dah-ing, to let go their own fears of death and dying, and because Ain-dah-ing is the source of compassion – *to extend this love out beyond self.*

Powerful Native American medicine[12] that resonates with Buddhism. Wisdom is indeed universal.

---

12   I have explored Blackwolf and Gina Jones's Native American healing wisdom in a paper entitled 'The caring dance' (2001).

Wednesday 3 July 2002

I walk Charlotte, my nine-year-old daughter, to school. It is a fresh summer morning, the sun is shining although rain clouds are gathering. We reach the recreation ground that leads to the school's rear gate. Before crossing the road we wait for a pickup truck to pass. It is driven by Maggie. She is bringing her daughter, Charlotte's friend Kristin, to school. A wave of trepidation ripples through me because it is the first time I have seen Maggie since her husband died, completely unexpectedly, in his sleep the Sunday night before last. He had picked Kristin up from our house that evening. He was the same age as me. I did not know him but I do know Maggie in a mutual parent way.

I move towards the pickup driver's door.

'How are you, Maggie?'

'I am having a better day today…yesterday was difficult.'

She cannot look at me in her grief. She is torn apart. We slowly walk our children across the recreation ground. I focus on her daughter, laughing that I had mistaken her school bag for a coat. I then say it's a tiger skin. Charlotte and Kristin laugh and say, 'No – it's a leopard's skin pattern.'

The children are a distraction from facing Maggie's torment. They represent life, hope, joy, light from behind the dark shadow his death has cast. We reach the school gate and say goodbye to the children and walk back. Alone, I ask how she is managing. Perhaps a banal sort of question but we have no intimacy between us. She is managing with the help of many people in the village where she lives. I express my shock and sympathy. We reach her pickup truck. Then she lets go her feelings; her suffering is intense. I stroke her arm and shoulder wanting to hold this woman but that's the best I can do without violating some unspoken rule. I am struck by the whiteness of her clean blouse in the sun. Maggie finally breaks away and says goodbye.

Although Maggie could not be comforted, I resisted the twinges of pity that pulled at me. It is never easy to know what someone like Maggie is feeling and sympathy always feels inadequate; often no more than a gesture to ease our own discomfort. Levine (1986) distinguishes pity from compassion:

> When you meet the pain of another with fear, it is often called pity. When you are motivated by pity, you are motivated by a dense self-interest. When you're motivated by pity, you're acting on the aversion you have to experiencing someone else's predicament. You want to alleviate their discomfort as a means of alleviating your own.

Pity creates more fear and separation. When love touches the pain of another, it is called compassion. Compassion is just space. Whatever that other person is experiencing, you have room for it in your heart. (p.168)

As I walk home, my feet feel lighter and the sun shines more brightly. It felt like a test of my ability to be compassionate outside my hospice role. It was more difficult to respond to Maggie's grief than with relatives at the hospice. The boundaries are different. I know it is simply responding to people in their human suffering, but I did feel more vulnerable.

Iris

Iris greets me with 'Am I tanned or jaundiced?' Her inner arms have a yellow tinge that give the game away. She is both. The whites of her eyes are a deeper yellow than before. I sense her fear – she says her healer is focusing on releasing the blockage...he has helped her this way before. Her legs are a mass of bleeding scabs as she scratches constantly in her effort to relieve the intense itching. Even as we talk she scratches at her skin, her nails clawing into the barely formed scabs, blood trickling across her jaundiced skin. A remorseless and distressing obsession. I wonder what it must be like to itch to distraction, to inflict such mutilation.

Iris is enthusiastic – 'I've persuaded Dr Brown to continue my dexamethasone... I've eaten so well. The holiday was a great tonic. I've stopped my non-dairy diet and I'm relishing the delights of chocolate again! Lena has just given me four Rolos, which were delicious. Dr Brown has prescribed a new anti-depressant that may also help the itching. The questran was useless. My shoulder's been more painful...the doctors are considering a nerve-blocking injection as an alternative to the destructive surgery...'

We play around the edges trying to dampen the distressing symptoms to improve the quality of Iris's life. Iris has retrenched from our previous conversation, no longer accepting that she will die soon. But when I ask her how she feels in herself she cannot completely mask the gathering gloom.

She finds comfort in the reclining chair. The tops of her feet are a scabbed mess but the bottoms of her feet are unscathed, just one sore under the second toe of her left foot. I decide to modify the reflexology to avoid much of the top of the feet so as not to disturb the wounds.

Iris is surprised that she fell asleep because she had been so tense. She expresses her relief that the reflexology retains its potency to take her to a calm place beyond the fear that constantly grips her. She is wiping the reflexology cream off her legs because it irritates her. I take over and carefully wipe it off. I will have to research whether any essential oils have a calming effect on itching skin. Rosemary is a renowned liver tonic which Davis (1999) notes helps in cases of jaundice. Perhaps rose – not just for its soothing and antiseptic effect on skin but also for its feminine qualities at a time when Iris's self-image is collapsing.

I admonish Iris for not drinking enough water, and urge her to drink more, especially after reflexology that is likely to release toxins into her body. She must rush off for her lunch date at the pub with a group of friends – perhaps the best tonic!

Monday 8 July 2002

Iris phones me to arrange another reflexology session. I give her my bad news – that I fell off a horse last week and fractured three ribs. The pain was excruciating. At least I can empathise better with Iris's bone pain and the side effects of analgesia! I have been prescribed the non-steroid anti-inflammatory drug meloxicam. As a consequence I developed indigestion and required ranitidine to counter that. I was also prescribed solpadol – a mixture of paracetamol and codeine phosphate-only to become immediately constipated. My bowel actions grounded to a halt for three days and then only a mighty effort laced with lactulose managed to shift things slightly. I switched the solpadol to paracetamol but the pain sharpened. I decided the pain was the lesser of the two evils. I wonder if bone cancer pain is the same severity as this? Perhaps it is even worse? Iris describes her bone pain as a deeper, more gnawing pain; a haunting pain that constantly reminds you of the cancer eating away. Yet the pain is only half of it alongside the distressing side effects.

What quality of life can people like Iris cling on to? Is it just the urgency to grasp life itself that is sustaining? Is it the thought of devastating loss that turns the head away from contemplating death? Such thoughts bother me because I have to say to Iris that my condition makes it impossible to give any treatments this week. I feel her disappointment down the phone and yet she suffers for me, anxious that I am okay. We make another appointment for Wednesday next week (17 July) and another appointment for Monday 22 July. Then the school holidays will be upon us and we must rethink our strategy. Perhaps I will need to go to her house rather than her coming to the hospice.

I reflect on my gut reaction to avoid touching Iris's bleeding legs. Instinctually, I had recoiled from touching Iris's legs. Did it show on my face? A stab of guilt wounds me. As I massaged Iris's legs and feet I could feel the scabs and sense the massage cream mix with the blood, yet it was no concern once I had seen the deeper beauty. Jill Jarvis (2002), in her reflection on massaging a woman's 'disgusting' skin, writes:

> With gentle circular movements my fingers attempted to coat the raw burning tissues of Sally's back lubricating the rippled surfaces. Feelings of sadness and hesitance are replaced by pleasurable sensations. The moist warmth infuses through the dryness of my hands creating suppleness and ease. In silence I continue covering any area of need, enjoying the experience of Sally's relaxation radiating through my fingertips. 'That's wonderful,' she whispers, 'You're not wearing gloves.' (p.11)

In this passage we can experience the exquisite beauty and significance of caring. Indeed it is beautiful because it is so significant, because Jill's action makes such a difference to Sally's care. The words are caught on the breath. Sally feels cared for, it is the essence of palliative care perhaps more than anything. Jill also had a sense of disgust at Sally's blistered and festering skin yet saw the deeper beauty. Sally had learnt that her skin was disgusting for the nurses to treat. She had embodied that knowing. Hence she expected Jill to wear gloves while applying cream. Jill was ambivalent – part of her wanted to wear gloves because the skin was disgusting. But another, deeper and more powerful part of her rejected the gloves because she knew tacitly that she was rejecting Sally and this engendered guilt. She could not easily live with herself if she chose to wear gloves. She writes:

> The disgust I felt on first seeing Sally produced intense guilt. The T-cell lymphoma had totally consumed her skin into a revolting, stinking mess. On reflection, I suppose as a nurse, it would have been normal to reach for gloves. However, I feel they create a barrier within the touching process preventing skin-to-skin contact. I wanted to communicate my acceptance of Sally despite her disfigured body. Autton (1996) describes how reassuring physical contact can be by transferring a healing massage (p.123). If I had created a barrier within the touching process, by wearing gloves, would Sally have received my message? No, I would have intensified her feelings of self-repulsion and ugliness. Sadly, when I tried to discuss this with my colleagues, they dismissed the idea and requested that we should all wear aprons as well to protect our clothes! (p.14)

The idea that Sally's skin was disgusting was Jill's false consciousness. Somehow, like her colleagues, she had learnt this. It was an illusion that she dispersed within the moment's recognition. Of course, to do a massage wearing gloves is an impossible equation. It never crossed my mind with Iris. Equally not massaging Iris's legs because they are so injured was not an option given the benefit that treatment gives her and that she might feel rejected, even behind a mask of understanding.

In terms of writing a narrative, Jill illuminates the feminine, the ability to light a torch in the dark chamber where caring has been invisible, hidden behind the heroic masculine of symptom management; a front that nurses hide behind in fear of such intimacy and repulsion, and yet a front that has obscured the sacred act of caring.

The gloves have a deeper meaning, because they also cover the soul. Jill draws on Estabrooks and Morse's (1992) words of *soul bumping*. And this is only possible because she does not wear gloves. Opening her unprotected self to Sally opens her soul and enables Sally to reciprocate. Sally can open her soul to Jill and in doing so their souls bump. The realisation of caring is profound. It shakes Jill to her core. She could touch the deep beauty of Sally and feel her soul glow in mutual realisation. Jill was not simply meeting some physical need in Sally but had touched on a spiritual level, a part of Sally that had been neglected, and a part of Jill that she had also neglected. Jill's reflection more than anything illuminates the mutuality of caring. As Jill quotes Kearney (1997), 'The way care is given can reach the most hidden of places'.

As Jill discovers, her presence helps Sally to find a sea of tranquillity beyond the horizon of the sea of torment. Jill is the ferryman who guides Sally to this place. Jill quotes Saunders (1978) that 'the real presence of another person is a place of security'.

To move beyond, Sally needed to feel secure, because to move beyond is an unknown place, perhaps more fearful than the fear we need to move from. It is letting go and Sally can only let go when she feels secure. The result was to unlock a miraculous self-healing process. Reading again Jill's story about working with Sally helps me to put my work with Iris into perspective and inspires me with confidence, courage and compassion.

Wearing gloves is a metaphor for resistance. How much do we nurses unwittingly resist our patients? We say we care, but how much of their care is conditional on our concerns? Jill's colleagues would wear aprons as well to protect themselves from Sally, not just Sally's disgusting skin and odour, but also from Sally's suffering. It is as if Sally's spirit is also festering and uncared for. On my work with Mary (p.54) I wrote that hospices are sanitised places, are sanitising, so much so that we dare to even talk about such things.

Perhaps then this is the real theme of my narrative, to become unconditional in my caring. And yet this requires such a deep knowing and letting go of a sanitised self.

Wednesday 17 July 2002

Iris

Standing in the nurse's room in day care, I turn and see Iris wave at me. Lena had just been saying how much worse Iris had seemed last Friday in day care. Robert had been with her. I say something facile like 'I suppose this is what we must expect…her gradual deterioration into death.'

Lena was upset to see Iris like that. Lena has been working with Iris for over two years and anticipates the grief of separation. It is easy to say 'we shouldn't become involved', 'not to allow our feelings to become entangled with hers', 'not to absorb Iris's suffering as our own' – but these are all clichés that pale in the emotional reality of the moment. I do believe that non-attachment is a virtue but I feel the force of Lena's distress. What goes around comes around. The wheel of life inexorably turns to face us.

I move towards Iris. She is deeply jaundiced. Her face is gaunt, as if etched with her suffering. Yet her smile is strong, vivacious almost. She wears a long summer dress. Her hair is carefully styled. Red lipstick smudged on her upper teeth gives a sense of the forlorn child. Full of sympathy she asks me how my ribs are? She immediately wants to care for me, putting aside her own concerns. She has brought me some chocolates for my injury. Perhaps it is a feminine thing of caring for others; perhaps by caring for another it helps distract her from the constant focus on being cared for.

As we move into the treatment room she unfolds her recent history. The name of her new chemotherapy drug just escapes her but she is pleased because her last liver function tests showed an improvement. Something positive like a ray of hope to clasp.

'What does your healer say?'

'He's confident that I have a blockage in the bile duct and he can shift it.'

I wonder about that, about offering such reassurance. Yet Iris does need hope …should it be false hope? Perhaps it was the best decision not to tell her about her lung involvement. It is too soon to pull down the veils of illusion to reveal the stark truth, even as she shifts to avoid its glare but deep down she knows it waits for her.

However, she has rejected the nerve block option to deal with her right shoulder. 'They said they could not isolate the specific nerve so they would have to block the lot...it would leave my arm useless. I decided against it. They increased my gabapentin and morphine – so the pain is better controlled...just a deep ache sometimes.'

I say: 'So you kept your car?' Iris looks slightly blank. 'You said you might use taxis instead?'

Iris twigs: 'I couldn't give the car up...it would be too much. I need my independence.'

'You can't let it beat you?'

Iris: 'No...not yet.'

Iris continues to scratch but says her skin is better. Many of the scabs have healed on her legs although plaster covers the latest wound. An appointment to see a dermatologist has been arranged for her.

'I've put on weight...staying on the dexamethasone has helped... They won't take me off that, will they?'

I reassure her that they will continue it. She feels it has also helped her mood. 'I still get some very dark days... I can barely move...'

'Like a fatigue?'

'Yes...the district nurse suggested she pops in on Mondays to keep an eye on me but said if anything came up then to let her know.'

I tentatively ask: 'Have you seen the Macmillan nurse?'

'I have. She came round the house to see me and the family. Charlotte asked her if mummy was getting better. She said no, that mummy was worse.'

'Did she say that in front of you?'

'Yes.'

'How did you feel?'

'In one way pleased that the kids and Robert have got someone to support them...everybody has been supporting me. I'm not sure about her coming to the house. I like to keep home and the hospice separate...so I'm not invaded.'

'Is it symbolic...the Macmillan nurse?'

Iris looks at me and then lowers her eyes: 'Yes, it is.'

Once again I visualise my recurring metaphor of the dark clouds gathering to obliterate her blue sky. These people offering help are harbingers of doom.

'Perhaps you still need to see me at the hospice rather than at home?'

Iris exclaims: 'No, I see you as different!'

Iris pauses: 'A friend of mine has offered to look after the children on Wednesdays through the holidays…everyone is offering help…so it might be possible to have the reflexology then?'

I say: 'Let's wait and see what's best at the time. I am happy to visit you at home.'

Iris relaxes in the chair. Thoughts of Jill and Sally come to mind as I gently move my hands over her feet and lower legs working the cream into her skin using rosemary and rose. This time I do not avoid the scabbed upper feet. I feel the warmth and rough surface of her scabs. I am so happy to do this for Iris. The music is beautiful, she closes her eyes and is soon asleep.

The skin on the bottom of her feet is like dry leather. It has lost its suppleness. It is also dark and brooding reflecting her embodied emotion. An hour later we finish. Iris awakened by the sound of one of the care assistant voices outside the room. Again, no respect for the healing inside the room. It is out of view and they cannot sense it. Her feet are again supple. She uses olive oil at home to soften them but has been neglecting them. The reflexology cream hasn't irritated her as before. In my massage strokes I visualised soothing the itching. Perhaps it helped? The mystery of aromatherapy.

Iris is not drinking enough. She says her urine is very dark but that is the jaundice – 'I promise to drink more…promise.' I say it will help to flush out the toxins as they accumulate. She laughs – 'I'll try.' We hug and say goodbye. I write Iris a poem.

> The clouds gather about you
> But your light still shines brightly
> Through the gloom
> The vigil begins
> And like moths
> The harbingers of doom
> Gather around

Monday 22 July 2002

Iris

Iris looks like a hippy chick, with metal necklace and leather studded belt and long denim skirt. She has always been careful about her appearance. The scabs have spread to her neck and face as the itching has continued unabated. The latest trick is to try phenergan. Trick or trial and error; the limitations of science when applied to the particular. Iris knows that phenergan can cause drowsiness. She slept fitfully last night. Tossing about. Mouth littered with ulcers and diarrhoea caused by the chemotherapy. She is on her third cycle.

I ask: 'How many do you have?'

Iris: 'It's continuous.'

I think to myself, no respite until the white blood cell count becomes untenable. The fine balance between treatment and the effects of treatment. What is better? Does treatment actually have any real benefit now? Perhaps in terms of sustaining Iris's hope. Should she be confronted with her reality? She is not ready to resign herself to her fate. Her healer feels her liver blockage is now clear. He is so confident of her survival that they have planned a supper on 20 December. Her healer insisted this is not 'false hope'. Either way, it seems to be a much needed boost to Iris's morale.

I gently hold her feet in my hands, these feet that I have nourished for nearly two years. They are less leathery than last time. The swollen liver feels shrunken. As I work her spine along the edge of both her feet and large toe, I pause at each chakra point to help mobilise and balance her diminished energy. At each point I work my own energy field, drawing up my breath through the spine and visualising each major chakra colour as a lotus unfolding in turn; red, orange, yellow, green, turquoise, indigo and violet for the crown chakra. There are many books to guide the reader to understand the chakra systems. My own use in reflexology has been largely instinctive. In Table 2.5 (p.232) I note the location of each chakra along the spine.[13] Afterwards, Iris says, 'I slept right through that... I needed that but I don't feel drowsy, I feel much better.' I admonish her for not drinking enough water. I will contact her in three weeks after my holiday.

---

13   My table follows Mercier (2000) except for the brow chakra which I feel is positioned midway between the tip and base of the large toe. The descriptors largely follow Myss (1998).

Ester

On the inpatient unit I ask Rosemary, a staff nurse, if any patients might benefit from therapy? She introduces me to Ester who is paralysed in her lower limbs due to spinal cord compression. She has been low although a 'girlie' day yesterday picked her up. Ester is open and welcoming. I feel an immediate attraction to her. She has a soft, moon-shaped face that belies her 53 years. I sit next to her and she unfolds her illness story. I wonder how many times she has told her story and yet she is eager to share it again to this stranger bearing gifts.

The spinal compression was caused by bone metastases from a malignant melanoma that was excised six years ago. Later she had a lymph node removed from her groin and subsequently 17 more removed resulting in lymphodeama to her left leg. Then the back pain and surgery but the cancer grew back and now there is no more curative treatment. She has just finished a course of radiotherapy that has given her violent indigestion. She feels the burning pain may last a few weeks. 'It's ruined my appetite. I'm taking large doses of steroids. Can you see my moon-shaped face?' She laughs easily.

'My fate is sealed…maybe I have six months, maybe a year.'

She's philosophical as she lies in bed, encased in a harness to support her spine. No more baths. She fears going home because she will be spending part of the day alone. Her husband can work from home sometimes but not always, and the care package will leave her vulnerable. Most of her friends live in Guildford where they used to live.

She apologises for her tears. 'I know I'm going to cry but it's okay, I'm okay.'

She seeks to reassure me. I smile in sympathy but I am touched by this brave woman. I take and squeeze her hand and then take on a journey through my aromatherapy case smelling different oils for her hand massage. We decide on frankincense, grapefruit and lavender mixed in jojoba carrier oil. She loves the smell, subtle yet intoxicating. As I work on her hand massage for about 30 minutes, we talk incessantly about life. She says, 'I need people to laugh and be positive. I was told I needed a positive mental attitude.'

Ester has been married just one year. Her husband is very supportive. I ask if she has any faith? No, but she senses things, senses something more beyond. At home, the dining room will become her bedroom so she can gaze across the garden. From her window we gaze across the hospice gardens. She says the gardens are beautiful.

I pick up the quip 'positive mental attitude' and suggest that might mean living in the now – she loves this idea. 'That's exactly it – living each moment fully.' I direct her attention to the beauty of a yellow flower in the garden, to each sensual note of the music I play, to the delicate touch of the massage...such small things but such beauty.

'With my arms I can paint and do things... If I should lose my arms...' Her words drift in silent angst at such a thought.

I move into TT, sensing that I might be able to alleviate a little of the burning chest pain. Working from the top of her head down her body I visualise a cool blue waterfall taking the heat out of her body. She opens her eyes and says that was so relaxing.

I have dwelt 75 minutes with Ester. It felt almost surreal, the way I can enter someone's life who will die of cancer and give a massage and TT while they reveal their secret life to me. This is such remarkable work. Yet, I hesitate to write I experienced joy because she suffers so greatly.

Thursday 25 July 2002

Ester

Ester's door is closed. Her husband and two friends are with her. I decide to pop in to say hello armed with a posy of lavender picked from my garden and Tolle's book *The Power of Now* (1999). Her friends exclaim at the depth of colour and strong scent. Ester's face is full of smiles. I am emotional seeing her, I want to reach out and wrap her in my deep compassion. Her husband realises I am the complementary therapist and warmly shakes my hand. Ester has enthused about me. I ask, 'Did the Therapeutic Touch help?'

Ester turns towards her husband. 'I have been calmer the past two days, haven't I?'

I find myself saying that if she needs therapy at home then to contact me through the hospice.

Later, reflecting on Ester inspires another poem within 'The stillness of the desert' series.

In the stillness of the desert/17

> In the soft light of the new day
> I see your smile
> Glisten across the lightening sky;
> I feel my heart will drown in compassion.
> Can you love too much?

Can you bear the ache
Of seeing death's tentacles slowly
Spread around you?
I brush my hand
Against your tear-stained cheek
And feel you let go
Just a little into the divine.

I hardly know you
Yet I am full of you
For you are simply love unfolded.

Ah little bird
As you hop about
Do you know I love you
Even as you fear me
Wrapped up in your little world?

Saturday 10 August 2002

I am on holiday in Le Racou, South of France, with my family.
Two days ago, Susan said my eyes were jaundiced in the fading light.
She was quite serious and I had no way of checking.
I sensed her fear and felt my own rise like a rising river.
Spontaneously I began to speculate what might the cause be.
Perhaps my NSAIDs[14] awash with alcohol?
Of course (of course?), worse fears tread in – cancer and death.
But what was my worst fear?
Not getting my journal published?
And indeed I would want to write about this sensation of being jaundiced.
How long do I have?
That question invades my mind;
A sense of panic that I will have no time at all.
I felt different.
A strange gnawing in my stomach as fear rippled through me.
Shock is the first response.
In the morning my eyes are clear.
Perhaps the jaundice has faded?

14   Non-steriod anti-inflammatory drugs.

Table 2.5 Position and description of chakras along the spine

Chakra	Indian name	Vertebra position	Colour	Descriptor
The seventh chakra: Crow chakra	Sahasrara	On top of the large toe	violet	Link with the divine, beyond self
The sixth chakra: Brow chakra	Ajna	Midway between first cervical and top of large toe	indigo	Consciousness, intuition, insight, meaning
Alma mater		First cervical	magenta	Balancing the energy systems
The fifth chakra: Throat chakra	Vishudda	Third cervical	turquoise	Self-expression, will power, self-control
The fourth chakra: Heart chakra	Anahata	Fourth thoracic	green	Emotional patterns, love/hate, compassion etc.
The third chakra: Solar plexus chakra	Manipura	Seventh and eight thoracic	yellow	Self-belief patterns, self-esteem, fear
The second chakra: Sacral chakra	Svadhisthana	First lumbar	orange	Patterns around relationships, sexuality, power, creativity, control
The first chakra: Base chakra	Mulhadhara	Fourth sacral	red	Patterns/group -thought forms that ground the person in the physical world

Perhaps it was never there – a trick of the light?
How do I feel?
Strangely nothing; perhaps a 'hmm' to myself.
Yet I sense its relevance to Iris.
Living that sensation gives me such a valuable insight
even as it was a false alarm…
And I think of Iris. How is Iris?

Wednesday 14 August 2002

Safely home from holiday. No more jaundice scares. No answer from Iris's phone. I leave a message to contact me.

Thursday 15 August 2002

Iris

Just after 9.00. Again no answer from Iris's home line. This time I let it ring until I hear Iris's voice on the answerphone. She tells me to ring her mobile. Again it is switched off. I phone the hospice to speak to Lena. Rea, the administrator, answers. Lena is at a meeting so I tell Rea I am phoning about news of Iris. A slight pause and Rea says that Iris 'passed away' the week before last. The funeral was last week. She died in the general hospital. Lena was with her. Rea is sorry that she's the person to break this news – would I like Lena to phone me when she is free from her meeting at 10.00?

'Please.'

Iris's death was inevitable but I am desolate that I was not there for her at that time. I can imagine Iris's fear as she slipped into death and the suffering of her children. I can imagine being in the hospital and not at the hospice, but then again I imagine Iris clinging to hope until the last moment. I imagine how Lena must have felt and must still be feeling. All this imagination but it does not take away the ache gnawing within. I work my emotions into poetic form.

To Iris

    Little bird
    They called your number early
    Yet how you held on
    To the raft of life
    As the storms gathered
    And battered you

And through it all
Your smile endured
Even as you suffered deep within
Brave for your children;
Parting must have been a great sorrow
It is hard for me to know
That you could be calm
Yet I must believe you did in your final breath

I close my eyes
And see your smile
And feel the joy of being with you
Flood through my being.
There is a place in my soul that is ever yours
As I absorbed your life within mine,
You who taught me so much about caring;
Yet I cannot dwell in sorrow;
I celebrate your life
And honour our time together.

Lena phones just after 10.00. I sit in the garden and feel the warmth of the beautiful day as Lena tells me about Iris's death. Iris had become exhausted from diarrhoea due to the chemotherapy which wasn't working. She came into the hospice on Sunday for respite care. On the Wednesday morning she became very breathless. It was felt she had a pleural effusion. She was shocked at this news – she asked, 'Where did that come from?' She didn't know she had lung metastases. So despite her poor condition she decided to go to the hospital to tap the effusion to ease her breathing. 'We were sitting in A&E when she went to the toilet and something must have happened. She came out looking totally drained. I knew she was dying. I told the staff and we moved her into one of the major trauma rooms but without any heroics to try and save her. The trauma rooms are very spacious and pleasant. Iris became a little agitated because of her breathlessness so she was given midazolam 5mg. It sounds awful but it was beautiful... I feel really privileged to have been there with her. She asked Robert, 'Am I dying?' He said 'Yes' ...he said later that was the hardest thing he's ever done. And she slipped away. Her mother died two days later while on holiday in Dorset. She also had a pleural effusion. They had a double funeral last Friday. The church was packed. Her daughter read a poem and her friend Mandy read something that Iris had written to be read at her funeral. She must have had a greater faith than we realised.'

I express my sadness that I couldn't have been there but Lena is quick to reassure me – I call Lena Iris…she laughs and says she did that with Sarah. Saying that, I feel the tears in my eyes. Talking to Lena has brought my grief to the surface…and I am thankful for that and that Iris did in fact find peace before she died and that her life was honoured. I wonder how Iris felt when she said those immortal words, 'Am I dying?' to Robert. Did she surrender to her God and feel at peace? Did she feel on a roller coaster about to plunge? The thought lingers with me.

To be touched by death is to feel life. We who work with palliative care must take death in our stride. It is our business but that doesn't make it any easier. Each death is a remarkable event. When you work with someone like Iris over two years it is more remarkable. We must learn to flow with the tide and feel the beauty of life about us and if it is painful then that pain is simply a reminder that nothing can ever be taken for granted. The sun still shines. Life continues. We try and make sense of things but ultimately there is no understanding, simply faith. We like to think we know, but we don't. We like to cling to the idea that we do know to feel secure in that knowing. Life is mystery unfolding.

> Rather than trying to control what can never be controlled, we can find a sense of security in being able to meet what is actually happening. This is allowing for the mystery of things: not judging but rather cultivating a balance of mind that can receive what is happening, whatever it is. The acceptance is the source of our safety and confidence. (Salzberg 1995, p.142)

Thursday 29 August 2002

Two weeks have passed since Iris's death and I have not been to the hospice. Penny, one of the team leaders, greets me. I confess that I was sad to be on holiday when Iris was admitted and to miss her funeral. Penny gently recounts Iris's admission and the circumstances in which she went to the hospital. She confirms my intuitive sense that Iris would have wanted to do anything to hold on to life…that it was her decision to go for the pleural tap. Iris was shocked she had a pleural effusion – and had asked where had it come from, unwrapping the collusion that protected her from this news.

Penny acknowledges my sadness – 'Working with her for two years I know you were close to her… I could tell you meant a lot to her.' Penny is good at this thing, helping staff to find the jewel of caring within the debris. It was nice to imagine Iris talking about me. It helps me to feel okay.

Debriefing with Penny helps me to work through my feelings and bring some sense of closure.

Monday 9 September 2002

Theo

I had met Theo last week as he arrived on the unit but had no real opportunity to meet with him and his family except in passing. His notes indicate:

- He had been suffering from morphine toxicity, possibly as a result of his MST (morphinse slow release tablets) being increased from 30 to 60mg by his GP. The night staff say Theo has had pain – they gave oromorph and heat pads which seemed to help. Their view is that Theo has not disclosed his pain to us.

- He has liver metastases with unknown primary. He has apparently given up, refusing aggressive intervention. He is deeply withdrawn and has been since admission. Why?

- He has cared for his wife through her own prolonged and ultimately successful battle with breast cancer.

I get caught up in the early morning paraphernalia of breakfasts. I check Theo's blood sugar. He's been an insulin-dependent diabetic for the past 20 years. Theo responds to my greeting in an abstract way, as if he's really somewhere else. He has no pain now…mumbling something about numbers. I translate this to mean the pain chart. 'Yes…numbers to ten.'

I encourage him to take his medication. He takes the tablets slowly with water and apple juice. A capsule gets stuck in his throat. He does not want breakfast. Blood sugar is 8.7 so we will omit his insulin. He closes his eyes. There is nothing he needs. I am dismissed. The rhythm of caring is staccato.

Later, Theo's bed is empty. He has made it to the toilet. He's okay so I ask him to ring the call bell before returning. Back in bed I ask if he would like the TV? 'Yes.' His eyes brighten. But he is not interested and would prefer a radio. He closes his eyes as FM Classics play. His favourite music is Bach.

Later again, he insists on sitting in a chair by the bed to wash and shave. He meticulously shaves himself and accepts a face wash and then carefully brushes his hair. Our conversation is functional, there is no obvious way to engage him on a deeper level. I am attentive for the signs but none are forthcoming. He says he worked as an administrator for DAF trucks. His only half laugh when he calls people outside his room 'customers'. He saw the funny side and changed it to visitors. And then in a moment of silence I ask him how is he feeling? Theo looks straight ahead. I sense the difficulty of this question and its immensity. After a few minutes I break the silence to say that was a tough question to answer – half-statement, half-question. But Theo responds, 'It is.' Enough said. I take his hand. He does not resist. I feel the immensity of the question in the touch. After a short while I say I will leave him now (unspoken 'with your thoughts'). Perhaps he has felt my concern. A tentative connection?

I share my thoughts with Kerry, the staff nurse I am working with this morning. She tells me how Theo was in floods of tears one evening but could not talk about his feelings – 'The reason I gave Theo to you was because I felt you might be able to reach him.'

Yet I too have struggled to flow with his staccato rhythm. His flow is jerky, twisted, reflecting his deep angst. His existential pain ripples about him. Perhaps I found his wavelength and flow with his jerky rhythm – reminding myself of Stephen (see p.144). I cannot kid myself I know Theo in any sense. Empathy is an illusion. I merely touch the surface.

Wednesday 11 September 2002

Theo

It is 15.20. When I glance inside his room I see Theo's wife Mary and another visitor. Mary catches my eye. I smile in acknowledgement although I have not yet met her. I decide not to intrude. Greta, a staff nurse, sits at the nurses' table. I quietly ask how Theo has been today. 'Not so good… Mary brought their wedding album in.'

The pictures show snow on the ground. The date was February 1963. A year of heavy snow that I remember well. The pictures are black and white. Theo was 23 years old. There is something very poignant about wedding photos when a partner is dying. My curiosity is burning, so I get brave and knock on the open door. I say, 'Hello, Theo' and then turning towards Mary say, 'I'm Chris, I looked after Theo on Monday.' Mary replies, 'I have seen you about.'

Relatives are very sensitive to the hospice environment and pay careful attention to what goes on about them. It is a vulnerable time. To my surprise, Theo is animated to see me. My doubt that I had not connected with Theo evaporates. Mary is smiling, welcoming and I move into the room to dwell with this family and friend for the next 30 minutes chatting about the weather in 1963 and their wedding.

I ask Mary how she is? She is tired. She has not slept well since last October when it started with Theo. She laments that Theo has given up fighting his cancer. Her weary eyes smile in acknowledgement. I think to myself, 'It must be hard for you to sit here watching Theo give up.'

Mary shares her anxiety that Theo may be discharged home – 'I really feel I could not cope.' She is exhausted. At least in the hospice she can share the burden with us. I reassure her that any decision about discharge would be made with her.

Dwelling with Mary and her friend gathered around the photographs felt very intimate, especially as I was almost a stranger. Her fears were able to bubble up to the surface. Perhaps she had mentioned her fear to other staff but it lay unresolved. The hospice does not like to commit itself to prolonged patient stay, expecting his morphine toxicity to be resolved and a new regimen for pain management established. Perhaps a week's admission will be enough to give Mary enough respite to recover her energy and resolve. Yet in the meantime Mary must suffer.

Saturday 14 September 2002

That weekend on a study course, I reflect on the meaning of *dwelling with*. Dwelling with is about creating a clearing amid the chaos of the unfolding illness drama, where myself and others feel relaxed and talk socially about whatever is unfolding. It is a spiritual and intimate space in which people feel cared for. In *dwelling with*, the practitioner appreciates the pattern of the whole and responds to guide the patient/family to find meaning and harmony.

Richard Cowling (2000) in his paper 'Healing as appreciating wholeness' asserts that wholeness is irreducible into parts yet the (whole) person can be appreciated as a merging and unfolding pattern in context of his or her environment. He states:

> My own view is that the nature of nursing is one of responding (with reverence) to the wholeness of human experience… In human terms, the pattern gives identity to and distinguishes one person from another. It is the essence of being who you are; thus, pattern appreciation is reaching for this essence in each individual and seeing the wholeness within pattern. (p.18)

I resonate with the idea of reverence, that what I do as a nurse is sacred and profound work. It is so important not to fragment wholeness for then we lose sight of the person. So appreciating someone's life pattern is a distant cry from assessing their problems. From the perspective of *dwelling with*, I become a part of the pattern, appreciating it from within.

Cowling further states:

> The transformative potential for practitioners rests within the way in which they learn to use themselves as instruments for pattern appreciation. Because the quest for pattern knowledge requires attention to all realms of data, one must develop data acquisition skills that allow the data to reveal itself. (p.23)

These words resonate with my belief that caring is nurturing growth through the illness experience. Through self-appreciation the person can move beyond suffering into new realms of being in harmony with life. Yet to guide the patient or relative the nurse needs to be skilled. Cowling acknowledges Wilber's work that to access and verify experience of a certain type requires adequate instruments. So for example, to access the spiritual realms of being, requires a practitioner to be suitably tuned into such realms within his or her life.

As noted previously, the hospice uses the Burford NDU Model: caring in practice. Its reflective cues are evident in the way I dwelt with Mary:

- Who is Mary?
- What meaning does Mary give to this illness experience?
- How is Mary feeling?
- How do I feel about Mary?
- How can I help Mary?
- How has Theo's illness/admission affected her/their usual life pattern and roles?
- What is important for Mary to feel more comfortable?
- What support does Mary have in life?
- How does Mary view the future for herself and others?

These cues have become internalised and are used naturally in response to the unfolding situation.

Friday 20 September 2002

Working an early shift. The morning is still and cloudy. Theo's name remains on the bed board. I am a little surprised but pleased to see that Theo is both alive and not discharged. I glance in – his face is sunken. Later I wash him with Christine. I love working with her because she embodies the spirit of the palliative care practitioner. She exudes the sacred simply in her presence.

I am mindful of 'dwelling with' and actually verbalise this to Christine: 'We are dwelling with Theo.' Just conjuring up the image of 'dwelling with' creates a sense of the sacred. I am mindful of bandying the word 'sacred'. What do I mean by it? First, it is an attitude of life – a reflection of the practitioner's own faith. I believe it is difficult to sense the sacred without faith in some higher consciousness or some being. Second, it is an attitude of reverence (to share that word with Cowling – see above) to what's unfolding – the mystery of life and death. Third, it is a reflection of the intense emotion within the situation that is experienced when the practitioner has tuned into and flows with the patient and family.

Washing Theo is a reflection of reverence, the slow rhythmic attention to each part of his wasted, jaundiced and bloated body in a flowing dance. I use body massage movements to wash his arms and legs, long sweeps, and massage his feet darkened with pent-up emotion. And when we finish there is stillness. Did Theo feel bathed in love rather than merely the soap and water? I hardly know, yet he is at peace.

Theo had asked to see the vicar a week ago 'as he has things that are troubling him'. The next day he was visited by a friend, Ted, with whom he rang the church bells. Both images suggest a faith. That afternoon he received an anointment. That night he was 'muddled'. Mary felt that he was trying to tie up loose ends. The next day (15 September) Mary was told that Theo could stay and die in the hospice. She expressed her 'utter relief'. The next day (the 16th), following a chat with Mary, Theo said he now had 'peace of mind' yet that night he became so restless that the nurses gave him midazolam. The next day Theo 'admitted to feelings of fear and wanting it over with'. His restlessness increased which increasing doses of midazolam failed to quell. On the 18th he commenced nozinan and haloperidol via a syringe driver which helped calm him, at least on the outside.

After lunch I catch Mary in the small kitchen preparing a tray of tea for herself and Theo's brother and wife. I ask her how she is. She had some reflexology last Tuesday in the day unit. The reflexologist suggested further treatments if she wished even after Theo has died. She expresses some anxiety that the therapist said the reflexology would reveal any underlying health problems – 'That was the last thing I wanted! I need to keep free from any such concerns, at least until it's over with Theo. He did help my twitchy eye though and I did feel more calm for the rest of that day…the twitchy eye is worse today. I did look for you, hoping you might give me the treatment.'

Therapists need to be sensitive to what they say. As I have experienced it is so easy to be careless when trying to be caring. This is one reason why I feel therapists should be nurses because the therapy becomes part of total care rather than something referred. The therapy becomes an extension of my care, chosen from my repertoire of appropriate responses to Mary's needs.

I smile at this woman who stands before me in her full vulnerability. Her words instantly reaffirm and take our relationship onto a more intimate level. She knows she can surrender into my care, that she can dwell comfortably in the space. I carry the tea tray back to Theo's room and meet the family. Theo is restless. I watch Mary struggle to make sense of what he is saying. Does he say pull the screen or asks Mary to scream? Once he turns to me and asks what I am looking at? A flash of anger or frustration at being misunderstood. Mary utters understated screams. I can feel her frustration and the anxiety this sort of event creates for her. The family look on uncomfortably. I know that Theo gets restless when he wants to use the bottle – this had happened twice during the morning. Perhaps the screen? Christine enters and we help Theo to use the bottle – and he is settled.

The family is relieved. They can now enjoy the tea and cake. Shortly afterwards I say goodbye. Theo will have died before my next shift next Wednesday.

Wednesday 25 September 2002

Wilf

A small red candle burns on the worktop. Its flame flickers in the half-light of morning. Eileen died during the night. Theo died yesterday. Christine expresses her amazement at Theo's determination to hold on for so long. Like me it is her first shift since we worked together last week.

After the shift report, I watch Brenda embrace Wilf, Eileen's husband. It is poignant. I can sense his anguish yet gratitude at the way she died. I feel deeply touched. I nursed her over the past few weeks as she slowly deteriorated, her jaundiced flesh wasting away. She loved a leg and feet massage. But I had only met Wilf once before, last Friday when I went to set up an aroma-stone to infuse Eileen's room with bergamot. Wilf was fascinated by my use of oils. We had not dwelt for very long and yet I had felt a strong connection with him.

As Wilf and Brenda disengage I move towards him and grasp his hand. He puts his left hand over mine as I offer my condolences. I touch his shoulder. He says Eileen died as she had wanted to do peacefully in her sleep and expresses his relief that she was now spared any further suffering. He was sleeping in another room when he arose just after 5.30 and went to see her. It was then she died. He had been with her at that moment which was so important for him. I wonder if she called him or whether he simply just knew?

Wilf asks if Eileen can remain in the room until midday...the grand-children are coming then. No problem. Through the morning various family arrive and congregate, and spill out about the hospice. They are very quiet, no dramatic tears. Half-smiles as we pass by or pause to acknowledge their loss.

Later in the morning Wilf and I meet again in the small kitchen. He has returned a tray laden with empty coffee cups. I cannot remember exactly how our conversation starts. Perhaps it is some throwaway remark about the flower on the tray. I ask him how long he had been married to Eileen.

'It would be 28 years next week.'

'Was this your first marriage?'

'It was for me but Eileen had been married before...the children are all from her first marriage...yet we have been, are, very close.'

'I met Alex...the youngest son? I guess he's in his mid-thirties?'

'Yes that's right. He had cancer you know...testicular cancer. Just a small lump that was found by chance. He's been a bit depressed these past months...he felt guilty that his cancer was cured and that his mother would die from hers. Eileen took him aside a while ago and talked to him, told him to pull himself together...that she was going to die and that she accepted that. He was much better afterwards. Eileen was good at things like that.'

'Did she have a strong faith?'

'She didn't.'

'I remember asking her that...she said she didn't.'

'It makes me doubt it as well...if there was a God, would he let people suffer like Eileen did?'

We pause, perhaps to let such words settle...and then putting my heart in my mouth, I ask Wilf: 'The home will be empty?'

Wilf takes my inquiry in his stride: 'Homes are very feminine...my sister is coming to stay with me as long as I need her to.'

Immediately I conjure up images of the woman as the homemaker and comforter. I imagine the house being empty and cold and that Wilf would miss Eileen very much. I am comforted by his sister coming to stay with him. 'That's good.'

Wilf says: 'Talking about these things is very helpful... I have had to learn to let them out rather than hold them in which is how I usually deal with difficult things.'

This is such a poignant moment. I am flooded with a tingly warmth that vibrates through me. I have an urge to hug Wilf and tell him what a brave, loving, wonderful man he is. I radiate my loving smile with my hand on his shoulder.

This moment seems to have opened a bright clearing amid his gloom. He searches my eyes and sees and feels only this love. He responds to the moment: 'Positive things have come from this...this hospice is a wonderful place. When Alex had cancer he did a charity ride from John O'Groats to Lands End and raised £5000 for charity.'

I laugh: 'You will be coming to our fetes then?!'

'Yes.' Wilf relaxes and laughs. 'Thank you, Chris. Thank you for this talk...talking helps so much. I had better be getting back.'

Suddenly I am aware that the small kitchen has become crowded as others jostle for refreshment and we manoeuvre for the exit.

I have been reading Andrew Cohen's book *Living Enlightenment* (2002). This morning, over breakfast, I read a passage that resonated with my experience of 'a tingly warmth that vibrates through me' with Wilf in the small kitchen. I dialogue with the text as it unfolds. Cohen says:

> But that's what enlightenment is – it is the liberating discovery of the
> profound mystery of our own self, a mystery that we will never be able
> to understand with the mind. (p.77)

I respond:

> My surge of love is the mystery I call compassion;
> I wonder at its source as it truly does liberate me from the fetters
> of self-concern.
> I do not seek to understand because it is already known,
> known, but a mystery – is this a contradiction?
> It is known because it has always been here
> though covered in ego layers
> and now revealed in a moment's glance.

Cohen says:

> The most important part of this mystery is the revelation of what I call 'true conscience' – the unexpected manifestation of intense compassion …it expresses a kind of care that the personality could never understand. It's the true heart, which is not the heart that we normally identify with the personality. It's the heart that breaks when we directly experience the one self that we are when we have no notion of being separate. (p.77)

I respond:

> I felt my heart break open to release the radiance of my
> compassion
> shedding light into Wilf's gloom,
> revealing vistas of possibility
> that had lain concealed in the half-light;
> Within the compassionate ripple grief turns into hope.

Cohen says:

> This true conscience, or this spiritual conscience, is experienced as caring. (pp.77–78)

I respond:

> My quest is to the realisation of caring,
> both as something I offer to Wilf
> and as something he experiences;
> Caring is the flood of compassion released across the ego's
> wasteland

Cohen says:

> And this caring is painful – a painful emotional experience – but it's this caring that finally liberates us, slowly but surely, from the attachment to the ego and its endless fears and desires. It is the emergence of this conscience that gives us the energy, strength, and inspiration to give ourselves to the most important task there is. (p.78)

I respond:

> If I do not feel pain have I not then broken open?
> Perhaps joy is pain simply inverted;
> My mind is still
> the body is light, energised and inspired

> freed from the ego's attachment
> In a moment of realisation.

Cohen says:

> So, if we want to be free, it's very important to ask ourselves: How much
> do I care? Because when our heart breaks in this way that I've been
> describing, we will, maybe for the very first time in our lives, experience
> a liberating distance from self-concern. (p.78)

I respond:

> How much do I care?
> I sense there is no boundary to constrain;
> It is true I had no concern other than to ease suffering;
> Perhaps that is self-concern,
> A narcissistic twist the ego has cunningly concealed;
> Yet I have been here before and glimpsed of the divine;
> Of love unleashed

Cohen says:

> Suddenly we will find that we are consumed by that mystery and we
> will spontaneously begin to express a passion for that which is sacred.
> It's only then that everything will begin to make sense. (p.78)

I respond:

> I am consumed, devoured
> and surrender joyously into its consequences;
> I ease along the sacred edge
> beyond the ego's grasping pull.

Cohen says:

> The degree to which we are able to liberate ourselves from self-concern
> will be the degree to which we are able to recognize that our true nature
> as human beings is love. (p.78)

I respond:

> I sense this balance between self-concern
> and concern for the other;
> It is a tug of love

Cohen says:

It happens automatically. This is one of the miracles of human life. When you have reached that point in your own evolution when you ready to leave self-concern behind, your heart will expand and you will know a love that is impossible to imagine unless you have experienced it for yourself. (p.78)

I respond:

> I have bathed in this deep well of love,
> within this mysterious place deep within;
> I do not imagine this love,
> but feel it ever present.

Cohen says:

The nature of this love is not personal; it does not have its roots in the personality. When our attention has become liberated from self-concern, this conscience is set free. Love is literally liberated from the depths of our own being and just emerges of its own accord...(pp.78–79)

I respond:

> Love is not a technique to refine or a tap to turn on;
> In response – love is ever present like a silver stream
> that finds its own level
> between the crooks and crannies where suffering lurks;
> To ease the way beyond

Monday 30 September 2002

Edward

Edward was transferred to the hospice from the hospital following investigation of grand-mal seizures. He is also a diabetic and has a known history of cerebral-vascular accident. He was diagnosed with cancer of the rectum in May with liver metastases reflected in his jaundice. The cancer was not operable and palliative chemotherapy was ruled out because of his heart condition. He had a seizure at the hospice on Saturday and is now in a prolonged post-ictal state. Before that he had been up and walking. In response he had been commenced on a midazolam 10mg infusion via a syringe driver. His wife Glenda had phoned early this morning. She is visiting around 10.00. I am told she is anxious, particularly about Edward having fluids.

He lies in bed picking at his sheets yet responsive to my greeting. His speech is rambling and apparently incoherent reflecting his clouded consciousness, yet there is some sense within the words.

A 10ml syringe lies on the locker which the staff had been using to give small amounts of fluid.

I fetch him some tea and give it via the syringe. He swallows reasonably well and indicates he enjoys the tea. His mouth is extremely dry suggesting he is dehydrated although the overnight urine bag is full. He has a conveen precariously in position.

I am working with Carol, one of the care assistants. This is an ominous sign because our last two shifts together were characterised by sorting out bowel problems. I call us the 'P' team – 'P' stands for poo and piss – a long way down a roll of honour that commences with the 'A' team. We discuss our patient management – one patient is going home whom Carol would like to get ready first.

I suggest we shift Edward's position from his 30 degree tilt onto his other hip. The conveen is off, the bed flooded. The urine smells offensive, or at least I thought it was the urine until we turn him onto his side and reveal his incontinence of faeces. Carol and I look at each other and smile knowingly – the morning is just beginning and we are immediately steeped in our reputation.

As I wash him I am very conscious of the way I move my hands in gentle massage movements. As if an expression of poetry. Being more conscious of touch is a revelation to my practice…helping me convert mundane acts of washing into a sacred dance. I know that sounds corny but it does make washing Edward more meaningful and helps me be mindful of my actions and their impact on Edward. I talked about massage movements when washing Theo. Staff had expressed strong interest in learning how they could do this.

Edward is clean and settled in his new position, that is until he opens his bowels again. Carol and me touched by our destiny. Shortly afterwards Glenda arrives. I am pleased Edward looks settled considering her anxiety. He is responsive and she is pleased. I take the initiative with the fluids and say Edward has drunk some tea, that I am encouraging him to drink and that we will constantly review his hydration.

I rest on Edward's bed sides. On the other side of the bed sits Glenda. Edward lies between us between the bed sides, in place because of the risk of seizure and injury. He is caged. We converse between us, and as we do I again feel that warmth of compassion rise within me…dwelling with these people at this time, talking about their lives, with its tragedies and hopes, feeling the edge of fear and easing it. I dwell with Glenda and Edward for about 15 minutes until I'm certain she feels comfortable. I bring her coffee and say I am about if she needs to talk more before she goes.

My feeling of compassion is a mixture of joy and sadness, as if I have an inscrutable smile on my face. Trungpa (1984) talks about the windhorse in the Shambhala teachings.

> The wind principle is that the energy of basic goodness is strong and exuberant and brilliant...that can be ridden...you can harness the wind of goodness. Discovering the windhorse is, first of all, acknowledging the strength of basic goodness in yourself and then fearlessly projecting that state of mind to others. (pp.84–5)

What a powerful vision and hope for all health care workers to dwell with patients and families! We need to scrape off layers of conditioning to reveal this goodness so it can radiate through our hearts, minds and hands. Trungpa says:

> If we are willing to take an unbiased look, we will find that, in spite of all our problems and confusion, all our emotional and psychological ups and downs, there is something basically good about our existence as human beings. Unless we can discover that ground of goodness in our own lives, we cannot hope to improve the lives of others. (p.30)

I imagine I am a windhorse. I dwell with Glenda and Edward without fear of what the moment might unfold. It is a wise and compassionate confidence that seeks to ease their suffering. Trungpa uses the Tibetan word *drala*, meaning beyond the enemy of ignorance, to describe the idea of a cosmic wisdom. It is the natural wisdom grounded in goodness and compassion that is revealed when the layers of ego concern are pulled away. It arms the warrior to fight ignorance and aggression in the world wherever it lurks. And in the midst of suffering is found joy, humour, warmth and gentleness. Again Trungpa:

> This kind of confidence contains gentleness, because the notion of fear does not arise; sturdiness, because in the state of confidence there is ever present resourcefulness; and joy, because trusting in the heart brings a great sense of humour. This confidence can manifest as majesty, elegance, and richness in a person's life. (p.86)

A few minutes later Carol suggests we shift Edward's position again. Again he is incontinent of faeces. This time I gently examine his rectum. It is nearly empty but my action brings out another stool. Perhaps he will be clear now.

His conveen remains firmly in position. Later I offer him some tea. This time he drinks from the beaker. He is more alert, more coherent in his speech. At lunchtime I wonder if he might manage drinking some tomato soup. Martha comes into the room with his medication. I am hopeful Edward can manage the handful of tablets. However, he fails to swallow the big tablet which Martha scoops out. He eats a few small spoonfuls of ice cream. I hold Edward's hand through the cot side and ask him how he feels about what's happening to him. He understands and says he knows he is going to die and that's okay. He is ready. He has been a staunch Catholic, he believes in God and an afterlife but he is in no hurry to go. He has no fear about dying. In response to his words I squeeze his hand and say, 'You're a good man, Edward.'

He smiles and says others have said that…then he softly laughs and says, 'We've had a good laugh this morning.' The moment is so poignant. I just wish I could capture it adequately in words. He says, 'The other one…thank her for me.'

In the shift report I try and express this moment, my voice a little choked, not because I am sad, but on the contrary because I am swollen with compassion. In preparation for the report I had read his notes. He had been diagnosed cancer of the rectum with liver metastases in May this year. They were unable to offer him palliative chemotherapy because of the risk of cardio-toxicity on Edward's damaged heart. They gave him one to two years but his jaundice suggests he will die soon.

I surface the dilemmas in his care. Should he be hydrated? Should he continue on midazolam? Some nurses feel the midazolam should be continued at least until this evening. I am keen that his consciousness is not impaired. He has been commenced on an anti-convulsant but are aware that anti-convulsants don't mix well with liver disease. We speculate about the cause of his seizures – is it due to hypoglycaemia, brain metastases, toxaemia? Should we know and aim to correct the metabolic or organic disturbance? And so we chew the fat without reaching firm consensus. Yet at least we have discussed and explored the issues even though they are left hanging in the air. Practice is indeterminate without easy answers. To pose the questions and explore our own partial views is mindful.

The art of dialogue is for each person to understand and suspend their own perspectives so we can listen carefully to what the other person is saying. Only then can we open our own perspectives for scrutiny and open ourselves to the possibility of changing perspective in the collaborative effort to give best patient care. We must loosen our attachment to our partial and often dogmatic views. The key to dialogue is being mindful – conscious of the way I am thinking and feeling in the moment; conscious of how I am defending my partial view and not listening; conscious of a need to let go of my attachment to my own perspectives. In letting go, I must gently enable others to let go so we can move into a clearing and find the best way forward. The art of dwelling this time with colleagues. I am the windhorse. The windhorse is such a powerful image to guide me. The caring practitioner evokes and rides the windhorse to ease suffering; with good intent, confident, fearless, compassionate, wise and with humility. Trungpa's book is subtitled 'The sacred path of the warrior' – perhaps an apt subtitle for the path I have journeyed within my narrative towards realising my caring self. Yet I am cautious writing about my practice as if the writing is leaving a trace that I can become attached to. Susuki (1999) says:

> If you leave a trace of your thinking on your activity, you will be attached to the trace. For instance, you may say, 'This is what I have done!' But actually it is not so. In your recollection you may say, 'I did such and such a thing in some certain way,' but actually that is never exactly what happened. When you think this way you limit the actual experience of what you have done. (pp.62–63)

A trace is an attachment to what has been done. Do I have a need to parade my practice for others to admire although people may doubt my sincerity and assume the story is lopsided or distorted to portray myself in a good way? Do I practise for myself in selfish ways rather than practise for others with compassion? Susuki (1999) says that the goal of our practice is to burn ourselves out completely, with our whole body and mind, so no trace is left:

> We should remember what we did but it should be without an extra trace. It is necessary to remember what we have done, but we should not become attached to what we have done in some special sense. What we call attachment is just these traces of our thought and activity. (p.63)

My stories are only a memory trace. They do not tell it exactly as it was. I am mindful of my intention in writing – to nurture compassion and become more wise in my practice. And I must always guard against becoming attached to my stories as being me. I shall leave the reader to dwell with words that resonate with the idea of mindful practice. 'When you are you, you see things as they are, and you become one with your surroundings. There is your true self. There you have true practice'(Susuki 1999, p.83).

PART 3

Postscript: Reflections from a Buddhist perspective

Bert Leguit

Buddha's most important message is that all life is suffering, and that the way of Buddhism is to free people from suffering. Human beings live with suffering, because it's in our nature to become attached to things, and to say: this is mine. But as we look at things as they really are, we will see that all things are changing from one moment to the next. All phenomena are born, live for a short while and then they decay. This happens to all the things in the world we live in. This is also the case with human consciousness. Some phenomena have a longer life than other phenomena, but not one thing is permanent.

In this senses it is not wise to cling to things: eventually we'll see that the thing we clung to has changed and is dying, and we don't want it anymore. We are always dealing with these two things: not wanting what we have, and wanting whatever we do not have. This is what Buddha means by suffering.

Suffering is not only great suffering when a loved one dies or when one gets a serious disease; the little suffering in thousands of our thoughts, too, shows us that human life is suffering. This is why the Buddha taught us to try to live without attachment and without aversion. If we accept the changing aspect in all things, we easily can let things come and go. Than we'll live in freedom and we'll be happy and liberated.

Being aware of every moment, it means living in the here-and-now; the present. When one is aware of this moment only, there is no thinking about the past or the future. History only exists in our memory, and is not really here. In the same manner we can only dream about the future in our fantasy.

The only thing that is real, is this moment. Only this. Living and working in the here-and-now gives a lot of pleasure. There are no sorrows from the past, there are no considerations about the future; there is only this one, clear, brilliant moment. A nurse who works only in the now-moment will give all her attention to the patient while she is there in that moment. The nurse is patient towards the patient, not disturbed by any thought of everything that needs to be done in her daily duty. That moment is for this patient.

In Buddhism the moment when one dies is very important. This is the time when a life transports from one body into another body. To secure a good, new life to follow the former life, it is important to die consciously. It is for this reason that people meditate: to train oneself towards eventually being aware of the moment of death. Besides this: meditating will give you a lot of wisdom in the present life.

In his reflective diary, Christopher Johns poses his cardinal question: how do you spend time with a dying person? From a Buddhist point of view, I will provide an answer: to be aware of all the changing aspects from one moment to the next. It's wonderful that reflective practice is a way to make a practitioner aware of all the things that happen to him, inward or outward. What reflective practice is, Johns explained in his earlier book, *Becoming a Reflective Practitioner* (2000). A reflective practitioner questions himself about everything concerning the why of every detail of his practice: what is happening? What is good and what is bad about this moment? How can I do this next time? Reflecting everything about the situations the practitioner comes across in his work, his practice will reach a higher level. This is the aim of reflective practice: how can I do it better next time? It is in this sense of observing every situation that reflective practice is a way of Buddhist meditation. Both direct you towards awareness of every moment and to being in the here-and-now. The difference between them both is that in reflective practice the aim is to increase the quality of your practice; Buddhism accepts the things 'as they are'.

I enjoyed reading Johns' reflective diary and reading about the honest questions he asks himself in difficult moments. 'How do I feel about him? Should I have been more sensitive? Why do I say these words? Did I yield or was I motivated to avoid conflict?' He also gives emphasis to the situation of the person he takes care of: 'What does she feel? What does she feel about being in the hospice? What does she feel about her life?' These questions make this reflective diary a very personal diary.

In ethical situations Johns makes use of a mixture of Buddhism and Christianity. He leads his practitionership by Buddha's eight-fold path, but when a patient dies, Johns hopes that the patient will go to God in heaven. In this sense also his diary expresses his personal view.

For me, a (40-year-old) student nurse from Amsterdam, the Netherlands, it was amazing to read about all kinds of complementary therapies that are practised in the hospice in Great Britain: reflexology, Bach Flower Consultation, Therapeutic Touch, Reiki, Indian head massage, bowel massage, breathing and relaxation therapy... I would already be happy if the hospital where I work would at least make use of one of these complementary therapies. So, for me Johns's diary is an example that shows me how you can work with seriously ill patients.

When I read this diary, I often asked myself: What would I have done in the same situation? What would I offer, what would I say? You start thinking about your own work on the ward and your own relationship with the patients. In this sense someone else's reflections boost your own reflections. That's why this diary can be helpful for every practitioner.

I enjoyed the way Johns made his diary. Not only did he write down his thoughts: he also added his poems, interesting thoughts from other authors and quotes from a lot of different books. This diary looks like a scrapbook of a journey Johns made with the people around him.

Christopher Johns also made this reflective diary as a teacher. He advises his students to write down their moments of reflection, so Johns made a good choice making such a document himself first. I hope that in this Johns can be a model for his students. Not only in writing a diary like this, but also in the way Johns deals with his patients, and the love and compassion he gives to the patients.

I wish every practitioner to think in full consciousness about his practice, why he acts the way he acts and how he feels when he acts. This way of reflecting will give you important wisdom. So be aware, every moment of your life.

Amsterdam, 13 May 2002

The Being available template

In the narrative introduction I noted that my transformative or developmental journey was marked by the *Being available template*. The template is used formally within the narrative as a way of pausing to take stock of what I have learnt through reflection. It also ripples between the lines throughout the whole of the narrative, giving the reader a point of reference to consider the extent of what being available means within each unfolding moment.

The Being available template was developed from analysing over 500 experiences shared in guided reflection relationships over a four-year period (Johns 1998, 2000) in response to the question: What is the nature of desirable practice? The question seemed significant to know (at least in some graspable form) in the quest to guide practitioners towards knowing and realising desirable practice.

The Being available template is centred in the core dynamic of being available to work with the other (patient/family) to help them find meaning in their health-illness experience, to support them to make best decisions about their lives and take appropriate action to meet their health needs. This description seemed to capture the essence of holistic caring practice with its emphasis on relationship, empowerment and health.

The extent the practitioner can be available to the patient and family is determined by six interrelated factors, as set out in Table A.1. Some of the factors have been explored adequately in the narrative introduction, for example the vision of easing suffering and nurturing growth, and compassion. Other factors require more discussion.

Knowing the person

In considering what it means to know a person I am influenced by Cowling's (2000) idea of appreciating the other's unique life pattern. This requires knowing how to read surface signs and pursue these into the deeper realms of the person's being, and then to find meaning in this information in weaving the whole pattern with the person. The Burford model cues help tune me into the other:

- Who is this person?
- What meaning does this health event have for the person(s)?
- How is this person feeling?
- How has this health event affected their normal life patterns and roles?

**Table A.1 The factors that influence the extent
the practitioner can be available to the patient/family**

Factor	Brief significance of each factor
The extent the practitioner has a strong vision of desirable practice	Intentionality – being mindful of easing suffering and nurturing growth at all times. Such vision gives meaning and direction to practice. It nurtures wisdom and focuses compassion.
The extent the practitioner is concerned for the other	Concern for the other or compassion is caring energy. I pay attention to the other because they matter to me.
The extent the practitioner knows the other	Knowing the other is empathic connection and appreciates the other in the pattern of their wholeness and the meanings they give to health. It is tuning in and flowing with the unfolding pattern of the person's experience.
The extent the practitioner can grasp and interpret the clinical moment and respond with appropriate skilful action (the aesthetic response)	To be wise in the event (rather than after it) in making judgements and how best to respond within the situation. To be aware of my own limitations and take responsibility for ensuring I am adequately skilled. To be confident in my intuition.
The extent the practitioner knows and manages self within relationship	Being mindful of my own concerns so they do not interfere with seeing, responding and flowing with the other's concerns, and ensuring my energy is 100 per cent available for caring work.
The extent the practitioner can create and sustain an environment where being available is possible	Ensuring I work in collaborative ways with my colleagues towards our shared vision and can act to maximise available resources for caring.

- How do I feel about this person?
- How can I help this person?
- What is important for this person to feel comfortable with health care?
- What support does this person have in life?
- How does this person view the future for themselves and for others?

Knowing someone can be just an unfolding moment in time especially within single encounters in acute hospitals. It requires a compassionate intent to know and connect with the other by tuning into the other's wavelength and flowing with them through their unfolding experience whether over 20 minutes or over weeks of deepening relationship.

The aesthetic response

When I enter into engagement with the patient or family member I am mindful to grasp and interpret what is unfolding. This involves appreciating the unfolding pattern of the other's experience while evaluating what has gone before and anticipating where we are moving towards. Based on this interpretation I make judgements and respond with skilled action, and evaluate its impact.

Knowing and managing myself within relationship

There are two major facets to knowing self; first, the Burford model cue 'How do I feel about this person?' prompts me to consider what issues I bring to the situation. To be available to the other I must windscreen-wipe my own concerns in order to see the person in terms of their experience and manage any resistance I may have towards the other person for whatever reason in order to flow with them. Naturally I need to be mindful of these concerns in order to manage them skilfully. Only then can I *truly* listen to the other person's story and connect with the other person in terms of their experience. If I am driven by my own concerns, these concerns will distort the viewing lens and consequently jeopardise my ability to connect wholly with the other person. To stay on the person's wavelength I must manage my resistance to that person, as difficult as that might be, when the demand of the situation takes me beyond my personal comfort zones. Resistance usually manifests itself as a sense of disquiet but might be taking place on a subconscious and prejudicial level.

Certainly within the narrative, I have been mindful of my resistance to patients. My reflective journal has been a space where I have been able to pay attention to and contemplate resistance. Through reflection I aim to focus and melt my resistance – to convert negative energy into positive energy. Newman (1994), drawing on the work of Prigogine and Stengers (1984), describes this as dissipating energy, the unique attribute of human beings as open systems with their environment. Second, and flowing out of the first point, by understanding and melting resistance, I can become intimate without becoming entangled or what Morse (1991) describes as overinvolved whereby therapeutic vision becomes blurred. To connect with the patient requires a deep intimacy that touches the other's soul with my presence. And yet, I must manage the space between myself and the other, so I do not become entangled in their story and overwhelmed. Mayeroff (1971) puts it like this:

> In caring as helping the other grow, I experience what I care for (a person, an ideal, an idea) as an extension of myself and at the same time as something separate from me that I respect in its own right. (p.7)

I must experience the patient's or relative's suffering without it becoming my own. If I am truly compassionate I can see the way we are both joined and separate. If I fail then my compassion may turn to pity as a reflection of my discomfort. If so, I will accumulate emotional baggage that will weigh heavy and sap my energy. To some extent this is inevitable, and requires I establish effective support systems to sustain myself. Without doubt, being open to the other's suffering renders me vulnerable to that suffering. It sparks my sympathy and so I must learn to manage my vulnerability in ways that do not constrain caring. In other words I need to express my sympathy. It cannot be rationalised behind the cold objective mask of empathy. So if I feel sad or angry I can pay attention to this feeling as if observing myself yet recognising that there is no difference between the observer and the observed. I might say to myself, 'I feel angry. Why is that?' and 'How do I best respond?' Perhaps I can generate the opposite emotion – in this example, compassion, and coming to realise that my anger is probably an inappropriate and unskilful response to any situation. Similarly if I feel pity, I can pay attention to this feeling and explore why I am uncomfortable with the other's suffering – again drawing on compassion to convert the negative energy, pity, into positive energy, compassion.

Creating an environment where it is possible to be available

Being mindful of creating an environment where it is possible to be available places my relationship with the patient firmly into the organisational context, necessitating my active engagement to secure a therapeutic environment. This means I must understand the nature of the organisational context, specially those conditions that constrain me, and become skilful at shifting those conditions to realise desirable practice. As Maxine Greene (1988) says:

> When people cannot name alternatives, imagine a better state of things, share with others a project or change, they are likely to remain anchored or submerged, even as they proudly assert their autonomy. (p.9)

Practitioners may not be able to respond differently because of social and cultural norms that are deeply embodied within us and embedded within normal patterns of relating. The world may not be amenable to change, locked as it is in turmoil. The best interests of practitioners are not necessarily the best interests of patients and families. Relationships between practitioners are often clouded by self-interest and determined by traditional power relationships that constrain the practitioner's ability to be available to be with the patient and family. When this happens, patients can easily become pawns in power games just as nurses can be pawns in games of more powerful others. To realise their caring vision, practitioners must be able to rise from any internalised sense of oppression to assert the interests of their patients, often against unsympathetic power gradients.

Perhaps the caring ideal has become diminished in a world driven by technology and organisational systems whereby the self has been reduced to some object. It is as if caring has been squeezed out of practice. Worse, it is squeezed out of practitioners. In Paramanda's (2001) words, we have been *trimmed*:

> When we start to look into our own nature we are always confronted with paradox. At the very centre is not something grand and magnificent but

> something rather grey and guarded, something unknown and neglected. This
> is how it is for most of us. The imagination has been trimmed. (p.81)

I sense that many practitioners feel that what they do as nurses is not valued within organisations. In the modern NHS business world the organisational focus is on outcomes, not the subtle nuances of caring that make such a significant impact on the individual patient's perceptions of being cared for. Practitioners struggle with the contradiction of their need to care within systems where caring has become trimmed. It hurts, and if you listen carefully, you can hear their cries across the wastelands of practice where nurses have perished for loss of caring.

Perhaps I paint an unduly gloomy picture but generally nurses do struggle to care. Working in a hospice has been my refuge from this harsh reality, although the insidious hand of NHS bureaucracy stretches out to insist on specific outcomes in return for funding, and increasing medicalisation results in an overemphasis on symptom-management within the palliative care vision of holistic care. Yet saying that, I chose to work in a hospice because caring *is* highly valued. I hear so many stories from patients and relatives grateful to be at the hospice because of the *un*-caring they have experienced in general hospitals. There should be no compromise of resources in enabling people to die in dignity and comfort, without fear and surrounded by love. Dying, after all, is our collective destiny.

The good news is that reflection and stories help us reconnect to our values, to recover meaning and sense of self as a caring person and to resist being trimmed. Empowered voices are not easily accepted within the status quo so I have also been coached to be political, stealthy and patient, chipping away at the conditions of practice rather than wholesale revolution. It is simply too hard to break out of the vicious cycle of suffering without help. As Fay (1987) notes:

> Coming to a radically new self-conception is hardly ever a process that occurs
> simply by reading some theoretical work; rather, it requires an environment of
> trust and support in which one's own preconceptions and feelings can be made
> properly conscious to oneself, in which one can think through one's
> experiences in terms of a radically new vocabulary which expresses a
> fundamentally different conceptualisation of the world in which one can see
> the particular and concrete ways that one unwittingly collaborates in
> producing one's own misery and in which one can gain the emotional strength
> to accept and act on one's own insights. (pp.265–266)

The idea that reflection can help us alleviate our own suffering is profound. It highlights to me that we do seem to go round and round in circles making the same old mistakes that cause us suffering and misery. In Buddhist language this is samsara, whereby the cock, snake and pig are biting each other's tail in a relentless circle within the centre of the 'wheel of life'. These three animals represent craving, hatred and ignorance. The opposite of these negative states is giving, love and wisdom – and these are the qualities the mindful and caring practitioner must nurture in order to ease both their own and others' suffering. And then perhaps, in the quiet dawn, I, we, may realise new ways of skilful being in relationship with our patients and colleagues. Ultimately, transformation must be communal, not simply individual, although I take personal responsibility to start with myself.

The reader will observe that I rarely use the Being available template in the narrative in an explicit way although it always ripples between the lines. So for example, the reader can always judge the extent I know the patient or the extent I respond skilfully, etc. However, the Being available template is not a prescription for plotting development within narrative. Any *congruent* schema can be used. By *congruent* I mean a scheme that adequately reflects the nature of the desirable practice. The risk of schemes is to fit experience to the scheme. This can create an impression of fragmenting the wholeness of practice into discrete themes. This is my criticism of phenomenological studies that claim to represent lived experience. They merely sanitise experience, representing it as if it were orderly and explanatory rather than being complex and contradictory. Markers are indicators of my growth and should be seen as a loose structure rather than a rigid structure that forces experience into arbitrary categories. Perhaps it would be better to simply tell the story without wrapping it up in interpretative frameworks. Perhaps, but my plot is to become a more effective practitioner and so I must seek feedback that I am realising this beyond just an intuitive sense.

Glossary of drugs

Co-danthrusate
A bowel stimulant only licensed within palliative care

Cyclizine
An anti-emetic

Dexamethasone
A steroid usually given to reduce inflammation associated with brain tumours

Diamorphine
Morphine-based opioid given for severe pain

Diazepam
A drug given to reduce anxiety

Diclofenac
An anti-inflammatory drug usually given as an adjunct to combat pain

Domperidone
An anti-emetic that aids gastric motility

Fentanyl
An opioid drug given for severe pain in patch/slow release form

Gabepentin
An anti-convulsant drug given for neuropathic pain

Haloperidol
An anti-emetic at low doses

Herseptin
A chemotherapeutic drug to combat liver cancer

Hyoscine
A drug used to dry secretions, often used to combat death rattle

Ketorolac
An anti-inflammatory drug usually given as an adjunct to combat pain

Meloxicom
A non-steroid anti-inflammatory drug

Metoclopramide
A drug given to reduce gastric mobility to offset nausea

Midazolam
Given to offset terminal agitation

Movicol
A combined bowel softener and stimulant given to combat constipation

Nozinan
An anti-emetic at low doses

Ocreotide
Used to reabsorb fluid from the gut

Oromorph
Morphine given in relatively small dosage to ease breathlessness and associated anxiety and for pain

Oxycodone
An opioid analgesic given as an alternative to morphine

Palladone
Like Oxcycodone, an opioid analgesic given as an alternative to morphine

Pamidronate
A biphosphonate give to strengthen bone and to treat hypercelcaemia

Paracetamol
A mild analgesic

Phenergan
An anti-histamine drug given to ease itching (among other uses)

Questron
A drug used to alleviate the itching associated with jaundice

Ranitidine
Used to protect the gut mucosa

Sevredol
Oral morphine in tablet form – a trade name for morphine

Sodium valporate
An anti-convulsant drug given for neuropathic pain

Spironolactone
A potassium sparing diuretic

Ventolin
A bronchial dilator to ease breathing

References

Allan, H. (2001) 'A good enough nurse: supporting patients in a fertility unit.' *Nursing Inquiry 8.1*, 51–60.

Autton, N. (1996) 'The Use of Touch in Palliative Care.' *European Journal of Palliative Care 3.3*, 121–124.

Batchelor, S. (1990) *The Faith to Doubt: Glimpses of Buddhist uncertainty.* Berkeley: Parallax Press.

Beck, C. J. (1989) *Everyday Zen.* London: Thorsons.

Beckett, T. (1969) 'A candidate's reflections on the supervisory process.' *Contemporary Psychoanalysis 5*, 169–179.

Belenky, M., Clinchy, B., Goldberger, N. and Tarule, J. (1986) *Women's Ways of Knowing: The development of self, mind and voice.* New York: Basic Books.

Benedict, S., Williams, R. and Baron, P. (1994) 'Recalled anxiety: From discovery to diagnosis of a benign breast mass.' *Oncology Nursing Forum 21*, 1723–1727.

Benjamin, M. and Curtis, J. (1986) *Ethics in Nursing* [Second edition]. New York: Oxford University Press.

Benner, P. (1984) *From Novice to Expert.* Menlo Park: Addison-Wesley.

Benner, P. and Wrubel, J. (1989) *The Primacy of Caring.* Menlo Park: Addison-Wesley.

Bohm, D. (1996) *On Dialogue.* London: Routledge.

Borglum, D. (1997) 'The long shadow of good intentions.' *Tricycle 7.1*, 66–69.

Callahan, S. (1988) 'The role of emotion in decision making.' *Hastings Center Report 18*, 9–14.

Carmack, B. (1997) 'Balancing engagement and detachment in caregiving.' *Image: Journal of Nursing Scholarship 29*, 139–143.

Chancellor, P. (1990) *Illustrated Handbook of the Bach Flower Remedies* [Revised edition]. Saffron Walden: C.W. Daniel Company.

Chödrön, P. (1997) *When Things Fall Apart.* Boston: Shambhala.

Chung Ok Sung (2001) 'The conceptual structure of physical touch in caring.' *Journal of Advanced Nursing 33*, 820–827.

Cixous, H. (1996) *Sorties: Out and Out: Attacks/Ways out/Forays.* In Cixous, H. and Clément, C. (trans. B. Wing) *The Newly Born Woman.* London: Tauris.

Cohen, A. (2002) *Living Enlightenment: A call for evolution beyond ego.* Lenox, MA: Moksha Press.

Cohen, M., Headley, J. and Sherwood, G. (2000) 'Spirituality and bone marrow transplantation: when faith is stronger than fear.' *International Journal for Human Caring 4.2*, 40–46.

Colyer, H. (1996) 'Women's experience of living with cancer.' *Journal of Advanced Nursing 23*, 496–501.

Corley, M. C. and Goren, S. (1998) 'The dark side of nursing: impact of stigmatizing responses on patients.' *Scholarly Inquiry for Nursing Practice: An International Journal 12.2*, 99–118.

Cowling, W. R. (2000) 'Healing as appreciating wholeness.' *Advances in Nursing Science 22.3*, 16–32.

Davis, P. (1999) *Aromatherapy: An A–Z.* Saffron Walden: C.W. Daniel Company.

De Hennezel, M. (1998) *Intimate Death* (trans. C. Janeway). London: Warner Books.

Diamond, J. (1998) *C: Because Coward's Get Cancer Too.* London: Vermillion.

Dreyfus, H. and Dreyfus, S. (1986) *Mind Over Machine.* New York: Free Press.

Rumi (2001) *Hidden Music* (trans. Azima Melita Kolin and Maryam Mafi). London: Thorsons.

Salzberg, S. (1995) *Loving Kindness: The revolutionary art of happiness.* Boston: Shambhala.

Sangharakshita (1990) *Vision and Transformation.* Birmingham: Windhorse.

Sangharakshita (1995) *Transforming Self and World: Themes from the sutra of golden light.* Birmingham: Windhorse.

Sangharakshita (1999) *The Bodhisattva Ideal.* Birmingham: Windhorse.

Saunders, C. (1978) *Appropriate Treatment, Appropriate Death: The management of terminal illness.* London: Edward Arnold.

Saunders, C. (1988) 'Spiritual pain.' *Hospital Chaplain* March.

Schön, D. (1987) *Educating the Reflective Practitioner.* San Francisco: Jossey-Bass.

Seedhouse, D. (1988) *Ethics: The heart of health care.* Chichester: John Wiley & Sons.

Simonton, O.C., Matthews-Simonton, S. and Creighton, J. (1978) *Getting Well Again.* New York: Bantam.

Smith, G. P. (1995) 'Restructuring the principle of medical futility.' *Journal of Palliative Care 11.3*, 9–16.

Spotted Eagle D. (1998) *Pray CD cover notes.* Malibu: Higher Octave Music.

Stein, D. (1995) *Essential Reiki: A complete guide to an ancient healing art.* Freedom, CA: The Crossing Press.

Stewart, I. and Joines, V. (1987) *TA Today: A new introduction to transanctional analysis.* Nottingham and Chapel Hill: Lifespace Publishing.

Street, A. F. (1995) *Nursing Replay.* Melbourne: Churchill Lingstone.

Subhuti (2001) *Madhyamavani 5.* The magazine of the College of Public Preceptors of The Western Buddhist Order.

Susuki, S. (1999) *Zen Mind, Beginner's Mind* (First revised edition). New York: Weatherhill.

Taylor, C. (1995) 'Medical futility and nursing.' *Image: Journal of Nursing Scholarship 27.4*, 301–306.

Tolle, E. (1999) *The Power of Now.* London: Hodder & Stoughton.

Trexler, J. C. (1996) 'Reformulation of deviance and labeling theory for nursing.' *Image: Journal of Nursing Scholarship 28.2*, 131–135.

Trungpa, C. (1984) *Shambhala: The sacred path of the warrior.* Boston: Shambhala.

Twycross, R. (1986) *A Time to Die.* London: Christian Medical Fellowship.

Walter, T. (1994) *The Revival of Death.* London: Routledge.

Wilber, K. (1991) *Grace and Grit: Spirituality and healing in the life and death of Treya Killam Wilber.* Dublin: Newleaf.

Wilber, K. (1997) *The Eye of Spirit: An integral vision for a world gone slightly mad.* Boston: Shambhala.

Wilber, K. (2000) *Sex, Ecology, Spirituality: The spirit of evolution.* Boston: Shambhala.

Wiltshire, J. (1995) 'Telling a story, writing a narrative: terminology in health care.' *Nursing Inquiry 2*, 75–82.

Woodward, V. and Webb, C. (2001) 'Women's anxieties surrounding breast disorders: a systematic review of the literature.' *Journal of Advanced Nursing 33.1*, 29–41.

Worwood, V. (1999) *The Fragrant Heavens.* London: Doubleday.

Yen Mah, A. (2000) *Watching the Tree.* London: HarperCollins.

Subject Index

A Way of Being Free (Okri)
60–4
aesthetic response (being
available) 160, 255, 256
with Ann 81–2
see also wisdom
afterlife, having a sense of
147–8, 174, 230
agitation 98–9, 192–3, 241

breathing difficulties 50, 71,
114, 120–3, 177–8
and incontinence 142, 167,
199–200, 241
sedative use 50, 71, 136, 142,
167, 235, 241
therapies for 114, 167, 184,
192
Ain-dah-ing 219–20
air
nature and caring 151
'need for' as metaphor for life
185
anti-depressants 49, 186–7
anxiety
about the future 37–8, 44,
149–50, 158–9
caregivers concerns 27–8, 89,
92, 156–7, 173
financial concerns 44, 207
panic attacks 149–50
and parent/child ego states
68–9
attachments
and suffering 253
see also losses; non-attachment
authenticity, in caregiving
156–8, 213
autonomy of the patient 85–6
concealing diagnosis 204–5
Awakening the Buddha Within
(Lama Surya Das) 83–8
awareness 20, 103
and right mindfulness 88
see also consciousness

Bach flower remedies 96–8
agrimony 96–7, 187
crab apple 98
oak 98, 188
olive 97–8, 187
red chestnut 97
scleranthus 97

star of Bethlehem 187
sweet chestnut 187
white chestnut 93, 187
'baggage', in our thoughts 24,
130, 260–1
bargaining with cancer 48–9,
202
Becoming a Reflective
Practitioner (Johns) 252
bedside manner, stereotypical
behaviours 156–7
Before I Say Goodbye (Picardie)
155–6
being with another, Five basic
modes (Halldórsdóttir) 93
'being available' template
255–260
use with Ann 78–88
use with Stephen 211–13
'being mindful' 18–20, 69
and the reflective process 7–8
belief systems 190–2
see also religious beliefs
The bluest eyes in Texas are
haunting me tonight (A
Camp) 215
Bodhisattva ideal 19, 32–3, 131,
192–3
body-image 70, 98, 148, 156–8,
175, 207
bone metastases, and pain levels
48, 222, 229
boundaries 151–2, 156–7
home life/hospice care 161,
194–5, 227
professional barriers 261–2
see also detachment
Brahma viharas 84
brain tumours/metastases 47,
69–70, 111, 112, 143
breaking bad news 203–4,
205–6, 226–7
ethical mapping 206
Kaye's ten steps 209
breast cancer
coping themes 39, 138
breathing difficulties 50, 71,
114, 120–3, 177–8
breathing techniques/treatments
36, 38, 169–70, 177–8,
219
buccal tumours 49–50
Buddhism
Bodhisattva ideal 19, 32–3,
131, 192–3
death 252
Eight-fold path 82–8

Phowa practice 76–8, 123–4,
192–3
practices to enhance
connectivity 57
v. reflective practice 255
Shambhala teachings 248–9
Burford Model cues 37, 136,
259
burn-out 27

caregiving
and beauty 24, 223–5
commitment and continuity
27, 58, 92
detachment and stereotypical
behaviours 19–20, 67,
81, 90, 92, 95, 102–3,
132–3, 151–2, 156–7
fears of own death 132–3,
166, 212, 219, 231–3
and guilt 24, 40–1, 107,
144–5
habits and blind spots 27
importance of reflection 24–5
importance of ritual 69, 108,
196, 198, 151, 217
and labelling 19–20, 67,
132–3, 147, 173
love in giving 99, 170–2,
183–4, 244–7
motivations and ego 48,
87–8, 99, 166
mutuality 72, 224
and nature 28, 151
and need for self-care 144–5,
159–60
numbness 183
and spiritual growth 17–18,
161, 219–20, 239,
244–7, 248–9
spiritual traps 166
to other caregivers 236
and transactional analysis
67–9
'caring dance' 18, 46, 63–4,
123, 125–31, 161, 172,
189
and music 38–9, 41, 52,
57–8, 180, 214
The Caring Dance (Johns) 125
chakra colours 47, 198, 228,
232
chakras 94, 96, 216, 232
children
communicating bad news
226–7

fear of loss 36, 40, 43, 46,
    47, 48–9, 114, 104–5,
    158–9, 207–8
  and healing 220
CHUMS 207
clothes and uniforms 156
communication
  avoiding 'death/dying' words
    213, 215
  breaking bad news 204,
    205–6, 209–10
  limits and boundaries 150,
    156–7, 194–5
  and listening 202, 258
  making connections 57
  name use and intimacy 151–2
  negative words 70, 173
  'perfect speech' and
    truthfulness 84–5
  talking about the weather 151
  and transactional analysis
    67–9
community care 89–92, 227
compassion (being available) 19,
    32–3, 73, 82, 103, 131,
    160, 163, 172, 258
  and Ann 79
  'idiot' compassion 166
  as spiritual conscience 244–7
  v. pity 221, 258–9
compassion fatigue 27–8
concern 79, 258
  see also compassion (being
    available)
conditional caring 161
confession 23–5
  and seeking forgiveness 107
consciousness
  balancing sedative use 167
  beyond death 147–8
  the human condition and
    suffering 250
constipation, management 41,
    42, 45, 71, 154
containment 181–2
  see also holding
continuity of care 58, 92
coping mechanisms
  for caregivers 64, 67–9,
    101–2, 132–3
  support from fellow patients
    38, 39, 105, 117, 136
  women with breast cancer 39,
    138
  see also detachment; labelling;
    non-attachment; self-care
courage 17

creating environments (being
    available) 82, 258, 259–60
  see also environments
critical social science perspectives
    17
cultural differences 182

dana 84, 194
Dancing with Shadows (Johns)
    18
  see also 'caring dance'
'dark side of nursing' 152, 173
day care, support from fellow
    patients 38–9, 105, 117,
    136
death
  and acceptance 147, 116, 177
  Buddhist beliefs 254
  caregivers fears 132–3, 166,
    212, 219, 231–3
  importance of ritual 69, 108,
    192–3, 195–6, 217
  and 'meaning' 177, 235
  patient fears 72, 75, 91,
    132–3, 136–7, 166
  and Phowa practices 76–8,
    123–4, 192–3
  the right to dignity 260
  sudden 69, 143, 192–3
  talking about it 116, 117–18,
    147–8
debriefing 236
Deep Peace (Donovan) 52, 56–7
A Deeper Beauty: Buddhist
    reflections on everyday life
    (Paramanda) 29
defence mechanisms 23–4
  see also denial; detachment
delivering bad news see breaking
    bad news
denial 150, 221–2
  see also Iris's journey
dependency 65–8, 112
depression 186–7
detachment 19–20, 67, 81,
    102–3, 132–3, 151–2
  and doing harm 90, 92, 95
  and non-attachment 159–60
Dharma, and the Eight-fold path
    82–8
dialogue 28–9, 250
  with literature 29
dignity, loss of 106, 112, 260
diuretic use 153
doing harm, through detachment
    90, 92, 95
doubts 17, 175, 212–3

dreams 42, 47
'dwelling with' 238–40
dying
  beauty 24, 29, 223–5
  and the 'caring dance' 18, 46,
    38–9, 41, 52, 63–4, 123,
    125–31, 161, 172, 189
  denial 150, 221–2
  distress at decay 50–1
  and holding 52–3, 78, 94,
    101, 181–2, 216–17
  and letting go 77, 100, 139,
    219
  odours 50–1, 53, 90, 154–5
  patient awareness 70, 105,
    147, 235
  and Phowa practices 76–8,
    123–4, 192–3
  tying up loose ends 240–1

ego
  caregivers fears of death
    132–3, 166
  'caring' for self-gratification
    87–8, 99, 166, 194
  parent-child states in caring
    67–9
  and restlessness 87–8
  and truth 60–4
  and yielding 132–4
Eight-fold path 82–8
emotional responses 84
enduring 15
energy fields, balanced state 56
enlightenment 17, 161, 244–7
  and perfect samadhi 88
environments
  importance in healing 214,
    261–2
  and noise 148–9, 163
essential oils
  inhalations 169–70
  for masking odours 51, 55–6,
    155, 182
  for positive thinking 88–9
  for relaxation 43, 163, 189
  for the spiritual journey 55–6,
    168, 180
  for stress 163, 171–2
ethical mapping (Johns) 205,
    206
existential suffering 14
  see also soul pain

faith 190–2
  in giving care 91, 100
  see also religious beliefs

family
    breaking the news/prognosis
        203–6, 209–10, 226–7
    as caregivers 71–2, 170–3
    exhaustion 91–2, 238
    and pain 73, 93
    saying goodbye 109–10,
        177–8, 179–82, 242
    stress manifestations 115,
        145–6, 171
    see also children
fatherhood 125, 178
fears
    about the future 38, 44,
        104–5, 162, 185
    of caregivers about death
        132–3, 166, 212, 219,
        231–3
    of the dying process 72, 75,
        91, 138, 174, 200
    of family about death 204–5
    and hope 218–19, 226
    and letting go 77, 100, 139,
        219
    of prognosis 70, 89, 193,
        203–4, 221–2
feedback 44, 194, 243
feminine v. masculine 'caring' 32,
    224
financial worries 44, 207
'flow freezers' 126
Four Noble Truths 83
The Fragrant Heaven (Worwood)
    55–6
frankincense 168
funerals 196
fungating tumours 49–50,
    115–16

gastrostomy/PEG feeding 71,
    122
Grace and Grit (Wilber) 40, 44
grandchildren 106
grief, and healing work 177,
    235, 243
growth see self-growth
grumpiness 66–7, 71
guidance 27–8
    and dialogue 28–9, 250
Guided Reflection: Advancing
    Practice (Johns) 9
guilt
    in caregiving 24, 40–1, 107,
        144–5, 176, 193, 223–4
    of surviving 118, 140

harm, through detachment 90,
    92, 95
healing attitude, Five aspects
    159–60, 160
holding 52–3, 78, 94, 101,
    181–2
    through Therapeutic Touch
        216–17
hope 218–19, 226
hospice care
    in the modern NHS 262
    philosophical basis 13–14
    see also caregiving
hostility
    grumpiness 66–7, 71
    as response to dependency
        64–9
    as response to despair 154,
        210–12
humour 197, 230

'in place' 58–9
In the stillness of the desert
    (Johns) 198–9, 231
incontinence 247–8
    and distress 142, 167, 241
independence, loss of 65–8, 112
Indian head massages 171–2
inhalations 169–70
inner conflict, of the caregiver
    23–5, 89, 176
integrity 85–7
intimacy 113, 151–2
intuition 22
    see also knowing the person
        (being available)
Iris's journey 35–47, 88–9,
    92–3, 96–8, 104–5,
    117–19, 134, 138–41,
    149–50, 158–9, 160–3,
    182–3, 186–9, 193–4,
    203–5, 214–16, 218–19,
    222–9, 233–6
isolation
    bodily decay and dying 50–1
    and rejection 223–5

journal writing 25–7
    see also reflective narrative

knowing the person (being
    available) 258, 259
    with Ann 79–80, 85–7
knowing self (being available)
    255, 257–8
    with Ann 80–1

see also self-growth;
    self-knowledge

labelling 19–20, 147, 173
    as coping mechanism 67,
        132–3
language use
    avoiding 'death/dying' words
        213, 215
    conventions and rituals 151
    names 151–2
    negative words 70, 173
learning, from the cared for 72,
    224
letting go 77, 100, 139, 219
literature, as guide 29
liver tumours/metastases 37, 40,
    42, 108, 196, 236, 247
    and toxicity 214–15, 221
Living Engagement (Cohen)
    244–7
living in the present 253–4
losses
    of dignity 106, 112, 262
    of independence 65–8, 112
    of loved ones 38, 44, 104–5,
        152, 207
    of mobility 173
    of roles 137
    sexuality and body-image 70,
        98, 156–8, 175, 207
love, in caregiving 99, 170–2,
    183–4, 244–7
lung cancer 112–13

Macmillan nursing 89–92, 227
managing self (being available)
    102–3, 255, 257–8
    and non-attachment 159–60
    see also knowing self (being
        available)
Marie Curie nursing 91–2
massage 111, 153
    coping with disfigured skin
        223–5
    feet 148–9, 159, 168
    hands 72–3
    head 171–2
    and intimacy 37, 111
    to restore body-image 158
    see also essential oils;
        reflexology practice
meditations 21–2, 198
    and imagery 199
    loving kindness (metta
        bhavana) 163
    see also poems

metta bhavana 163
midazolam use see sedative use
mindfulness 18–20
Model for Structured Reflection,
    guidance and cues 25–6
Mortally Wounded (Kearney)
    211
motherhood and breast cancer
    Iris 36, 40, 43, 46, 47,
        104–5, 158–9, 207–8
    Maisie 48–9
motivations for caring 48, 87–8,
    99, 166
motor neurone disease (MND)
    71–2
mouth care 71–2
MRSA 116
music and the caring dance
    38–9, 41, 180, 214
    Deep Peace (Donovan) 52,
        57–8
    Lost Blues 38
music and massage/reflexology
    Chaco Canyon (Rusty
        Crutcher) 36, 153
    Oceans Eclipse (Rusty
        Crutcher) 172
    Peace of Mind (Brahma
        Kumaris) 42
    Walk in Harmony (Brian
        Carter) 189

naming, first names and intimacy
    151–2
narrative research 9–10
Native American medicine 18,
    219–20
nature and caring 151
nausea control 111, 148, 179
negative feelings 23–4, 27–8,
    173
    about the future 37
    analysis through the reflective
        framework 25–6
    and projection 27–8, 145
    see also guilt
negative language 70, 173
neroli 170
NHS, and the caring ideal 262
No Man Is An Island (Merton)
    99–101
noise 148–9, 163
non-attachment 103, 159–60
    and the authentic response
        213
nursing roles 156–7

objectivity
    in dialogue/communication
        28
    v. subjectivity 7
    see also truth
odours
    from pressure sores 90
    in hospices 50–1, 53, 154–5
oedema 153–4, 202
oesophageal cancer 65, 135–6
pain
    from temporal bone invasion
        48
    of the soul 79–80, 82, 136–7,
        191, 210–13, 237
pain ladder (WHO) 210
pain relief 54, 69, 135, 170–1,
    203, 236
    and consciousness 167
    see also sedative use
palliative care 14–16
    WHO definition 14
    within hospices 13–14
    see also caregiving
pancreatic cancer 108, 165, 167
panic attacks 149–50
paralysis, spinal cord
        compression 89–92,
        229–30
partners see family
patchouli 88–9
patient-caregiver relations 46
    parent-child ego states 67–9
peer support 236
    see also guidance
pettigrain 172
Phowa practice
    with Ann 76–8
    with Josie 192–3
    with Rose 123–4
pity, v. compassion 221, 257–8
play 31–2
poems
    for the dying (Johns) 75–8,
        80, 227–8
    In the stillness of the desert
        (Johns) 198–9, 231
    for love and grief (Rice)
        183–4
    To Iris (Johns) 234
The Power of Now (Tolle) 230
pressure sores 65, 90
professional boundaries 261–2
    see also boundaries
prognosis delivery 205–6
    and ethical mapping 205, 206

patients wish to know 70
projections, of negative feelings
    27–8, 145, 147, 173
prostrate cancer 89–92
rectal cancer 247, 249–50
reflection
    accuracy of recollections 22–3
    guidance 27–9
    key attributes 27
    suspending ego/value
        judgements 28–9
reflective narrative
    author's own writing
        experiences 9, 25, 255
    and coherence 29–30
    and dangers of
        self-gratification 87–8
    the process 7–8, 10, 29–33
    prompts and cues 25–6
    as research into 'self' 9–10,
        29–33, 37
    transformation and
        transgression 29–33
reflective practice
    as a communal responsibility
        263
    and importance of feedback
        249–50, 263
    v. Buddhism 255
reflexology practice 36–7, 42–3
    and visualisation 37, 47, 204
    see also massage; Therapeutic
        Touch
regrets, over treatment options
    40, 44
Reiki 36, 52–3, 96
religious beliefs
    asking the question 37, 52,
        54, 56–7, 90
    faith and fear 72–3, 75, 91
    patient vulnerability to carers
        beliefs 86–7
    and the process of dying 52
    and secularism 190
    and universality 101, 219–20
research into self 9–10, 29–33
resonance see music and the
    caring dance
'right or perfect speech'
    (Sangharakshita) 60
ritual
    conversational routines 151
    importance of 69, 108,
        192–3, 196, 198, 217
'running in place' 21–2

saddah 84
sandalwood 180
Sangha 82
sedative use 50, 71, 136, 142
    v. alternative therapies 167,
        184, 192–3, 250
self, and mortality 15–16, 212
self-blame, in caregiving 24,
    144–5, 176
self-care 144–5, 159–60
self-distortion 8, 23, 27–8, 60
    and spiritual traps 164–5, 251
self-doubts 175, 212–13
self-gratification, through 'caring'
    87–8, 99, 166
self-growth 15–16, 178
    being 'in-place' 59
    of caregivers 17–18, 59, 251
    finding goodness within
        248–9
    finding life's patterns 239
    finding true consciousness
        244–7
    through all experiences 161
    see also knowing self (being
        available)
self-knowledge 130
    in caregiving 20, 22–3, 27–8,
        257–8
    through narrative research 10,
        27
    see also knowing self (being
        available)
self-presentation
    behaviours 156–7
    clothes 155–6
sentimentality 166
sexuality and body-image 70,
    98, 156–8, 175, 207
Shambhala teachings 248–9
Sister Kathleen 11, 185
'soul bumping' 224
soul pain 79–80, 82, 211
spirituality 16, 190
    appropriateness in care
        settings 58–64, 191–2
    as essence of being human 16,
        188
    'inflation' and 'traps' 164–5,
        166
    reality, truth and reason
        59–64, 164–5
'stages of dying' (Kübler-Ross)
    212
steroid treatment 47–8, 153,
    218, 229

storytelling, and transgression
    30, 60–4
'stuff', in thoughts 24, 130, 260
subjectivity
    and assumptions 22
    v. objectivity 7
    see also truth
suffering 14–15
    absorbing from patient 44, 53,
        80–1, 101, 213, 215–16
    detachment v. non-attachment
        159–60
    doubts about meeting needs
        73–4, 103–4
    and emotional release 15
    research perspectives 9
    and soul pain 79–80, 82, 211
support systems, fellow patients
    38, 39, 105, 117, 136
Sweat Your Prayers (Roth)
    125–31
symptom management
    balances and trade-offs 153–4
    sedative use v. alternative
        choices 167, 184, 192,
        192–3
    see also individual symptoms

Therapeutic Touch (TT) 44–5,
    91–2, 94, 181, 216–17,
    230
therapy v. nursing care 43
thinking processes, suspending
    ego/value judgements
    28–9
touch
    significance of 217
    see also Therapeutic Touch
Transactional Analysis 67–9,
    147
transgression, in the narrative
    process 29–33, 60–4
treatments, tyranny of
    'programme management'
    158, 228
A Tribute to the Patron Saint of
    Love (Rice) 183–4
truth 250–1
    and avoidance 213
    in narrative 59–64
    and perfect speech 84–5
    see also denial
TT see Therapeutic Touch

uniforms 156

value judgements 20, 28–9

vision (being available) 78, 83,
    160, 258
    importance of sharing 169
Vision and Transformation
    (Sangharakshita) 83–8
visitations 174
visualisation
    in meditation 199
    and reflexology 37, 47
    and Therapeutic Touch 91,
        109, 208
    to dissipate fears 140

'windhorse' (Shambhala
    teachings) 248–51
wisdom 160
    grounded in compassion 249
    v. knowing 19–20, 129–30
World Health Organisation
    (WHO), on palliative care
    14
writing practices
    prompts and cues 25–6
    timing issues 25

yielding 132–4
    see also letting go

Zen meditation practices 21–2

Author Index

Allan, H. 101
Autton, N. 224

Batchelor, S. 17, 26–7
Baron, P. 39, 138
Beckett, T. 20
Beck, J. 21–2, 53, 219
Belenky, M. 29
Benedict, S. 39, 138
Benjamin, M.
Benner, P. 9–10, 22, 81
Bohm, D. 28
Borglum, D. 164

Callahan, S. 81
Carmack, B. 80, 102
Chancellor, P. 98
Chödrön, P. 161
Chung Ok Sung 37
Cixous, H. 32, 59
Clinchy, B. 29
Cohen, A. 244–7
Cohen, M.190
Colyer, H. 39
Corley, M.C. 152, 173
Cowling, W.R. 9, 37, 137, 239, 257
Creighton, J. 47
Curtis, J. 85

Davis, P. 55, 171, 189
De Hennezel, M. 53
Diamond, J. 114
Downie, R.S. 73–4, 85–7, 146
Dreyfus, H. 22
Dreyfus, S. 22
Dunniece, V. 7

Engebretson, J. 191
Estabrooks, C. 224
Evans, D. 214

Fallowfield, L. 50
Fay, B. 17, 27, 259
Flaming, D. 213

Gerber, R. 56
Glassman, B. 13
Goldberger, N. 29
Goldstein, J. 19
Goren, S. 152, 173
Greene, M. 258

Halldórsdóttir, S. 92, 93
Headley, J. 190
Heidegger, M. 81
Henderson, A. 10–31, 95
Howard, J. 96–8

James, N. 173
Janssens, R. 213
Jarvis, J. 214, 223
Johns, C. 80, 125, 136, 158, 206, 212, 252–3, 255, 256
Joines, V. 68
Jones, B. 23, 33, 59, 101, 133–4, 144–5, 219
Jones, G. 23, 33, 59, 101, 133–4, 144–5, 219
Jourard, S. 156–7

Kaye, P. 209
Kearney, M. 79–80, 82, 211, 224
Krishnamurti, J. 28–9, 129
Kübler–Ross, E. 212
Kuuppelomäki, M. 191

Lama Surya Das 83–8
Landmark, B. 158
Lawton, J. 14, 51, 54, 105
Leguit, B. 251–3
Levine, S. 19, 103, 221
Longaker, C. 52, 57, 76–7

McCaffrey, R. 214
McNamara, B. et al. 14
Macrae, J. 44
Marris, P. 177
Mathews–Simonton, S. 47
Mayerhoff, M. 15, 58, 72, 257
Mercier, P. 229
Merton, T. 99–101, 103
Morse, J. 9, 15, 80, 224, 260

Newman, M. 15, 38–9, 257
Nightingale, F. 59

O'Donohue, J. 27, 189
Okri, B. 30, 31–2, 60–4, 187

Paramanda 20, 24, 96, 217, 258
Pettigrain 172
Picard, C. 125
Picardie, R. 155–6
Plager, K. 82
Polanyi, M. 22
Prigogine, I. 257

Quinn, J. 42

Randall, F. 73–4, 85–7, 146
Reed, P. 16, 190
Remen, R.N. 7
Rice, H.S. 183–4
Rinpoche, S. 24–5, 87, 110
Roth, G. 18, 124, 125–31
Rumi 46

Salzberg, S. 19, 235
Sangha 82
Sangharakshita 23, 60, 83–8, 159–60, 178, 194
Saunders, C. 15, 211, 224
Schön, D. 55, 63, 81, 154
Seedhouse, D. 212
Simonton, O.C. 47
Sherwood, G. 190
Slevin, E. 7
Smith, G.P. 143
Spotted Eagle, D. 188
Stengers, I. 257
Stewart, I. 68
Street, A.F. 25
Subhuti 27
Susuki, S. 250

Taylor, C. 143
Tarule, J. 29
Ten Have, H. 213
Tolle, E. 123, 131, 133, 139, 144, 230
Trexler, J.C. 67
Trungpa, C. 248–9

Wahl, A. 158
Walter, T. 190–2
Watson, J. 15
Webb, C. 158
Wilber, K. 40, 44, 60, 102, 239
Williams, R. 39, 138
Wiltshire, J. 59
Woodward, V. 158
World Health Organisation (WHO) 14
Worwood, V. 55–6, 89, 168, 170, 180
Wrubel, J. 81

Zylicz, Z. 213